CHANGING PATTERNS OF EMPLOYEE RELATIONS

CHANGING PATTERNS OF EMPLOYEE RELATIONS

Mick Marchington and Philip Parker

HARVESTER WHEATSHEAF

New York   London   Toronto   Sydney   Tokyo

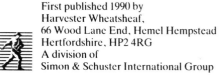

First published 1990 by
Harvester Wheatsheaf,
66 Wood Lane End, Hemel Hempstead
Hertfordshire, HP2 4RG
A division of
Simon & Schuster International Group

Printed and bound in Great Britain by
Billing and Sons Ltd, Worcester

British Library Cataloguing in Publication Data

Marchington, Mick, *1949–*
    Changing patterns of employee relations in Britain.
    1. Great Britain. Industrial relations
    I. Title   II. Parker, Philip, *1962–*
331'.0941

    ISBN 0–7450–0532–2
    ISBN 0–7450–0533–0 pbk

1 2 3 4 5   94 93 92 91 90

CONTENTS

PREFACE

This book is concerned with the management of employee relations in the British private sector during the late 1980s. It comprises three parts: first, we review a wide range of literature which analyses the changing nature of employee relations, the meaning of management strategy, and the links between management style and the product markets within which companies compete. Second, we move on to present four in-depth case studies of companies in the private sector drawn from different industries, namely: chemicals, food, retail and engineering. The data for each case was collected over a two-year period of longitudinal study, during which time we were able to interview key personnel at various levels within the companies, as well as observe their interactions and analyse written documentation. In the third part of the book, we interpret the empirical findings as a whole, relating our ideas to contemporary theory in the field of employee relations and modifying this as appropriate. In addition, we suggest a simple model which can assist our understanding of employee relations in its managerial and organisational context.

The book should appeal to students and lecturers specialising in industrial relations, personnel and human resource management and organisation studies; its most specific target is the final-year undergraduate or postgraduate student, who is undertaking a course in any of the above areas, perhaps as part of a degree in Management or Business Studies, or as a professional qualification such as at Stage Two of the Institute of Personnel Management's examinations. We trust that it has been written in a way that is easily understandable, even though we may at times be delving into literature with which students are unfamiliar. Equally, it has been our intention to present the case study data in sufficient depth to enable readers to get a feel for the reality of employee relations management in these four companies in the late 1980s.

As ever, we owe a considerable number of debts to people, many of whom must go unmentioned for the sake of space and confidentiality. The research would not have been possible without the aid of a three-year grant from the Economic and Social Research Council (F 0023 2226) which paid the salary of Philip Parker, refunded travelling expenses and various associated costs. In addition, our employer (UMIST) provided the infrastructure which allowed the study to take place, as well as a good environment in which to work. People at the four companies that were most extensively involved in the research project gave generously of their time and patience, even though we probably overstayed our welcome on a number of occasions. In particular, we should like to thank the principal contact people in each organisation: Steve Abbott, Keith Ballantyne, Ken Barrett, Stuart Coppen, Joe Dewhurst, John Edwards, Jane Fenner, Bob Morton, Nicola Standring, and Julie Tuz. In addition, we should like to express our gratitude to Professor John Goodman (of the Manchester School of Management at UMIST) who read the whole manuscript, made a mass of detailed suggestions, and reoriented the direction of some of the early chapters. Peter McGoldrick, another of our colleagues, provided a number of comments on the chapter about Multistores, which were helpful for that particular case and industry. At Harvester Wheatsheaf, Stephen Rutt and Peter Johns were responsible for progressing the manuscript along its various stages, and we are grateful to them for this.

Finally, we would like to thank our families for putting up with us during the period of the research. Although we undertook the fieldwork phase of the research jointly, Philip was responsible for writing up the raw case studies into a manageable size, and I then refined them for this book. Since it was my responsibility to write the book, the major burden (if my isolation in the study could be perceived in that way!) fell upon the Marchington household. Whilst Lorrie already knew what it was like to be an academic 'widow' during the writing-up phase of a research project, Jack and Lucy had to be inducted into the experience of fatherly neglect, and even helped to print out the manuscript from my word processor. Any errors or inconsistencies which remain after all this assistance are due solely to my shortcomings.

Mick Marchington
Manchester

PART I

EMPLOYEE RELATIONS IN THEORY

1 · INTRODUCTION

This book is concerned with the management of employee relations in the British private sector during the late 1980s. It is based around empirical work undertaken over a two-year period in four companies, drawn from a range of industries – chemicals, food, retail, engineering. Our principal area of interest is the way in which management style develops in relation to the product market in which the company operates. Relatedly, we are keen to assess the role which trade unions play within companies which are initiating schemes for employee involvement, and in the precise meaning of management strategy in such circumstances. Before providing a review of relevant literature, as a forerunner to the empirical work, we shall first expand on the background to the study and the methodology employed in it.

1.1 BACKGROUND

The ways in which employers choose to manage their employees have long been a source of interest and concern for academics and practitioners alike. Over the course of this century, different approaches have gained prominence in line with a variety of pressures, both internal and external to employing organisations, such as the growth of trade unionism, changing product and labour market conditions, labour law and new technology. In addition, policy pronouncements by governments, and the proposals emanating from bodies such as the Donovan Commission (1968), the Commission on Industrial Relations (1973) and the Advisory Conciliation and Arbitration Service (ACAS) (1981) have also sought to guide employers in certain directions. Indeed, over the last twenty years, managements have been repeatedly encouraged to adopt a more proactive and strategic stance in relation to labour, and to integrate this with general business strategy wherever possible.

The 1970s and 1980s are also significant because they provide a range of highly contrasting features in the economic, legal, political and social environment. During most of the 1970s, employers were encouraged to recognise and work with trade unions, required to improve the floor of employment rights for the majority of workers, and prompted to conciliate rather than confront in the event of a dispute. In the 1980s, the political and legal climate changed to the extent that many of the statutory rights of trade unions have been removed, the legal protections available to employees have been reduced, and confrontational stances have been openly utilised and supported by government. In addition, of course, the level of unemployment in the United Kingdom during the 1980s, especially in certain parts of the country, has remained at a much higher level than in the previous decade. There is little doubt that the combination of these factors has given employers greater freedom to manage employee relations in a manner which suits their own requirements. In particular, these conditions would appear to facilitate a more assertive approach by employers, one which is aimed at reinforcing managerial prerogatives in the workplace. The well-publicised cases of 'macho management' provide adequate illustrations of employers who have chosen to transform their labour relations practices by sacking senior shop stewards, withdrawing recognition from trade unions, enforcing tighter disciplinary standards and demanding greater labour flexibility, for example (Mackay, 1986). Although there is a superficial plausibility about the connection between a harsher economic and political context and 'macho management', there are also considerable doubts about its accuracy. First, it has never been properly defined, and is often interpreted so broadly as to encompass just about every action taken by management in the 1980s, whether this be a head-on assault on the unions, or more sophisticated attempts to increase employee commitment to the enterprise. Second, the evidence for 'macho management' often rests upon a number of highly specific cases which have attracted media interest, and may consequently be relatively unusual.

Third, as we shall see later in this book, the notion of macho management implicitly assumes that labour relations form the central preoccupation of employers, and that the actions of the latter are primarily directed towards this particular aspect of management. Finally, the link between contextual factors and management practice is far too deterministic, leaving no room for choice, disagreement and mistakes within the enterprise.

In contrast to ideas about macho management, there is now a sizeable body of evidence which suggests that workplace trade unionism and the established institutions and procedures of industrial relations – such as collective bargaining – have survived remarkably well during the 1980s. As we shall see in the next chapter, the Workplace Industrial Relations Survey undertaken in 1984 demonstrates a considerable element of stability and continuity in British labour relations (Millward and Stevens, 1986). This has even led some analysts to suggest that the 1980s, far from being a decade of major transformation, as governmental rhetoric would imply, have in fact seen a deceleration in the rate of change, compared with the 1970s (MacInnes, 1987). Other commentators, drawing on large-scale interview material, suggest that workplace trade unionism has weathered the economic and political onslaught rather better than expected, but at the same time point to developments in employee involvement and workforce flexibility as also being evidence of change (see, for example, Batstone, 1984; Edwards, 1985, 1987). Of course, it may well be that the institutions remain relatively intact, but their character has altered significantly so that they are now less central than in the 1970s (Brown, 1986; Terry, 1986).

A third view has also gained in prominence during the 1980s, that of human resource management (HRM). Unlike the perspectives outlined above – which point to an increasingly aggressive management approach to employee relations, or stability and continuity in the institutions of job regulation – this suggests that employers have sought to develop employees, treat them as resources or investments, and integrate personnel policies more closely with other strategic decisions (Armstrong, 1987). HRM is considerably different from earlier conceptions of the personnel role and profession, which focused on welfare, employment administration, negotiation, and legal expertise (Watson, 1977; Legge, 1978; Thomason, 1981). However, the extensiveness of HRM in reality, as well as its precise meaning, is still largely unknown (Guest, 1987; Tyson, 1987).

Each of these themes provides a springboard for the rest of this book, which has three principal objectives. First, there is a need for more in-depth, qualitative, case studies to extend the growth in data of a quantitative nature which has emerged over the last few years. Whilst it is clearly valuable to have a comprehensive and representative body of information about workplace employee relations, data of this nature is never sensitive and detailed enough to enable researchers to evaluate changes in individual work-places, especially on the shop floor. Moreover, with data of this kind, we are unlikely to discover the views of 'ordinary employees', as opposed to those of managers or shop stewards, about the everyday practice of employee relations. In short, we shall provide an analysis of four case study companies, drawn from different parts of the private sector, which aims to balance the trend towards quantitative data in the subject.

Second, we propose to test a number of hypotheses about work-place employee relations which have emerged in the last decade against the evidence from our case studies: for example, the idea that managements sponsored the development of steward orga-nisations in the 1970s and have subsequently rolled them back in the 1980s; the argument that employers aim to separate the level (or function) which deals with collective bargaining from that which makes strategic decisions; the proposal that schemes for employee involvement undermine collective bargaining and trade unionism. More broadly, we shall reconsider views about the meaning and existence of management strategy, and the degree to which labour relations concerns form a central part of employer objectives. We are particularly keen to explore beyond the policy pronouncements made by corporate headquarters about new in-itiatives, and to consider in depth the way in which employee relations is practised on the shop floor.

We also intend to focus on differences between companies, as well as noting similar developments across these organisations as a whole. Our final objective follows on from this, namely to identify the factors that are associated with differences in employee rela-tions management, and in particular to analyse the way in which the nature of the product market is intertwined with the manage-ment of labour. This is seen as increasingly important by employers, as well as by students of industrial relations, and although much has been written on the subject it does not tend to be in a form that allows for accurate comparisons between organisations. Futhermore, we also wish to emphasise that the link between product market conditions and employee relations practice is highly complex.

1.2 THE RESEARCH PROGRAMME

The programme commenced late in 1985, with the aid of a grant from the Economic and Social Research Council to investigate developments in joint consultation within large, multi-plant, heavily unionised private sector companies in the United Kingdom. This was stimulated by survey evidence which indicated a resurgence in joint consultative committees (JCCs) during the 1970s when previous theorising would have suggested a decline. More important than evaluating the extent of JCCs, however, we felt it was crucial to assess whether or not they had undergone a character change as well. In addition, we wished to incorporate into the analysis developments in direct employee involvement. Consequently, our study was originally broadly defined as participation, so including concepts such as involvement and communications, and to a lesser extent collective bargaining. As the research progressed, it became apparent that to restrict our analysis to employee involvement alone would severely limit the value of our findings, since other aspects of management–union relations are so inextricably bound up with employee involvement (EI). Because of this, we broadened the study to include an analysis of employee relations more generally, thus incorporating issues relating to union recognition and support, collective bargaining, work organisation and flexibility, and management style, as well as employee involvement.

Why use the term 'employee relations' rather than the more traditional 'industrial relations'? The use of employee relations has become more common in recent years for at least three reasons. First, through slippage, whereby the term becomes fashionable, and enters the language for no positive reason other than it is used elsewhere. Second, because it is a term increasingly used by practitioners to label that part of the personnel function concerned with the regulation of relations (collective and individual) between employer and employee. For example, some companies now refer to employee relations officers or managers when a number of years ago these people would have commanded the title of industrial relations. Similarly, one of the Institute of Personnel Management's (IPM) three Stage Two examinations is Employee (rather than Industrial) Relations. Third, the term may be used because employee relations has actual academic differences from industrial relations, most notably in the focus on management alone (rather than all the parties to the employment relationship) and on contemporary practices (rather than on history and development as well as current activity). There is also the greater emphasis on informal and individual aspects of management–employee relations rather than on collective bargaining and representative institutions. We have chosen to use 'employee relations' principally for the second reason, although we also have some sympathy with the perspective that there are more fundamental differences between the two terms.

The second key feature of the investigation was its focus on specific types of company. We deliberately chose to analyse developments in the private sector because this offered more scope for variation between organisations than did the public sector. We wanted to examine unionised establishments because this was felt to represent a harsher terrain in which consultation or other forms of employee involvement could operate, and it also provided us with the opportunity of evaluating the extent to which trade unions were able to sustain former levels of influence over the conduct of employee relations. Our decision to concentrate on multi-plant companies provided us with another advantage, namely that of comparing practices between different establishments within a single firm, and of assessing the influence of senior management beyond the plant on shop floor practice. As indicated above, we were keen to discover the extent to which the practice of employee relations accorded with the intentions of policy makers.

In seeking appropriate case study companies, we secured initial interviews with personnel practitioners at over fifty different establishments, some of which – though not many – were part of the same parent company. All were located in the North or North West of England. Our objective at these initial meetings was to collect basic information about the company, especially its employee relations systems, and about EI in particular. We only followed up these leads in the event of the company's fulfilling the desired criteria (unionised, multi-plant, evidence of EI), which reduced the size of the sample. Equally, of course, a number of the companies were unwilling to continue with research beyond this stage. Further interviews were arranged in about twenty cases; in the case of our initial contact being at divisional or central HQ, we followed up leads at individual plants; in some cases, we pursued contacts at other plants within the same company, whilst in others, we talked with other managers at the establishment. Again, some dropped out at this stage, leaving about a dozen which offered the potential of continuing with the research. In each of these organisations, we then made contact with the senior shop stewards on site in order to gain their commitment to the research.

We had also determined at the outset of the research that a longitudinal study was preferable to a series of discrete case studies in which the researcher spends no more than a few weeks in contact with each of the companies. This approach gave us the opportunity of analysing relations over a period of time (albeit only up to two years), getting to know key individuals very well, and following through initiatives as they were put into practice. This approach also meant that when the time came to interview shop floor employees, we were well aware of the key issues at the establishment, could focus our questions much more specifically and could be reasonably assured of their cooperation. Of course, there are problems with a longitudinal approach owing to wastage, since establishments are 'lost' for a variety of reasons; for example, the closure of one plant at which we were doing our study, a merger between two multinationals which prevented us from completing our study in another, or the long-term absence of a principal contact which made our study less relevant to yet another company. Also, we were unable to conclude our research at several plants because of insufficient time to undertake an analysis of shop floor opinion. Eventually we interviewed our target range fully in four companies (six establishments), and these form the basis of the empirical material in subsequent chapters.

In each of the case study companies, we used a range of methods in order to generate the information required to produce a comprehensive and meaningful case study (see Denzin (1970, p. 13) for a discussion of 'multiple triangulation'). Interviews comprised the principal method of data collection, although these varied considerably in form and detail between establishments and respondents. We conducted loosely structured interviews with senior personnel managers and shop stewards in each establishment so as to help us focus on the key issues; a checklist was used so as to ensure that all the areas were covered in the interview, but we generally left respondents free to develop their own ideas, picking up on outstanding questions later in the interview or at a subsequent meeting. Such interviews could last up to a couple of hours at a time, and several of these people we saw on numerous occasions. The most structured interviews were with shop floor workers, supervisors and line managers, since we had more specific questions to address to them, for example, about the regularity of team briefing in their department, its message, its impact, and its acceptance on the shop floor, or about the precise nature of the jobs they did. These interviews tended to be shorter, usually between half an hour and an hour. At each site, we interviewed a cross section of staff from different departments and levels, thus resulting in fifteen to twenty-five respondents in each case, in addition to those with personnel management and the senior stewards. It was not our intention to interview a statistically representative sample of respondents, but rather to ensure that the coverage was sufficient to write a soundly-based case study.

Besides conducting interviews, we also collected a mass of information from company documentation, such as minutes of consultative and negotiating meetings, copies of management letters to employees, management reviews of EI techniques, as well as formal agreements between the company and the unions. In some cases, we were able to inspect minutes of meetings going back over a number of years, and these allowed us to appreciate the way in which employee relations had developed over the last decade. For the companies which had them, we also received copies of their newspapers and house journals (including those printed at the site), and a copy of any statements on corporate philosophy. Wherever possible, we 'grounded' the data gained from the interviews by observing committees, team briefing, or people at work. We had extensive tours of each workplace, and plenty of opportunity to stop and talk with staff on an informal basis. In two of the companies, we attended a number of JCC meetings, and were therefore able to gauge the way in which the meetings operated in practice, rather than having to rely on minutes or participants' assessments. Unfortunately, we were not able to observe meetings or presentations at every site, either because the information disclosed was felt to be commercially sensitive, or because the meetings were held *in camera*; however, we were allowed access to most activities at the establishments, and we did manage to achieve an extremely high level of cooperation in all cases.

A further component of our research design was to get access to personnel beyond the level of the specific establishment in which our work was concentrated. This was important for two reasons; first, we wanted to assess the influence of corporate or divisional head office over employee relations at the individual plants. In all four companies we were able to interview managers from higher levels, whether this were central, divisional or regional, or a combination of these. Second, we were keen to compare employee relations practices at other locations within the company with the one in which we undertook our detailed investigation. In the case of the chemical company, we interviewed at three other production plants, and observed the JCC at one of these. This proved helpful in assessing the degree to which the establishments really were autonomous from higher levels or whether, even with a highly centralised system, there was still room for manoeuvre between sites. In a final effort to minimise any inaccuracies in our knowledge of these companies, we wrote feedback reports for the personnel involved, and this led to further corrections and insights, as well as some disagreement about our interpretation of events. Overall, we feel that the range of techniques used and personnel interviewed provided us with a relatively clear picture of employee relations within these companies, although we are fully aware that there are bound to be gaps in our knowledge of these locations. In the accounts which follow, we have also inserted a number of insignificant inaccuracies in an attempt to preserve the anonymity of the companies involved.

Before moving on to outline the structure of the book, we also need to comment on the typicality of the four case studies. Our final 'sample' was drawn from four different industries which between them cover a large spectrum of manual employment in the private sector; chemicals, food, retailing and engineering. There are also differences between the establishments in terms of the number of staff employed at the time of our research, as well as growth or decline over the course of the 1980s. Two of the sites employed few women on the shop floor, whilst in the other two, women formed a significant proportion of the workforce. In addition, there were many other differences between the companies; for example, in the type and number of unions recognised, the level at which collective bargaining took place, the techniques used for employee involvement, and the product markets in which the companies competed. However, we cannot claim that the results of this study are representative of British industry as a whole, or that grand generalisations can be made from its findings. Nor can we argue that these companies are typical of the industry from which they are drawn, and in some cases (for example, the retail firm) they are patently not. But it was never our intention to construct a representative sample, rather to adopt a methodology which allowed us to examine four companies in depth, so as to provide detailed case study information, as well as to test out the validity of recent hypotheses about the nature of employee relations in the 1980s. In short, we view this qualitative study as a valuable complement to, and extension of, recent quantitative surveys of British workplace employee relations; both serve quite different and necessary purposes.

1.3 STRUCTURE OF THE BOOK

Basically, the book can be divided into three parts: a literature review, which comprises three chapters; an examination of the four case studies; and a reanalysis of previous research in the light of the findings from these cases. In Chapter 2, we review survey and case study material reporting on changes in the nature of employee relations over the last two decades, and in particular that relating to the 1980s. Specifically, we examine ideas about management support for and opposition to union organisation in the workplace, the character of collective bargaining, the nature of flexibility at work, and the effect of employee involvement on the role of trade unions. By focusing our analysis on employee relations, it is easy to assume that this constitutes the predominant concern of employers, and that all their actions are aimed at resolving the 'problem' of labour. In Chapter 3, we consider these arguments in greater depth, and attempt to define the term 'management strategy' more precisely by breaking it up into its constituent parts. We also deal with questions concerning the centrality of labour relations to corporate decision-making, and the way in which management policies are amended, thwarted, resisted, or approved, as they work their way down the hierarchy. But strategies and styles vary between organisations, and they are also influenced by the context within which the company operates; this is the subject of Chapter 4, where we specifically analyse the notion of management style, and theorise about the connection between this and the product markets in which the company competes. In addition to considering the effect of product markets on the management of employee relations, we also point out the ways in which senior managers can influence the market, as well as utilise arguments about competitive conditions in order to legitimise actions which they would have taken in any event.

In the next four chapters, we provide details on the case study companies, following a broadly similar format in each. We describe the way in which work is organised and the degree to which flexibility is achieved at each site, the nature of the product market(s), the philosophy and style of management, collective bargaining, workplace union organisation, and forms of employee involvement. In each case, our objective is to provide a fairly full picture of employee relations in the company so that, within the space constraints available, readers will be able to form their own impressions of the sites under investigation. Each company was of interest for a variety of reasons; the chemical plant (Ichem) was the most progressive in its approach to employee relations, had gone further to harmonising conditions between blue and white collar employees, and was the nearest to HRM in our study. Foodpack (the food plant) had introduced a whole range of policies and practices to reform its employee relations – including a three-year pay deal and a variety of initiatives to disclose information to the shop floor – but it still recognised five separate unions. The retail outlet (Multistores) is relatively unusual for that sector in that it recognises unions, but the company has also recently implemented team briefing, customer care committees, and other EI techniques in order to supplement its JCC structure. Typeng (the engineering company) differs from the rest of our case study sites in a number of ways; it retains many of its adversarial traditions, the unions maintain a monopoly over formal channels of communication in the factory, and it has least direct EI.

In the final part of the book, we reanalyse the case study material and compare it with the available literature on the subject. In Chapter 9, we focus on the issues raised in the first two chapters, concluding that the evidence from these case studies offers relatively little support for recent theories of workplace industrial relations. Accordingly, we question the basis and applicability of a number of these proposals: sponsorship, roll-back, institutional separation, or the use by employers of EI for the direct undermining of trade unionism in the workplace. Finally, in Chapter 10, we re-examine the material on management style, before suggesting a number of ways in which this can be improved. We also attempt to clarify our understanding of product market circumstances so as to allow for comparisons between organisations. In conclusion, we propose a model that analyses the links between product markets, management style, trade unions, employees, and product quality. It is hoped that this will provide a basis for more comprehensive and realistic evaluations of the way in which patterns of employee relations are changing, as well as revealing the reasons behind these changes.

2 · EMPLOYEE RELATIONS IN TRANSITION

2.1 INTRODUCTION

In Chapter 1 we outlined two particular themes in the management of employee relations, namely 'macho management' and 'human resource management', both of which appear to have gained in currency over the 1980s. We also urged caution in their usage, given that there has been so little firm evidence to assess the applicability and extensiveness of such approaches within British industry, although there is much rhetoric about their presence. In this chapter, we shall analyse the survey and case study data that has emerged over the past two decades and argue that, whilst there have clearly been changes in the character of employee relations over this period, there has not been the substantial realignment which proponents of Thatcherism would have us believe.

We are fortunate that a number of surveys of employee relations have been carried out since the early 1970s which enable us to chart the principal changes in practice. In 1978, Brown conducted a survey of industrial relations managers in 970 *manufacturing* establishments employing more than fifty people, and this allows for an 'assessment of change over the intervening decade', that is, between 1968 and 1978 (1981, p. 1). Two surveys by a consortium of organisations (the Department of Employment, the Economic and Social Research Council, the Policy Studies Institute and ACAS) were undertaken in 1980 and 1984, thus enabling us to analyse changes between 1975 and 1984 (Daniel and Millward, 1983; Millward and Stevens, 1986). These were more representative of the economy as a whole, since they involved interviews with representatives of management and unions in the service sector (public and private) as well as manufacturing, and also smaller workplaces (n=25) were covered. In addition, information from two other studies will be used as appropriate; Batstone (1984) undertook a postal survey of 133 personnel managers in manufacturing in 1983, getting comparisons with the earlier Brown survey by reweighting the sample; secondly, Edwards (1987) interviewed 229 factory managers in large manufacturing plants (employing 250 or more) in order to assess the extent of change between 1981 and 1984. This study is also useful because it taps the opinions of general managers, rather than relying solely on personnel and industrial relations specialists.

To help organise the remainder of the chapter, we shall deal with the literature in relation to three key questions:

- To what extent have employers continued to recognise and deal with trade unions in the workplace, given the much changed economic, political and legal circumstances of the 1980s?
- How have the institutions and outputs of the collective bargaining process, including workforce flexibility, changed since the 1970s?
- Is there any evidence to support the view that employers are using mechanisms for employee involvement – such as joint consultation, team briefing and quality circles – to undermine the activities of trade unions?

2.2 WORKPLACE UNION ORGANISATON

Although they differ to some extent, all of the surveys and much of the case study work indicates that the 1970s was a decade of change for the organisation of management and unions in the workplace. The personnel function increased in importance, especially if measured by the likelihood of board representation (Brown, 1981, p. 32; Daniel and Millward, 1983, pp. 286–7), largely owing to the employment protection legislation of the decade and the activities of trade unions (see Batstone, 1984, p. 195 for a counter argument). Tied in with an enhanced role for the personnel function was an equally significant increase in the number of shop stewards, particularly those who were full time on union business. For example, Brown estimated that almost 12 per cent of large manufacturing establishments had someone occupying such a role in 1978, which represented a fourfold increase over the decade (p. 64). Not surprisingly, these full-time union representatives tended to be concentrated in the largest workplaces, with more than two-thirds of establishments employing over 1,000 people having at least one steward who spent all of his or her time on union business (Daniel and Millward, 1983, p. 34). All the other indicators of management–union activity showed similar tendencies, with increases in time off for training, check off arrangements, and joint shop steward meetings, either on their own or with management (Daniel and Millward, 1983, pp. 37, 74, 101; Brown, 1981, p. 79). Without doubt, the position of workplace union representatives had been formally strengthened by the end of the 1970s.

At the same time, there is considerable agreement that the closed shop became more extensive between the mid-1960s and 1980, not only within manufacturing but also in other sectors (Brown 1981, p. 56; Daniel and Millward, 1983, p. 280; Dunn and Gennard, 1984, pp. 15–16). In 1978, for example, Dunn and Gennard estimated that over five million employees were covered by closed shop arrangements, that is in excess of 40 per cent of union members. Over 80 per cent of these closed shops were of the 'post-entry' type, whereby employees are required to join a recognised trade union within a specified period of commencing employment (Gennard *et al.*, 1980, pp. 16–22). In addition, the closed shop had also spread into what had previously been regarded as 'open' industries, such as food, drink and tobacco, clothing and footwear, transport and communications, and public utilities, as well as into non-manual occupations (McCarthy, 1964, p. 52; Gennard *et al.*, 1980, p. 18). It appears that the closed shop also changed in character over the 1970s, and the newer arrangements were much more likely to be written, formal, openly-agreed documents which had been negotiated by management and unions, rather than imposed by the latter (Gennard *et al.*, 1980, p. 21). As Brown noted, 'the closed shop as a reflection of workplace solidarity may be increasingly replaced by an institution which is seen by management and the wider union primarily as an instrument of procedural discipline' (1981, p. 59). In short, it could be argued that some of the traditional indicators of union strength, such as the closed shop, owed their existence more to management acquiescence or encouragement than to union power.

This view is most explicitly presented in Purcell's elaboration of a 'strategy for management control in industrial relations', pulled together with only a little embroidery from the activities of large corporations in the late 1970s (Purcell and Smith, 1979, pp. 27–58). His argument largely revolves around Fox's description of a 'sophisticated modern' style of industrial relations management (we shall return to this in Chapter 4). Within this approach, management legitimises the union's role as 'conducive to its own interests as measured by stability, promotion of consent, bureaucratic regulation, effective communication or the handling of change' (Fox, 1974, p. 302). Purcell categorises this strategy into eight elements, of which three are relevant to this discussion since they relate to workplace union organisation. First, the corporation should encourage union membership and support the closed shop where appropriate, even though the latter may be distasteful to some senior managers, since this 'may give some stability to industrial relations, reduce the risk of inter-union membership squabbles, and provide a useful bargaining counter (Purcell, 1979, p. 29). Aside from the pragmatic advantages of the closed shop in preventing unrecognised unions from gaining toe-hold in the company, it may also positively influence the character of relationships with the union(s) already recognised (pp. 31–2). Secondly, given that some employees may feel they have been forced into union membership against their will, the corporation should encourage membership participation in the union(s), since the 'uninterested majority' can be a source of strength for the company in 'controlling' the leadership if it fails to represent rank and file interests. In this connection, the company ought to allow for full-time senior stewards, give time off for union activities, and encourage representatives to be adequately trained (pp. 32–4). Thirdly, the corporation should encourage inter-union cooperation and the development of joint shop steward committees in order to ensure that the unions work together; it may even go so far as to 'seek to engender a feeling of company unionism' (p. 35). The aim will to be ensure that industrial relations are centralised at establishment level, partly via explicit support for the senior stewards, but also by the careful design of payment systems which inhibit the development of sectional bargaining (p. 36). Although such a 'strategy' inevitably begs many questions, not least in terms of management omniscience and omnipotence (see Chapter 3 for a discussion of this wider question), it does provide a useful vehicle for assessing the place of trade unionism within companies at the end of the 1970s, and in particular the extent to which management may have encouraged the development of shop steward organisation and the closed shop.

The notion that managements actively 'sponsored' the growth of shop steward organisation during the course of the 1970s is not confined to Purcell, and indeed the major exponents of this thesis were Terry (1978; 1983) and Willman (1980), to some extent supported by Brown (1973; 1981). Terry differentiates between an engineering paradigm (which included other conventionally well-organised industries such as printing), wherein shop stewards emerged independently of management, and a non-engineering paradigm, in which management played a significant part in the development of the steward netwwork (pp. 5–6). In the case of the 'sponsored' organisations, management have influenced the shape of this body by the judicious granting of facilities, as well as more indirectly by the choice of particular forms of procedural machinery and wage payment systems (p. 10). However, it is inaccurate, according to Terry (p. 10) to view these organisations as nothing more than extensions of the personnel management function, and it is also clear that management influence was more likely to be indirect than 'for its own sake'. In other words, the centralisation of shop steward organisation was a consequence of unions adapting their plant level structures in the context of the innovations and reforms pursued by management (pp. 12–13). Although Willman criticises certain aspects of Terry's approach (1980, pp. 42–3), he broadly follows the same line of reasoning; for Willman, the crucial distinction between sponsored and 'independent' shop steward organisations is in the kinds of policy which are pursued by them. Independent organisations seek to exert influence on the effort bargain *and* assist in the rationalisation of the personnel function, whereas sponsored organisations merely pursue the latter (p. 45). However, both Terry and Willman suggest that there will be little difference in the configuration of these two types of body, for example in terms of hierarchies or in the number of full-time stewards.

Whilst it is clear that managements did substantially assist the development of steward organisations, both directly and indirectly if it suited their own interests, the sponsorship argument can be overplayed. At the very least, it seems to conflate managerial activity regarding shop stewards with other aspects of their employment and more general business practices, and to give primacy to a consequence – intended or otherwise – of changes elsewhere (such as in the payment system). Furthermore, the thesis of managerial sponsorship isolates the analysis of shop stewards from other factors in the environment, for example those relating to the strength of the workers involved. As Batstone suggests, 'an analysis of "sponsored" steward organisations has to pose and answer the question of why stewards did not previously develop autonomously: the answer is likely to relate to the inherent weaknesses of the workers concerned' (1984, p. 108). Indeed, it is unlikely that managements would encourage developments in shop steward organisation without some form of worker pressure; as Batstone notes, in reinterpreting Terry's evidence, there seems to have been 'some challenge from the shop floor which induced management to engage in sponsorship. This fusion of sponsorship and worker pressure appears to apply more generally' (1984, p. 107; see also Spencer 1985, p. 24). More fundamentally, the evidence does not support the view that sponsored organisations are more likely to comply with managerial actions either. Batstone found that greater union involvement had not made stewards more sympathetic or less obstructive towards management (1984, p. 257). It is also accepted that these organisations may change their character over time, thus casting yet more doubts upon the significance of sponsorship as an explanatory device (Marchington and Armstrong, 1983, p. 39; Batstone, 1984, p. 108).

A somewhat similar set of arguments can be applied to an analysis of the closed shop, typically seen as a prime indicator of union power. At the time of McCarthy's survey in the early 1960s, this view was probably an accurate reflection of the nature of such arrangements, given that they were concentrated in a relatively small number of industries; moreover, many were of the pre-entry type, whereby potential applicants were required to be union members in order to gain an interview for a job (McCarthy, 1964; Dunn and Gennard, 1984). The character of the closed shop had changed so extensively by the late 1970s that Hart could write of an institution 'loved' by employers (1979, pp. 352–4). The managers in her survey felt that the principal advantages of the closed shop to them were those of order, predictability and discipline, thus reinforcing a tendency towards greater formalisation and regulation (p. 354). Paradoxically, she argues, it is unions who should be anxious about the spread of compulsory membership.

Whilst Dunn and Gennard lend some support to this explanation for the growth of the closed shop, they also suggest an alternative view. Broadly, they put forward two theories of the closed shop, the 'hard' and the 'soft' (1984, pp. 41–55). The hard theory views the closed shop as a creature of either union power or a joint union–management agreement to promote order and stability in the workplace; whatever the motivation, it is seen as 'having a significant impact upon industrial relations', likely to produce significant benefits (p. 41). The soft theory, conversely, views the closed shop as 'a marginal factor in industrial relations, a side effect of procedural reform, perhaps playing a tidying role where union membership is already high' (p. 89). Whilst the hard theory is said to account for the development of the closed shop in the late 1960s and the early 1970s, it is reckoned that the soft theory became more relevant in the latter part of the decade. The authors argue that managements 'continued to concede UMAs where union membership was high because they could see few disadvantages and accepted that it fitted with the logic of formal joint regulation' (p. 89). Whatever the explanation, the closed shop changed in character as it became more extensive.

In totality, therefore, the 1970s saw substantial changes in the nature of workplace industrial relations, along the lines promoted by Donovan and the CIR, although not necessarily because of their attempts at reform. As Brown (1981, p. 79) suggests (about manufacturing, though it could have been applied more broadly), 'the rapid spread of closed shop agreements, check-off arrangements, full-time stewards . . . all tell of a management involvement in workplace union administration which was unthinkable a decade ago'. Following the 'managerial sponsorship' argument, he then queries the ability of steward organisations to sustain this enhanced position in a worsening economic climate, especially where their facilities and procedures owe more to 'the administrative needs of management than to the bargaining achievements of the workforce' (p. 120). However, as we have seen above, whilst management may have become much more involved in the development and form of workplace union arrangements during the 1970s, the pressure (potential or actual) of workers themselves should not be discounted. Thus, rather than expecting a significant decline in workplace union organisation during the 1980s (as the pure sponsorship argument might suggest), these institutions may show themselves more resilient to a managerial onslaught, should one be forthcoming. Indeed, applying Dunn and Gennard's 'soft' theory of the closed shop to the position of workplace union organisation as a whole, there must be doubts as to whether management would actually *want* to remove the institutional bases of the unions even if they had the opportunity.

Despite the sweeping changes in the political, economic and legal environment in Britain over the course of the 1980s, all the surveys indicate a remarkable degree of continuity and stability in the extensiveness of workplace union organisation. Whilst union membership has fallen considerably over the decade, this loss can largely be explained by shifts in the distribution of employment (by sector and workplace size) as well as higher levels of unemployment. According to Millward and Stevens (1986, p. 303), 'managements in those workplaces with [union] members present were no less likely to recognise the appropriate unions' over the period between 1980 and 1984, and there has been little evidence of employers withdrawing recognition from those unions which already had it at the start of the decade (p. 69). Overall, there was only a slight fall in the percentage level of union membership in the large establishments covered by the Batstone (1984, pp. 209–11) and Edwards (1987, p. 117) surveys of manufacturing industry. From other quarters, there is evidence of a growth in the number of new plants which are non-union (Beaumont, 1986, 1987), although a contrary view is expressed by Sproull and MacInnes (1987).

The total number of shop stewards increased slightly between 1980 and 1984, but this does in fact mask a decline in manual representatives within manufacturing and the private service sectors; conversely, the numbers in the public sector increased substantially (1986, p. 84). Similarly, the number of full-time stewards remained at the 1980 level, but once again, those in manufacturing fell by 35 per cent, and in the private service sector the absolute number of manual stewards halved over the period. Edwards' survey provides support for this view of decline (p. 117), although Batstone's does not (p. 216). The decline in the number of full-time stewards has been described as the 'roll-back' of workplace organisation, since there is 'well documented evidence from particular companies of determined management efforts to reduce the number of full-time shop stewards' (Terry, 1983, p. 55). Although this was associated with other attempts to restrict the activity of shop stewards (such as in their ability to move around the workplace without permission), Terry concedes that management was not concerned to destroy workplace organisation as a whole, but rather to 'achieve a reduction in the scope and power of shop stewards while maintaining much of the formal structure' (p. 55).

Other anecdotal experience confirms this, but it is difficult to determine the precise extent of these more aggressive approaches (Marchington, 1988a, pp. 213–14). More seriously, it cannot be assumed that a decline in the number of full-time stewards automatically means that management is seeking to reduce the role of the workplace union, as Terry's terminology implies. Indeed, as plant size declines, it would not seem unreasonable for employers to question the cost or need for a representative who is full-time on union duties, without this being interpreted as part of the 'roll-back' of workplace organisation. Some reduction in the number and type of stewards may be expected, given the drop in union membership during the 1980s, and the evidence indicates that 'the number of representatives has declined more slowly than the number of members' (Millward and Stevens, 1986, p. 87). In short, the conventional wisdom of 1980s industrial relations is that the majority of employers have not mounted a direct attack on workplace union organisation even though, perhaps for other reasons, there has been some reduction in certain facilities (Batstone, 1984, p. 260; Batstone and Gourlay, 1986, p. 107; Edwards, 1987, p. 116).

Although the surveys point to a large element of continuity in relations between managements and shop stewards, the closed shop has been subject to a rather more vigorous legal and political onslaught during the 1980s. Given the variety of attempts by the government to alter the nature and extent of union membership agreements, employers have certainly had the opportunity to retract from agreements signed during the previous decades. The

Millward and Stevens survey confirms that the closed shop has become less extensive, with a fall of one-third in the number of employees covered by such arrangements, although the number of establishments with a closed shop has not declined to the same extent (pp. 102–7). As with stewards, the closed shop has declined most in the private manufacturing sector, and large establishments in all sectors (employing over 1,000 manual workers) have suffered more than average. Conversely, Edwards (1987, p. 117) finds that large manufacturing plants (in his case those with over 250 employees) were just as likely to have 100 per cent manual union density in 1984 as they had six years before, although it should be recalled that this is not strictly the same thing as a closed shop agreement (Gennard *et al.*, 1980, pp. 16–17). Support for Edwards' view comes from Batstone and Gourlay's survey of shop stewards, which indicated little management opposition to the closed shop where it already existed (1986, p. 60).

It is clear from the Millward and Stevens survey that there have been changes in the extensiveness of closed shop arrangements since the 1970s, but the exact nature and location of these changes is more difficult to determine. Apart from well-known exceptions in the public sector, most employers who entered the 1980s with a closed shop have been unlikely to try to remove this (Dunn and Gennard, 1984, pp. 149–50); however, it is equally true that very few new closed shop agreements have been signed during this period either (Millward and Stevens, 1986, p. 306). Many employers appear to have maintained a *de facto* arrangement with shop stewards that new starters will be encouraged to join the appropriate union, whilst at the same time refusing to sack any individual who refuses to join or who resigns his or her membership; to some extent, this saves employers the trouble and difficulty of balloting in order to 'legalise' their closed shop arrangements (Roberts, 1984). More broadly, this also seems to strengthen the 'soft' theory of union membership agreements put forward by Dunn and Gennard, particularly in the context of 1980s employee relations.

There is, therefore, broad agreement that the institutions of workplace union organisation have held up remarkably well during the Thatcher years (see also MacInnes, 1987). However, we also need to offer an explanation for this level of continuity at a time of considerable economic change and upheaval, as well as make an assessment about whether the *nature* of shop steward organisation has changed in those companies which continue to deal with trade unions, even if its extensiveness has not.

Two sets of arguments seem to be relevant here; these relate to the *desire* and the *ability* of employers to initiate adjustments. There are at least three sets of reasons why employers may not wish to change their arrangements with the trade unions in the workplace. First, employers may feel that trade unions represent a useful channel through which to deal with collective affairs – such as pay bargaining, the introduction of new technology, or dispute resolution – and that they consequently assist in the maintenance of order and stability in the workplace (Marchington, 1988b, p. 64). Secondly, it can be argued that employers are more concerned with issues other than those relating to trade unions and, provided the latter do not present too great an obstacle to the achievement of more important goals, their presence can be tolerated. This is even more relevant if trade unions are not engaged in a continual struggle with employers, but see cooperation as a more appropriate stance in difficult economic circumstances (Chadwick, 1983, p. 10; Batstone, 1984, p. 310). As Terry (1986, p. 177) suggests, the interests of workers and managers may be temporarily aligned, and both worker and management power may be directed along the same lines, for example to ensure company survival or avoid compulsory redundancies. Cooperation may therefore represent 'an optimum strategy for the present and for maintaining strong formal workplace organisation, and its potential for the future' (Batstone and Gourlay, 1986, p. 265). Whether or not this is an indication of shop steward weakness or resilience is, of course, an empirical question to be addressed in different workplaces, but on the basis of a variety of case studies, Terry (1986, p. 176) suggests extremely tentatively ('hedged about with qualifications') that they are now weaker. Part of his argument relates to the link between collective bargaining and joint consultation, which is considered in a subsequent section. Finally, employers may desist from using their potential power at a time of comparative advantage, for fear of a future backlash from the trade unions, should conditions change and stewards seek to settle old scores (Marchington, 1988b, p. 64). Indeed, it might be argued that 'responsible' workplace union organisation and 'responsive' management are mutually reinforcing.

Even if they have the desire to remove the institutional base of trade unionism from the workplace, employers, of course, may lack the ability to effect this in the short run. Whilst the state of the national labour market (that is, the level of unemployment) may give signals to employers that a more forceful approach is possible, it is not usually a simple matter to withdraw union recognition, still less to sack all workers and replace them with equally qualified individuals at short notice. Labour market surpluses at a macro level frequently coexist with shortages at a local level, and there is often a lack of suitable substitute labour available to the firm (Batstone, 1984, p. 312; Kelly, 1987, pp. 279–80). Secondly, many employers are likely to show caution in their dealings with trade unions – unless they are convinced that they will win, or they perceive no alternative to a fight – for fear they might encounter new forms of resistance or give workers a focus for struggle in the workplace (Batstone, 1984, p. 311; Marchington, 1988b, p. 64). Finally, rather than enhancing employer strength, competitive product markets may actually reduce it, since companies are even more dependent upon continuity of production or service to ensure that orders are delivered on time (Kelly, 1987, p. 279). In other words, a more competitive product market is a source both of strength and weakness for employers in their dealings with employees.

Although there have been some institutional changes in the position of workplace trade unionism during the course of the 1980s, and there have been a number of well-publicised and highly successful assaults on unions in certain organisations, what is more significant is the extent of continuity since the 1970s. At first sight, this appears strange. However, the foregoing analysis makes this appear more plausible; in particular, whilst not denying the role of management in encouraging the sophistication of steward organisations during the 1970s, it is clear that their influence has been overestimated. Moreover, it is also apparent that decisions to extend and formalise the position of unions in the workplace, through closed shop agreements for example, may have been less proactive than previously assumed, and have constituted a rather low-key response to a matter of minor significance. If this was the case in the 1970s, when unions were generally acknowledged to have greater power than in the current climate, it is more likely to be relevant now. In short, even if employers now have the ability to dismantle union agreements, it may not appear to be worth the effort, given other more pressing needs both within and outside the employee relations arena. In the case of the former, appropriate levels for collective bargaining, workforce flexibility and employee involvement appear to have been particularly central to the interests and concerns of employers during the 1980s (Edwards, 1987, p. 195; Batstone, 1988, p. 190); we will now turn our attention to an investigation of these.

2.3 COLLECTIVE BARGAINING AND WORKFORCE FLEXIBILITY

For the twenty years preceding and following the end of the Second World War, the principal method for determining the pay of manual workers was collective bargaining conducted on a multi-employer, industry-wide basis. By the end of the 1970s, Brown noted that in private sector manufacturing this pattern had changed substantially, and he could write of 'the rise in significance of single employer bargaining' (1981, p. 24). Nevertheless, of those employers who engaged in collective bargaining (fewer than one in ten of his sample did not), approximately 40 per cent still regarded multi-employer arrangements as the most important level for the determination of manual worker pay. Of the remainder, the vast majority reported that negotiations at establishment level were more important than those covering the company as a whole (p. 8).

However, despite this general picture, a crucial observation from the Brown study of manufacturing is the extent of *diversity* in arrangements between different industries and types of establishment. For example, even though the establishment was the most important level overall, in five of the eleven industries surveyed, multi-employer arrangements were considerably more important. Similarly, the size of the establishment also showed a significant association with bargaining structure, with multi-employer arrangements proving more important to smaller workplaces; the converse applied in larger companies, although corporate level bargaining appeared particularly significant in this situation (p. 9). Brown therefore concluded that 'British manufacturing industry is likely to have a mixture of single and multi-employer bargaining for the foreseeable future' (p. 25). The 1980 Workplace

Industrial Relations Survey broadly confirmed this picture for manufacturing, and also demonstrated that the system of pay determination in Britain showed even greater variation between sectors. For example, national bargaining remained predominant within the public sector, and to a lesser extent in private services; at the same time, single employer bargaining in private services was twice as likely to be at corporate level than at the establishment (Daniel and Millward, 1983, p. 188). The size factor was again important, with single employer bargaining more likely in larger workplaces, whilst the larger the enterprise the more importance was attached to corporate bargaining (p. 190).

By 1984, collective bargaining was the principal method of pay determination for manual workers in fewer manufacturing establishments than in 1980 (55 per cent compared with 65 per cent); this was partly due to the smaller proportion of large workplaces in the sector, but also to the reduced likelihood that smaller establishments would engage in collective bargaining (Millward and Stevens, 1986, p. 229). For the remainder, there had been a slight shift from establishment to corporate level, but this was only significant for non-manual employees (p. 231). Little change had occurred to the structure of negotiations within private services as a whole since 1980, with multi-employer arrangements continuing to be the most important, despite the increasing significance of both corporate and establishment arrangements (p. 238). In line with the marginal trend towards corporate bargaining, the survey also illustrated the influence of more senior managers over pay negotiations at establishment level; in almost two-thirds of the cases, consultations with higher level management took place before negotiations commenced, and in half the cases after bargaining had started (p. 243). This led Brown, in a review of the survey findings, to comment: 'In the metaphor much-loved by frustrated trade union officers, the management monkey with whom they negotiate is kept on a short chain by the corporate organ grinder.' (1987, p. 293).

Before discussing the possible reasons for employers choosing different bargaining structures, we also need to say something about pay increases. Data from the CBI Databank has been analysed in depth for the five years up to 1984 by Gregory and her colleagues, and they identify consistent 'winners and losers' over this period (1985, p. 347); of relevance to the case studies analysed later in this book, chemicals and FDT (food, drink and tobacco) had significantly higher than average settlements, whilst mechanical engineering was a consistent loser (p. 348). However, there was no evidence that winners and losers could be differentiated on the basis of the level at which bargaining took place; conversely, the authors argue, 'the pay settlement has been largely shaped by the economic circumstances of the industry and the firm' (1986, p. 229). Moreover, they suggest that 'employers who are reasonably secure in the product market are rewarding those well-established employees who are relatively secure in the labour market' (1986, p. 230). Indeed, according to the CBI respondents, the most significant upward pressures on pay – aside from the cost of living – have been company profits and the need to recruit and retain staff (1985, p. 350). As Roots (1986, p. 7) reminds us, 'employers are not interested in wage rates, but in labour costs. Firms are willing to grant wage increases if their labour costs do not go up (and) the average company has a rapidly falling wage bill.' Pay settlements are clearly conditioned by the circumstances confronting an employer rather than any 'national interest'.

As we indicated above, a key feature of employee relations is the choice of bargaining levels, that is plant/establishment, division, corporate, or multi-employer, or indeed a mixture of several of these. Lists specifying the relative advantages and disadvantages of centralised or decentralised bargaining arrangements can be found in a number of publications (Beaumont et al., 1980, pp. 136–9; Thomason, 1981, pp. 469–71), but these tell us little about the reasons why a particular company manages to achieve the structure it does, nor how this was put into effect. As with many 'best-fit' contingency approaches, the analysis of how bargaining levels are chosen almost becomes a straightforward technical decision, with no allowance for the role that political processes within companies play in determining such issues. There is also the associated drawback that multi-employer and corporate arrangements are merged into one category, as are those at and below plant level, thus reducing the value of such lists yet further.

An alternative and potentially more fruitful line of inquiry has been to focus on the notion of 'institutional separation' (Purcell, 1983, p. 8). This can take two forms; first, it can be applied to functional distinctions between personnel and other managers at the same – usually corporate – level. Collective bargaining is dealt with by specialist industrial relations and personnel managers, who perform a 'buffer' or 'gatekeeper' role, thus keeping trade unions away from other senior managers who are therefore free to take strategic decisions without the need for bargained solutions (Purcell, 1983, p. 9). Alternatively, it can relate to a distinction between the levels at which bargaining and strategic decision-making take place. Thus, Kinnie (1986, p. 17) suggests that there is a

> mismatch or inconsistency in common between the levels at which strategic industrial relations decisions are taken and the level of collective bargaining. This incongruency or lack of fit is not the result of accident, but is a policy pursued consciously by management to maintain their prerogative.

He proposes at least four patterns of industrial relations management based upon this distinction, the most typical being the making of strategic decisions at group level with collective bargaining confined to the plant (Kinnie, 1985, p. 23). However, it is also possible, according to Kinnie, to have bargaining at a higher level than strategic decision-making if the latter is more appropriately dealt with by establishment level management. In the more common case (plant bargaining and corporate decision-making), an illusion of plant autonomy is maintained by head office management and local industrial relations managers who mask 'the actual degree of control . . . from others in the plant by the appearance of freedom presented by decentralised bargaining structures and other controls' (1987, p. 464). Despite this appearance of plant autonomy, head office monitors bargaining closely, requiring plants either to adhere to a model agreement or to submit proposals to the centre for approval prior to circulating these to other plants for information (1987, p. 467). In short, according to Kinnie, 'the function of collective bargaining is to "parochialise" industrial relations so that (trade union) attention is focussed on local issues even though key decisions are taken at a higher level' (1987, p. 476), so aiming to neutralise the deleterious effects of unions (Purcell, 1983, p. 8).

Although they disagree with Kinnie in certain respects (notably his distinction between operating and strategic decisions), Marginson and his colleagues also stress the extent of head office involvement in collective bargaining at establishment level. Their survey results indicate that in more than 90 per cent of the cases where establishment bargaining occurred, corporate officers reported that they were 'either directly involved in negotiations or pay determination, or indirectly involved through the issuing of guidelines or instructions or the convening of meetings to discuss offers. In short, corporate office involvement was widespread' (1988, p. 238). Ahlstrand and Purcell (1988, p. 7) provide further support for this when they note that the freedom to operate autonomously at plant level is severely circumscribed via 'considerable pressure to reach settlements based on guideline "budgeted" figures, employed within the logic of the financial control system'. In addition, within the companies they studied, there were frequent informal inter-plant discussions in order to ensure a 'patterned' settlement (p. 7). In contrast to these findings, Edwards finds rather less evidence of corporate control from his survey of factory managers in large manufacturing plants; indeed, where establishment bargaining took place, this only involved consultation or influence from outside the plant in 25 per cent of the cases, a much lower figure than for the other studies (1987, p. 100). He suggests, therefore, that 'plant autonomy is not entirely illusory: local managers are given the power to make decisions, even if their range of choice is limited and the consequences of their decisions are closely monitored' (p. 92). For him, the word 'constraint' is preferable to 'illusion'. Part of the difference in this interpretation may well reside in the nature of the respondents, since it is plausible to assume that factory managers would be more influential than their personnel counterparts, especially if financial considerations are central to decisions on labour costs.

This literature is useful because it provides us with a number of insights into the possible rationales behind employer policies towards collective bargaining. However, there also exists a variety of shortcomings which need to be addressed more carefully; in particular, implicit assumptions are made about the omniscience and rationality of management strategy, about the centrality of labour relations considerations to management decision-making, and there is no allowance for the role of trade union or worker influence over decisions about bargaining structures and outcomes. Moreover, it is difficult to conceive of how companies can alter their bargaining levels, and so maintain 'institutional separation', unless they amend their systems for decision-making at the same time. We shall take up these issues more fully in subsequent chapters, but the case study work of Ahlstrand and Purcell casts further light on this. They note that political in-fighting is associated with choices about 'appropriate' bargaining levels, and in one of the companies they investigated decentra-lisation did not occur owing to the influence of the central person-nel department (p. 7). Internal tensions developed within manage-ment to the extent that decisions were 'resolved primarily through a political process of argument, persuasion and power, rather than through rational, planned deliberate choice' (p. 10). In other words, whilst certain senior managers may prefer to keep trade union negotiators away from strategic decision-makers, others may have different objectives which prevent the achievement of institutional separation.

Another factor that has entered the language of 1980s employee relations is the notion of workforce flexibility. Since it has attracted interest from a wide variety of circles, it has been interpreted as incorporating just about any new initiative in work organisation, such as the removal of restrictive practices, shift-working, profit-related pay, job sharing, self-employment, and even flexible specialisation (Piore and Sabel, 1985). For the pur-pose of this book, we shall examine contemporary practice utilis-ing the model of Atkinson *et al.* (1984, 1986, 1987), whereby flexibility is divided into the categories of functional, numerical and distancing. In addition to the contributions by Atkinson *et al.*, we can also draw upon results from the surveys undertaken by Daniel (1987) and ACAS (1988) in order to assess the extensiveness of flexible working practices in the United Kingdom.

Functional flexibility

This has been defined as the 'ability of firms to reorganise jobs, so that the jobholder can deploy his or her skills across a broader range of tasks' (Atkinson, 1987, p. 90). This flexibility may be horizontal – that is, between jobs at the same skill level, as with multi-skilled craftsmen or production operatives – or vertical – for example, between process and maintenance workers, such that the former undertake limited repair work, or the latter do semi-skilled jobs. Of course, there may also be combinations of the two. Functional flexibility enables an organisation to make 'more effec-tive use of its permanent full-time employees by varying the tasks they undertake to meet the changing requirements of production' (Rubery *et al.*, 1987, p. 131). The evidence from Atkinson and Meager's survey of seventy-two companies, drawn at random from four parts of the private sector (engineering; food, drink and tobacco; retail; financial services), suggests that the shift to functional flexibility has been restricted largely to manufacturing firms; in retail and financial services only about one-fifth of the sample had tried to introduce such changes. Within manufacturing, nearly all the companies that had sought horizontal flexibility amongst process workers had been able to achieve this, and most had been able to gain a limited degree of overlap between craft workers. However, very few (15 per cent) reported flexibility across trades, and even fewer had any vertical flexibility (pp. 27–8). Of the works managers in Daniel's survey, a little under half reported some attempt to modify working practices in their companies over the previous four years; more precisely, 29 per cent had taken initiatives to promote the relaxation of craft demarcations, and 20 per cent had instigated steps to develop great vertical flexibility. Only a few had tried to create a multi-skilled or enhanced category of craftsman (1987, p. 175). The ACAS survey (584 companies) also illustrates that some relaxation of demarcation lines has been achieved by employers during the 1980s, with one-quarter of respondents reporting vertical flexibility, and approximately one-third indicating that some horizontal flexibility had been achieved between craftsmen (1988, p. 15). Certain industries (for example, metal goods/electrical engineering/vehicles) had achieved more than others, as, too, had certain regions (for example, the North West of England).

Whilst the surveys can help us to appreciate the extent of functional flexibility, case study material can provide us with information about how this operates in practice, albeit in limited detail. For example, at British Leyland (now Rover), the principle of mobility has been agreed whereby 'any employee may be called upon to work in any part of his employing plant and/or carry out any grade or category of work within the limits of his abilities and experience with training if necessary' (Manwaring, 1983, p. 18). The Nissan agreement is similarly broad, and allows for 'complete flexibility and mobility of employees'; this is enhanced by having only two job titles in the plant, and a philosophy which emphasises teamwork and quality, as well as flexible working practices and continuous development (Wickens, 1987, pp. 43–4). At Ford, there are moves towards teamworking, and the employment of skilled workers on production processes to operate and maintain automated production facilities. Mobil has introduced flexibility at its Coryton plant via the concept of the 'refinery craftsman' who will be 'fully flexible without any demarcations or restrictions, subject only to limitations imposed by individual skill levels' (Young, 1986, p. 377). Perhaps the most extensive of the flexibility deals has been at Shell Carrington whereby all manual workers have been reclassified as technicians; with appropriate training, these workers will eventually be able to undertake all tasks on an individual plant, irrespective of the exact nature of these tasks. Unlike most other arrangements, this provides for both vertical and horizontal flexibility, at least in principle, although there has not yet been any independent re-evaluation of the scheme.

Numerical flexibility

This denotes the ability of the firm 'to adjust the number of workers, or the level of hours worked in line with changes in demand for them' (Atkinson, 1987, pp. 89–90). Included within this category would be arrangements such as part-time working, temporary workers, shift patterns, annual hours contracts, and overtime working, for example. For the Atkinson and Meager sample, numerical flexibility had been extended in 90 per cent of the companies; part-timers were more extensive in the service sector, as were temporaries in manufacturing, but much of this arose from traditional reasons, that is, companies with a variable demand for labour over the course of the year or the week/day would use temporaries or part-timers as appropriate. Again, there are massive sectoral differences, with less than 10 per cent of the manufacturing firms using more part-timers, whereas 90 per cent of the retailers had made more use of this form of labour contract (pp. 26–7). Results from the ACAS survey give us some idea about the extent of change in numerical flexibility within individual firms over the last three years; for example, whilst part-time workers were twice as likely to have increased as decreased, well over half the companies reported that their numbers had remained about the same (1988, p. 7). The number of temporary workers on fixed-term contracts were much more likely to have increased than decreased in the three years up to 1987 (a ratio of over 3:1), but still about half the respondents reported no great change in this area (pp. 9–10).

There have been various reports of how numerical flexibility has been introduced into specific organisations, although once again it is usually the written agreement which is described, rather than any analysis of actual shop floor practices. For example, in 1984, Petrofina introduced new arrangements for its drivers and depot workers, organised around a standard working week of 37.5 hours spread over five rather than six days. Hours worked on any one day can vary from six to eleven, with any excess in one week being given as time off in lieu during the next (Curson, 1986, p. 275). New forms of shiftworking have been initiated by employers, partly to cope with reductions in the length of the working week, but also to ensure that capital equipment is used over longer periods each day and week (see Brewster and Connock, 1985, pp. 73–6). Different forms of part-time working have also been described, whether this be categorised as classical, whereby the nature of the job largely determines the hours worked (such as school dinner staff); supplementary, in which part-timers are employed in addition to full-time staff (for example, on a twilight shift); substitutes, in which part-time workers are employed in preference to full-timers, although there does not appear to be much direct evidence that this is occurring. Finally, there is temporary work, although of course this has always been used in certain organisations to provide cover for seasonal variations in demand or one-off events. A well-known recent example of this is at a Xidex plant, where about 20 per cent of the 1,000 people employed at the site are 'supplementals' whose contracts are of varying lengths depending on market requirements (Curson, 1986, pp. 333–6).

Distancing

The third form of flexibility is distancing, which represents 'the displacement of employment contracts by commercial contracts ... an alternative to flexibility [whereby] a company may simply contract out peaks in workload to another individual or organisation' (Atkinson, 1987, p. 90). In this case, the company reduces the proportion of its own direct employees, attempting to maintain control over the quality and performance of subcontractors by commercial pressures. Nearly three-quarters of the respondents in the Atkinson and Meager survey reported a greater use of distancing in recent years (p. 29), and Hakim confirms the growth in self-employment during the 1980s (1987, p. 551). Similarly, ACAS illustrates the increasing tendency for companies to use subcontractors (40 per cent had increased their use compared with 7 per cent who had decreased use), but once again the majority of employers reported no real change in this area. Homeworking was also on the increase (1988, pp.11–12). One example of subcontracting is at Rank-Xerox, for its external transport operations, cleaners and a number of engineering trades. In this case, most of the former employees were recruited by the new contractor companies (Curson, 1986, pp. 287–92).

There has been a good deal of rhetoric about the growth and extensiveness of flexibility (MacInnes, 1987, p. 124), as well as a tendency to fuse description, prediction and prescription into a self-fulfilling prophecy (Pollert, 1988, p. 50). What is often lacking from surveys purporting to examine the increased incidence of flexibility is an analysis of change within individual companies, rather than across the economy as a whole. Consequently, it is highly likely that the greater incidence of certain forms of working (say, part-timers) is to some extent a reflection of sectoral adjustments from manufacturing to service industry. The ACAS survey does at least provide some firmer evidence on managerial assessments of change within particular firms; whilst generally this suggests there has been a growth in flexible working practices of all types, as opposed to a decline, it also clearly indicates in each category that a larger proportion of workplaces report no real change between 1984 and 1987. More serious perhaps is the paucity of data which analyses the actual implementation and operation of flexibility on the shop or office floor, rather than the formal agreements or intentions of employers. Of course, there is often a considerable difference between written agreements and custom and practice on the shop floor. In addition, the espoused policies of management are regularly thwarted or amended before they become operational reality (Brewster et al., 1983, p. 65).

A further problem is the tendency to assume that 1980s flexible working arrangements are new, a product of the specific environmental features of Thatcherite Britain. MacInnes (1987, p. 5) is particularly critical of this perspective, arguing that the 1980s has been a decade in which the rate of change has *slowed down* rather than increased. Data from Hakim's survey also lends support to this view of longer-term developments in numerical flexibility and distancing, especially in relation to part-time working, temporary contracts and subcontracting (1987, p. 555). In addition, a number of writers have also drawn parallels between the current interest in functional flexibility and the UK experience with productivity bargaining in the 1960s (MacInnes, 1987, p. 118; Blyton and Hill, 1988) and even to the latter part of the nineteenth century (Pollert, 1988, p. 46). There are many similarities with productivity bargaining, not least in the kind of flexibilities sought by management and the inducements offered to accept them; for example, relaxing demarcations between crafts or greater mobility between departments, in return for higher wages and harmonisation of conditions (Royal Commission Research Paper Number 4, 1967, pp. 11–24). But there are also some fundamental differences between the two periods, most clearly in the labour market context within which the deals have taken place. During the 1960s, for example, unemployment was much lower, so that the scarcity of labour forced employers to find ways to be more efficient rather than 'hire and fire at will' (p. 5). Moreover, it was argued that, since wages were expected to rise in any event, employers ought to seek some concessions in return (p. 4). Furthermore, the incomes policy in operation throughout the latter part of the 1960s also encouraged employers and unions to find ways around the rules in order to justify high wage increases; this meant that many of the deals were ineffective or short-lived (Young, 1986, pp. 368–70).

2.4 VARIETIES OF EMPLOYEE INVOLVEMENT

As we saw above, it has been argued that the impact of collective bargaining is minimised by maintaining a clear separation between trade unions and strategic decision-making. A further (and possibly parallel) view is that collective bargaining has been undermined by a resurgence and upgrading of joint consultative committees (JCCs), its role progressively reduced to 'form without content' (Terry, 1986, p. 175). That is, joint consultation has been 'upgraded' principally in order to undermine the scope and effectiveness of collective bargaining. Such a view is in direct contrast with that put forward by McCarthy (1966, pp. 33–4), wherein the post-war decline and transformation of formal consultative machinery could be directly attributed to the growth of shop steward organisation. In order to survive, it was argued, such bodies had to change their character and become indistinguishable from negotiating committees. If JCCs were not transformed, they would be boycotted by shop stewards – aware that power resided elsewhere – before eventually falling into disuse. The McCarthy thesis has been re-examined in a number of publications during the last decade, and the full argument does not need to be repeated here (Cuthbert and Whitaker, 1977; Marchington and Armstrong, 1983; Joyce and Woods, 1984, for example). In order to assess the validity of the 'upgrading' thesis, however, we first need to provide data on how the distribution and character of JCCs has changed over the last two decades.

The survey by Brown, undertaken in 1978, showed that over 40 per cent of manufacturing establishments had JCCs, and he estimated that 60 per cent of these had been introduced over the course of the previous five years (1981, p. 76). Daniel and Millward's finding is broadly similar although, given the broader nature of their sample, the absolute figures are somewhat lower; they found that 37 per cent had committees in 1980, 20 per cent of which had been established in the previous two years, and 40 per cent in the previous five (1983, pp. 129–33). Almost half of the JCCs were in workplaces in which there was no union representation, thus indicating the width of coverage, as well as the variety of purposes which may be served by consultation. Most commentators were in agreement that there had been an increase in the extent of formal consultation over the 1970s, although MacInnes dissents from this position, arguing instead that 'the high birth rate and apparent renaissance of consultation is paralleled by an equally high but less visible death rate' (1985, p. 106). Daniel and Millward's finding of an introduction to abandonment ratio of 9:1 between 1975 and 1980 seems to point to some expansion, even allowing for fairly severe lapses of memory (1983, p. 132).

The 1984 Millward and Stevens survey evidence indicated no change in the overall proportion of workplaces with a JCC over the period from 1980; it was 34 per cent in both cases (1986,

p. 139). However, this does mask a decline in the extensiveness of formal consultation within the manufacturing sector from 36 per cent to 30 per cent of establishments over the four-year period. The figures reported by Batstone (1984, p. 254) and Edwards (1987, p. 117) in their separate surveys are much higher than this, but that is largely explicable by the fact that they excluded small establishments, and JCCs are much less likely in smaller firms. A large proportion of these JCCs cover both manual and non-manual workers on the same committee, rather than one group alone, and a substantial minority have JCCs based on non-union channels (Millward and Stevens, 1986, pp. 143–5); that is, unions did not nominate any of the representatives for these committees, although this does not mean that these individuals are not union members. The decline in the number of workplaces with JCCs is, according to Millward and Stevens, due to structural changes in the economy (by sector and size of workplace) rather than any tendency for establishments with committees to abandon them (1986, p. 138), a finding reinforced by the panel interviews which they conducted as part of the study.

Whilst all these findings point to little change within individual workplaces in terms of the extensiveness of JCCs, they are not sensitive enough to establish whether or not there has been any change in the character of these committees. There are competing views about this. First, it has been argued that managements have been introducing or upgrading their JCCs in order to deal with issues previously the province of the negotiating arena (Terry, 1983; Chadwick, 1983; Edwards, 1985). These 'new style' JCCs are supposedly different from their earlier counterparts in that they 'occupy themselves with the key strategic decisions of the plant or company' (Terry, 1983, p. 56). Thus, 'one intention of managerial moves towards increased joint consultation seems to be to reduce the influence wielded by shop stewards through collective bargaining' (p. 56). By involving the stewards more closely in an understanding of company problems, it is felt that they will come to accept the 'logic and inescapability' of management solutions (although see Batstone, 1984, p. 257 on a related point). For Chadwick, this represents 'a clear and well-thought-out strategy, based upon the introduction of consultative arrangements to settle many of the issues previously determined by collective bargaining or custom and practice' (1983, p. 7). It is further assumed that managements are successful in their pursuit of such a strategy to the extent that they feel no need to confront trade unions 'head-on' via policies of a more aggressive nature.

The 'upgrading' thesis is disputed by MacInnes (1985) and his colleagues (Cressey *et al.*, 1985), who argue that in recent years quite the reverse has occurred; consultation has in fact been downgraded, becoming even more marginal to the regulation of affairs in the workplace. They suggest that many consultative committees merely go through the motions, surviving on a diet of trivia, before eventually one or other of the parties decides that there is little point in continuing with the arrangement. As Mac-Innes (1985, p. 104) indicates, committee members find they have more pressing priorities which take precedence over their attendance at the JCC, and eventually 'someone not only forgets to organise a meeting, others forget they have even forgotten'. The authors' conclusion about consultation in the six companies in which they researched, is that the process is marginal and un-stable, as well as contradictory, because of the difficulty of recon-ciling the distinct and differing aims of managers and employee representatives (pp. 102–3). Indeed, much of this echoes the view of Ramsay (1980, p. 49) about the degeneration of many consulta-tive schemes over time.

Futher criticisms have been levelled at the 'upgrading' thesis by Marchington (1987a), though it should be noted that this does not imply support for the 'downgrading' model. In the case of the former, whilst items of key strategic importance may appear on the agenda of JCCs, this is usually for the purpose of information-passing, often about issues of which stewards are aware prior to the meeting. Moreover, to assume that stewards will necessarily be convinced by the managerial 'logic' of such information is to misjudge their ability to treat with caution data which is received from employers. In addition, it is not altogether apparent why managers should automatically adopt oppositional stances in relation to labour, nor is it clear that control over the labour process is a central and primary concern of employers. What also appears to be lacking from this approach (and also the 'downgrading' model) is an awareness of the contextual (especially product market) arrangements within which companies operate, which might (and do) lead to consultation fulfilling different purposes in different workplaces (pp. 350–1).

A third model has been proposed by Marchington and Armstrong (1986), in which consultation operates as an adjunct to negotiation, as complementary to each other rather than working as competing processes in the regulation of workplace affairs. Negotiation is used for the determination of wages and working conditions, whereas consultation acts as a sounding board, helps to lubricate relationships, and generally fills in the gaps needed to administer employee relations. In some of the companies they researched, trust appeared central to this approach, since both sides 'had taken the view, mistakenly or not, that working together would enable them to satisfy their own objectives more adequately than would trying to destabilise and undermine each other' (Marchington and Armstrong, 1986, p. 165). Despite criticisms of the 'upgrading' thesis, however, this is not to deny its relevance to particular workplaces in certain contextual circumstances, as is also the case for the other models. The relationship between consultation and collective bargaining is more appropriately seen as an empirical question for futher investigation, rather than a generalisable law, as we shall see in the following case studies.

During the 1980s, employee involvement has also grown in other ways, via the use of communications exercises, and initiatives such as team briefing and quality circles, techniques which have often been viewed with suspicion by trade union negotiators. To what extent have these constituted an indirect threat to collective bargaining and unions?

The survey evidence indicates a growth in direct employee involvement (EI) throughout the 1980s, although it is not possible to compare this with the previous decade because the appropriate questions were not asked in the earlier studies; the results of the later studies therefore need to be treated with some caution when evaluating the degree of change in the extensiveness of this form of participation. Despite this, Millward and Stevens concluded that the biggest distinction between the 1980 and 1984 surveys was the 'very substantial increase in the number of managers reporting that in their workplace there had been an increase in two-way communication' (1986, p. 165). The stewards in the sample were less convinced about the extent of this change, although they did agree that this had been the biggest development since 1980 (p. 167). Whilst Batstone (1984, p. 263) supports this view, he does suggest that such strategies have a marginal impact, largely because managements have been trying to introduce EI techniques into workplaces in which steward influence is particularly strong, and in such cases may parallel moves to increase the participation of stewards as well (p. 272). Edwards also finds that the factory managers in his survey made regular reference to consultation, communication and involvement in the personnel policies of their firms. He notes two things from these replies:

> one is the stress on communicating with workers and generating a sense of commitment to the goals of the organisation. The other is the detail and the specificity of the replies. It is not just managers picking up the currently fashionable language, for they were able to point to concrete arrangements such as works councils and quality circles which had been introduced or extended. (1987, pp. 139–40)

More recently, Storey (1988) has analysed 'people-management' programmes in six typical UK companies, all of which have introduced some elements of direct employee involvement into their organisations during the 1980s.

These schemes have generally been introduced in an attempt to gain worker commitment for plans put forward by senior managers. Broadly, the initiatives take two separate and quite distinct forms; the first are attempts to communicate more information to employees, to make them aware of organisation-wide initiatives, and consequently persuade them to accept company plans and proposals. These take the form of mechanisms such as team briefing or employee reports supplemented by videos. All the surveys indicate that this is a growth area; for example, Batstone found that briefing groups existed in 63 per cent of establishments, and about half of these had been introduced in the previous five years. Company or plant reports to employees on financial affairs were, if anything, slightly more common than briefing groups, having increased at roughly the same rate over the same period (1984, pp 268–9). Since this is the one area within the participative arena in which there has been statutory intervention (Section 1 of the 1982 Employment Act, which requires large companies to report on steps taken to introduce, maintain or develop employee involvement during the previous financial year), it might be expected that this would have had an influence on management actions. However, the evidence has shown this to have been a somewhat toothless piece of legislation, even though some companies have operated according to the spirit of the law by reviewing and updating their practices and reports each year (Institute of Personnel Management, 1988, pp. 5–6).

Team briefing is the system which appears to have been most widely used to communicate information to employees (for further details of this, see the Industrial Society's publications or Marchington, 1987b, pp. 166–9). The basic principle behind briefing is that communications are cascaded down the organisation via a number of management levels. Employees should thus find out about information relating to the company as a whole, as well as that relating to their own department or sub-unit. According to the Industrial Society, the purposes of team briefing are to increase workforce and supervisory commitment, to reduce misunderstandings, to reinforce the role of line managers, to help people to accept change, and eventually to improve upward communication (Grummitt, 1983, pp. 3–7).

These grand objectives are not always easy to achieve, and some of them appear to rest upon highly questionable and unestablished assumptions. There are suggestions that the regular delivery of information via the briefing system cannot be taken for granted (Storey, 1988, p. 24). There are also cases of trade union opposition to team briefing where they regard it as a potential threat to their own role in the communications chain, and especially so where it is viewed as part of a deliberate managerial attempt to marginalise the unions within the workplace (both of which occurred at the Post Office during 1988, for example). Consequently, it could be argued that team briefing has the least chance of success in precisely those situations where management feels that it is most needed, and the greatest chance of success where it is least needed by management (Marchington, 1987b, p. 169). Nevertheless, despite these examples, relatively little research has been conducted into team briefing, and most of the publications are either short on detail or uncritically supportive. Alternatively, team briefing techniques are conflated with other EI initiatives, and dismissed as part of a wider strategy to mask the assertion of managerial control (for example, Littler, 1985, p. 235).

The second sort of initiative is of the quality circle type, that is, where management set up a system based upon small groups of employees which meet voluntarily to identify, analyse and solve work- and quality-related problems. Although team briefing and quality circles are often grouped together under the head of direct EI, there remain significant differences between them. Basically, the former are downward communications techniques, the contents of which are initially formulated at the top of the appropriate managerial chain, whilst the latter are established as creative, problem-solving bodies which examine issues relating to the workplace. Despite the amount of media attention devoted to circles, they are thought to exist in no more than 500 workplaces in Britain, in sharp contrast to the Japanese experience where the estimates are over one million. Batstone did find a substantial growth in the number of circles operating in large manufacturing plants between 1978 and 1983, but even so this still only accounted for under one-fifth of the establishments surveyed (1984, p. 266). Moreover, it should be noted that, even in situations where circles have been introduced into establishments, the coverage is often far from complete; for example, Black and Ackers report that the twenty-three circles at Browns Woven Carpets only involved six per cent of the workforce (1988, p. 13), and indeed given the principle of voluntary membership, total participation could hardly be expected.

As with the literature on team briefing, much of that on quality circles tends to be prescriptive and managerialist in nature, often identifying reasons for success and failure, and providing guidelines for more effective operation (see, for example, Collard and Dale, 1985; Hill, 1986.) In contrast to the literature on briefing, however, there are some publications on quality circles which enable us to assess whether they do have an impact on trade unions and collective bargaining. Bradley and Hill remind us that British unions have traditionally been suspicious of quality circles (1983, p. 295), although their research did not offer support for the view that unions 'might be undermined by this new form of collective organisation. Indeed, quality circles could *enhance* shop floor power ... [moreover] there is little to encourage managers who see in QCs the means to weaken trade unionism' (p. 302, emphasis in original). However, it should be stressed that the organisations in which Bradley and Hill conducted their research both had 'enlightened personnel strategies' and 'harmonious industrial relations' (p. 307), so it would be unlikely that managers in these companies would actually *want* to use quality circles to weaken the unions. Conversely, Black and Ackers (1988, p. 13) note that 'union hostility and indifference has been an important reason for the limited development of quality circles' in the carpet factory which they studied. Yet, even here, they suggest that the quality circles may only have 'marginally weakened the unions' (p. 16). Indeed, one of the principal findings of Bradley and Hill (1987) concerns the limited impact of circles within the organisations they studied: in terms of decision implementation (pp. 77–8), patterns of industrial relations (p. 79), and managerial prerogatives (pp. 73–5). Since the evidence indicates that employers' primary motives in introducing circles were concerned with improving product quality and cost control (p. 71), perhaps it should come as no surprise that their impact on trade unions and collective bargaining is so slight. Conversely, it appears that the correlation might hold better in the opposite direction; that is, trade unions can limit the development and effectiveness of quality circles if they suspect managerial motives for their introduction.

2.5 CONCLUSION

There is little doubt that there have been changes in employee relations over the course of the 1980s, but rather less substantial than some commentators would seem to suggest or than special cases such as Nissan or Wapping would appear to imply. Despite the potential for an employers' offensive, there remain doubts about management motivation to make such a move, and the likelihood of this being successful if attempted. To aid our understanding of 1980s employee relations, we need further detailed case studies on specific companies over a period of time.

Two other cautionary points remain to be made; first, the focus on employee relations may have given the distorted impression that it is the principal and sole concern of management, when it is clear that many other matters are likely to be just as, if not more, central to strategic decision-making. Secondly, on the basis of this chapter, there may be a temptation to view management as omniscient, omnipotent and cohesive, as well as rational in all respects; clearly, this does not necessarily represent a realistic picture of the management process. To put such views into a more accurate perspective, we need to analyse management strategy in rather more detail. This is the subject of the next chapter.

3 · MANAGEMENT STRATEGY AND PRACTICE

3.1 INTRODUCTION

Since the mid-1970s, it has become rather more common for industrial relations researchers and writers to focus on the role of management as the principal character in the employment relationship. There are a number of reasons for this interest. On a practical level, given the economic and labour market context of the 1980s, managements have tended to adopt a more proactive stance in seeking to shape employment relations within individual firms. Similarly, evidence from overseas (most notably the United States and Japan) has illustrated the way in which managements there have taken the lead in adjusting or reforming their industrial relations which, it is argued, has put British companies at a competitive disadvantage. At the same time, a number of theoretical developments have also contributed to this emphasis on management strategy; the post-Donovan orientation in British industrial relations and personnel management has shifted the location of analysis, as too has the reinvigoration of the labour process debate following the publication of Braverman's *Labour and Monopoly Capital*.

Rather than present each of these practical and theoretical sources as quite distinct bodies of literature, however, our intention is to integrate them as far as possible. This will enable us to address a series of key questions about the existence and nature of management strategy in employee relations. In particular:

- To what extent is *labour control* central to or important in the development of corporate strategy?

- Is it accurate to assume that employers actually do have overarching strategies for the management of people at work, which are formulated with clear objectives in mind, or are managements more likely to be pragmatic or opportunistic in their actions?
- If employers do have employee relations strategies, how likely are these to be achieved in practice, especially in the face of supervisory or worker resistance?
- Rather than engaging in an automatic and continual struggle with employers, to what extent do employees support managerial actions within the enterprise?

Before tackling these questions, however, we need to make a few comments about the various contributory disciplines, and the way in which their interest in management has developed. In industrial relations, relatively little was written specifically about the function of management before the end of the 1970s. The standard text up until the end of that decade was Clegg's *System of Industrial Relations in Great Britain*. Although there was a chapter on management in this book (as well as one on employers' associations), this focused on aspects such as a description of work study techniques, a history of personnel management, and a brief consideration of the role of the foreman (1970, pp. 155–99). The updated version of this book contained a section on management style, but nevertheless Clegg concluded that the 'study of management in industrial relations is in a primitive state' (1979, p. 164). This is a rather strange conclusion, given that elsewhere the same author has argued convincingly that the main influence on union behaviour is collective bargaining, which in turn is heavily influenced by the structure of management and employers' organisations (1976, p. 118). Other textbooks written during the 1970s offered little more sophistication in their treatment of management (see, for example, Cooper and Bartlett, 1976; Jackson, 1977).

By the 1980s, the management function was being treated more explicitly and with a sensitivity to the realities of industry. Wood, for example, suggests that whilst management might have suffered from an empirical neglect in earlier analyses of industrial relations, many unanalysed assumptions had been made about the role of management. Accordingly, he argues, 'we should concentrate criticism on the lack of systematic study of management, not its neglect' (1982, p. 51). A number of publications have appeared since then which are rather more explicit about management strategy, most notably Thurley and Wood (1983) – although it should be recalled that the contributions to this book were first written in the late 1970s – and Gospel and Littler (1983); we shall return to both of these later, and to my own text on managing industrial relations (Marchington, 1982). Purcell also develops the line taken by Wood, arguing that there has been plenty of em-phasis on management in shaping industrial relations priorities but, he suggests, 'we know little about the process of management and the way in which management initiatives are formulated and carried through' (1983, pp. 1–2). His final plea is that the agenda for research should lead to a broadening of the boundary defini-tions of industrial relations to 'include corporate decision-making and its effects on labour, and be more concerned with the whole gamut of employee relations policies and actions ... the multi-disciplinary roots of the subject must spread yet further' (p. 12). This has been echoed by a number of others (Timperley, 1980, p. 38; Armstrong et al., 1981, p. 13; Kinnie, 1985, p. 24).

The debate on the labour process was revitalised following the publication of Braverman's book in 1974. His principal arguments are well known; what capitalist employers buy and labour sells is not an agreed amount of labour, but the power to labour over an agreed amount of time (1974, p. 54): the basic distinction between labour power and labour. Therefore, the essential function of management in industrial capitalism is 'control over the labour process' (p. 63), this being achieved by Taylorist methods of separating the execution of tasks from their conception. He was in little doubt that employers successfully achieved this objective, arguing that the 'labour force' becomes just another factor of production (p. 171). A whole range of assumptions underlies this work, principally concerning the omniscience of management and the uniformity of its approach to labour.

Since Braverman, a number of theorists have suggested mod-ifications to his thesis. For example, Friedman's major contribu-tion has been to indicate that management control cannot be reduced to a single unilinear approach, but needs to be seen in context as a simple distinction between what he terms 'direct control' (basically Taylorism) and 'responsible autonomy', although neither strategy is seen to be achieveable in its pure form (1977, p. 101). Burawoy's principal criticism of Braverman is that he became so obsessed with the separation of conception from execution, and with the narrowing of the scope for discretion, that he overlooked the 'equally important parallel tendency toward the *expansion* of choices within those ever narrower limits. It is the latter tendency that constitutes a basis for consent' (1979, p. 94; our emphasis). Contrary to Braverman, Burawoy's intererst is in why workers work as *hard* as they do, and how consent can be introduced via the internal labour market and the 'internal state' to ensure that the likelihood of struggle is reduced (pp. 104–10). R. Edwards (1979) also suggests that employers have used different strategies at different times, as well as in different parts of the system at the same time; he identifies three forms of control – simple, technical and bureaucratic – with the latter establishing the 'impersonal force of "company rules" or "company policy" as the basis for control' (p. 131). We shall return to each of these below in the appropriate sections; what they all have in common, though, is an implicit assumption that employers *do* have strategies, which are directed at increasing their control over the labour process, often with the associated but unarticulated belief that labour control is central to the task of management.

More recently, the labour process debate has to a large extent revolved around the annual UMIST/Aston conferences, papers from which have been published in a variety of volumes edited by Knights and Willmott (1985, 1986, for example). Although there has been some splintering, both in terms of the specificity of the contributions (e.g. gender and the labour process) and the degree to which researchers utilise Braverman as their starting point, it has maintained an integrative approach, and one which is wedded to the value of empirical work as a guide for and test of theory. Not surprisingly, it has attracted its critics, most notably Storey (1985a) and Thompson (1986), who argue that the theory is in a state of crisis, having 'run into the sand' (Storey, 1985a, p. 194). Paul Edwards (1986) also has worries about the recent debate, arguing amongst other things that the focus should be on *patterns* of workplace relations rather than on strategies or the construction of ideal types. Once again, we shall return to these below. We shall now move on to consider the questions posed at the beginning of this chapter, commencing with the degree to which management objectives are reducible to control over the labour process.

3.2 MANAGEMENT OBJECTIVES AND CONTROL

For some of the earlier writers on the labour process, such as Braverman and R. Edwards, increased control over labour was seen as the overriding and fundamental imperative for capitalist employers. For Braverman, the introduction of Taylorist techniques was seen to provide employers with an answer to 'the specific problem of how best to control alienated labour' (1974, pp. 89–90). Moreover, in order to 'ensure management control and to cheapen the worker, conception and execution must be rendered separate spheres of work' (p. 118). The practice of management therefore becomes synonymous with control over the labour process. R. Edwards is somewhat less forceful about the centrality of control, and indeed he prefaces his book with an acknowledgement that employers do have profit-making as a principal goal. However, he assumes that employers desire control and that profits will be increased if employers have control over labour (1979, p. viii). His elevation of labour control to a (or *the*) central objective of employers re-emerges at various stages in the rest of his book; for example, he suggests that employers may opt for a more costly technology, even if this leads to an increase in labour costs, provided that this will 'facilitate the transformation of the firm's labour power into useful labour' (pp. 111–12).

In recent years, this perspective has attracted a good deal of criticism from a variety of quarters. For example, Wood and Kelly note that the 'tendency to inflate control to the point at which it becomes the central problem of capitalist management is at variance with most analyses of capitalism . . . which emphasise the pursuit of profit as the directing aim of capitalist management.' It should be recognised, they argue, that 'management in general does not revolve simply around labour' (1982, p. 77). Or, as Littler and Salaman put it, 'capitalists are not, after all, despite the insistence of some recent writers, interested in control *per se* (1984, p. 64). Similar points are made by both Coombs (1985) and Jones (1982, p. 191) in relation to the debate about the introduction of new technology, which need to be seen in the context of product market, technical or efficiency arguments, rather than in terms of labour control. As Coombs notes (pp. 150–1), for many labour process theorists, technology tends to be seen as 'a fairly plastic instrument in the hands of management'. Again, part of the problem stems from a confusion between objectives and consequences, a transposing of cause and effect; just because certain decisions have significant implications for the management of labour does not mean that these have been 'formulated with a conception of the desired labour process prominently, or even clearly, in mind' (Child, 1985, p. 108). If labour control or labour relations is not the central purpose of management, what place does it occupy within the decision-making process? In broad terms, there are three different perspectives.

First, there is the view that labour is one factor amongst many which are necessarily considered by senior managers, all of which assume roughly equal prominence. Storey, once again, is dubious about the view that 'managers seek always to secure more control over labour . . . managerial action is in fact directed along a broader front. Labour is but one facet of economic activity' (1985b, p. 286). Moreover, he argues that extraction of surplus value is only half of the problem, because 'surplus value also has to be realised in the product market' (p. 287), points also made by MacInnes (1987, p. 96) about recent changes in industrial relations practice. Fidler, drawing upon interviews with a sample of British business leaders, proposes that directors manage their organisations via the 'ethos of balancing interests', to include satisfaction of customers and looking after labour, as well as serving the interests of shareholders and, of course, the generation of profit (1981, pp. 119–22). Their rather paternalistic concern with labour can be interpreted as 'control' only in the sense that happy workers mean fewer problems, although the directors themselves would certainly not have ascribed such a manipulative meaning to their actions; we shall return to this below.

The second view, which is rather more common, sees labour as a factor of secondary importance within the strategic decision-making process. In her survey of companies which were introducing new technology into their enterprises. Rothwell found that product market, profitability, and efficiency arguments were central to the decision to automate. She concludes that 'employment policies are of a lower order; the priorities are to meet the needs of customers and thus of shareholders, rather than employees' (1984, p. 118). Many other writers also subscribe to this view of labour as a lower-order feature of managerial activity, its importance to some extent being consequential on the setting of higher order priorities (see, for example, Edwards, 1986, p. 2; Rose and Jones, 1985, p. 91; Knights and Willmott, 1986, p. 8; Child, 1985, p. 108; Timperley, 1980, p. 42). Whitaker's case study on relocation illustrates this point clearly:

> in the last resort financial and technical factors were paramount in the decision to relocate . . . industrial relations considerations, although subsidiary at this stage, were by no means unimportant. In the choice of the actual site (rather than the decision to relocate), we can see the significance of organisational and industrial relations considerations. (1986, pp. 661–2)

Two recent surveys also indicate the extent to which labour relations considerations tend to be of second order importance in corporate or strategic decisions. Wilson and his colleagues, as a subsidiary to their main investigation, examined the extent to which trade unions were involved in strategic decisions. Although they caution that there is no reason to believe that involvement actually means influence, nonetheless trade unions were only involved as an interest group in fewer than 20 per cent of cases (1982, p. 326). Even in those cases where they were involved, their impact was assessed to be 'slight' (p. 328). A similar view emerges from the work of Hill and Pickering, with their finding that industrial relations and personnel decisions (along with those in production and marketing) rarely become the subject of corporate level interest, generally being taken at operating level (1986, p. 38), although Marginson and his colleagues (1988, p. 243) would question the simple distinction between strategic and operating decisions.

A number of more detailed studies lend further support to the view that labour relations is typically consequential to or downstream of other decisions. The most explicit version of this thesis can be seen in the work of Kochan and his colleagues in the United States, in which the potential for choice in labour relations is limited – though not determined – by previous decisions in the enterprise. Shocks sent through the system, for example an increase in product market competition or a technological advance,

require senior managers to formulate plans to counter or adapt to
these developments. Although decisions made at each level have
implications for the future of labour relations, the latter are not
central to the more strategic discussions. Decisions relating to
'whether or not to stay in a market' or 'whether to compete on the
basis of low prices and high volume, or go for a specialised market
niche' are essentially made without any explicit labour element to
them. At a lower level of decision, 'whether to go for new
investment in the same sites or for a greenfield site', labour
relations considerations become much more critical. As they
argue, 'the decision is influenced by the state of industrial relations
in existing plants and by the potential situations at alternative sites'
(1984, p. 25). The authors illustrate their model with reference to a
variety of industries. See, for example, its application to the tyre
industry (Kochan *et al.*, 1984), and to airlines (Cappelli, 1985).

Of course, there may be objections to using these as examples,
given that they are concerned with fundamental shifts in market
conditions (that is, the shift to radials and Japanese penetration of
the US tyre market, and deregulation in the airline industry) which
threatened corporate survival. At such times, it is likely that
employers will be obsessed with commercial objectives (Marchington and Loveridge, 1983, p. 78), although why these should
assume *less* prominence during periods of organisational calm is
not altogether clear. When capital is not under threat from labour,
it is probably even less likely that labour control would be of
central interest to employers. A further objection might be that
these are US cases, and because American labour has for the most
part been rather less powerful than its British counterparts (see
Cappelli and McKersie, 1987, p. 458), we need to examine
whether similar processes have been observed in the United
Kingdom.

Evidence from studies of the British car industry suggests that
parallels may be drawn. Marsden *et al.* note that 'although managers think ahead systematically about change in industrial relations
practices and procedures, this problem appears to be fairly well
downstream in corporate planning' (1985, p. 33). Examples from
both Ford and British Leyland are quoted in support of this; at
Ford, the *After Japan* campaign implied reforms in work organisation as well as employment reductions, but these were 'only as
necessary prerequisites for the achievement of specific targets on

market penetration, return on investment, and internal economies'. At British Leyland, the parameters of change in employment practices were 'related directly to *prior* decisions about
investment in new technology and new products which comprised
the "product-led recovery"' (p. 179, our emphasis). Whitaker
describes recent changes at Cadbury in a similar type of language
(1986, p. 673), whereby industrial relations adjustments are necessary to ensure that the objectives of an investment programme could be achieved. In other words, whilst labour issues may be
seen as important by many senior managers, they are not usually
as crucial as financial or technical decisions. However, this does
not imply that labour relations activity can be 'read off' from these
higher context-creating decisions, such that there is no scope for
choices to be made by management; we shall return to this point in
the next chapter.

A third view is that the importance of labour control varies
according to the issue, and it becomes more important at times of
crisis. According to Littler and Salaman, for example, whilst
control is not the first priority of capital, it does become a concern
when profitability is threatened (1984, p. 64). Purcell links the
importance of labour as a factor in strategic decision-making to the
level of unrest being experienced or anticipated by the corporation. Otherwise, he argues, we are 'deluding ourselves' if we
assume that industrial relations activities are central to the concerns of employers, unless the level of labour unrest is 'of such
magnitude to deflect the organisation' (1983, p. 4). In this context,
we need to recall Winkler's observations on directors' lack of
involvement and concern about strikes; he notes, in relation to
their non-contact with industrial relations affairs, that

> the pattern of directors' isolation prevailed in times of confrontation
> as well . . . . Boardrooms in the midst of a strike retained an un-
> expected (by me) placidity, a matter-of-fact atmosphere that ranged
> from manifest unconcern in one company to fatalistic doom-
> watching in another. (1974, pp. 195–6)

Although this may be the picture at corporate headquarters, our
own experience with a strike at Kitchenco in the mid-1970s indicates that senior and middle management at plant level become
almost wholly concerned with this issue during and just after a
dispute. What this implies, however, is that priority cannot be

assigned to 'a single factor in management strategy, whether it be labour, technology or markets, but that this must be determined empirically' (Wood and Kelly, 1982, pp. 88–9).

Wickens initially casts his support for the argument that labour is a factor of secondary importance, stating that

> companies are not in the employee relations business . . . they are in business to sell profitably a product desired by the customer . . . good employee relations can help but cannot create a market where none exists. It is sometimes salutary to remind ourselves of this (1987, pp. 5–6)

However, later in his book, he notes that the issue of union recognition was always at the forefront of the Nissan management's minds when deciding on whether and where to invest in Britain. He argues that 'for any inward investor, a comprehensive review of labour relations in the various potential locations forms a significant part of the investment decision-making process' (p. 127). Within Cadbury, Whitaker notes that the search for a 'suitable' site, bearing in mind the company's dependence on this one factory for supplies to other parts of the group, moved into 'sharper relief as a key strategic consideration' (1986, pp. 670–2). A more forceful statement of the perceived need for employer control over the labour process comes from Edwardes, when he reports that

> the real problem was that management [at British Leyland] was still striving to get into the driving seat, having been out of it for many years . . . we had to win the hearts and minds of the workforce . . . we needed to re-establish management authority. (1984, pp. 78–9)

Although this seems to inflate the position of labour control to central prominence, we also need to recall the specific and in some ways unusual circumstances in each of these cases. Nissan was an inward investor into a high profile and sometimes controversial industry, whereas British Leyland was subject to considerable financial and political pressures at the time these statements were made. In the case of Nissan, it may be difficult to find out how important the question of labour control was in comparison to other central concerns. In the Cadbury case, whilst it is argued that labour considerations became crucial in the decision to relocate, presumably if they had outweighed other factors, the company would have built more than one plant in order to minimise the disruptive potential of the workforce, irrespective of the initial financial outlay. Serious though the labour control problem may appear to senior managers, it tends to take a back seat in comparison with other issues at most times, at least in its *explicit* contribution to strategic decisions.

However, we also need to be aware that labour control considerations may be implicitly incorporated into management decisions, owing to the value systems held by directors. Winkler illustrates British directors' 'anti-concern' for labour relations issues, and their '*expectation* that the labour-intensive functions of the firm would operate *smoothly* and relatively without trouble'. Moreover, they made the '*maintenance of order* part of the job description of their subordinates and/or personnel specialists' (1974, pp. 199–200, our emphasis). According to Winkler, such a stance is deliberate, fulfilling a useful function as a strategy for remaining isolated from and ignorant of many of the internal problems confronting the company. In a similar vein, Fidler suggests that directors construct a psychological boundary within the firm, which effectively excludes all but senior managers and a few 'hired deferentials' – such as secretaries, chauffeurs and waitresses in the directors' dining room – from whom they construct a picture of employee attitudes (1981, pp. 151–3). In other words, their views of labour relations are formed with very little knowledge of labour, and especially their own employees, in mind. It is assumed that labour should not interfere with the primary objectives of the business.

Although early proponents of the managerialist thesis believed that the separation of ownership from control would lead to the new professional managers pursuing quite different policies from the old entrepreneurs, more recent analysis suggests that their objectives have remained much the same (Nichols, 1969, pp. 61–76). Mansfield *et al.*'s survey of British Institute of Management members in 1980 illustrates the extent to which the interests of shareholders and owners are still seen as central to the management task. Among private sector managers, the interests of owners are seen to take precedence over those of all other groups, themselves included. Both for Board members and their more junior colleagues, employee interests rank a poor fourth – just above those of the public at large. The authors suggest, 'the contemporary executive considers that the interests of employees ... should be disregarded in the overall policies of the company' (1981, p. 16). Furthermore, as Marchington and Loveridge (1979, p. 180) note, managers justify the non-involvement of their subordinates by reference to the pressures exerted by the external environment which are felt to leave managements no time to seek the views of their employees if decisions are to be made, and by a firm belief that subordinate employees do not have the professional abilities required to contribute to such decisions in any event. Given their adherence to what Parkin (1972, p. 81) terms the 'dominant value system', it should come as little surprise that managers operate in a manner which implicitly expects labour to conform to management plans, chosen in the 'best' interests of the company.

3.3 FORMULATING EMPLOYEE RELATIONS STRATEGY

In contrast to much of the earlier writing on industrial and employee relations, when fire-fighting was adjudged to be the norm, more recent contributions have tended to assume that managements have developed coherent and carefully-planned strategies for managing their employees. It is particularly apparent from much of the labour process literature that researchers make the implicit assumption that employers are all-powerful in their approach. For example, in criticising not just Braverman but also R. Edwards and Friedman, Wood argues that 'they still present management as omniscient, conspiratorial, and able, at least for a period of time, to get its own way – that is, to solve successfully its problem of control' (1982b, pp. 16–17). However, this assumption of unfettered management power is not just restricted to labour process theorists; for example, Kochan and his colleagues (1984) readily slip into a similar tone when describing the creation of new forms of industrial relations in the United States. As we saw in the previous chapter, many UK writers on the subject have also assumed that changes in labour relations since the late 1960s have been brought about by more proactive and strategic management stances; in relation to union recognition (Purcell, 1979), collective bargaining (Kinnie, 1985), sponsoring of shop steward organisation (Terry, 1978; Willman, 1980), employee participation

(Ramsay, 1977), and workforce flexibility (Atkinson, 1984), for example. So, too, did observers of the UK labour relations scene in the early 1980s, when each managerial offensive was viewed as part of a broader strategy to subordinate labour via direct confrontation (Marchington, 1988a, pp. 166–7). Of course, there are probably many cases in which managements do have conscious and predetermined strategies, but we still need to question the automatic assumption that employers act in such a purposive and long-term manner. Part of the problem undoubtedly lies in the looseness with which the word 'strategy' is employed, as well as the failure to treat strategy as an empirical concept to be determined in particular circumstances (Wood and Kelly, 1982, p. 89).

Definitions of strategy, at least in recent times, stem from the work of Chandler (1962). For him, strategy related to action which was long-term in its time horizon, proactive, and encompassing the entire enterprise. This has been criticised by Mintzberg (1978, pp. 945–6) for neglecting strategies which were unintended by the decision-makers, that is those which emerge in no purposeful way from a pattern of actions and decisions within the organisation. Whilst recognising that it would be overly restrictive to make a definition conditional on clearly articulated intentions in all cases, nevertheless some limit has to be placed on the breadth of this meaning. Alternatively, we fall back into the trap of imputing rationality from the consequences of actions which, with the benefit of hindsight, appear as conscious and intentional. It should also be noted that such a definition means that very few labour relations decisions can merit the title 'strategic', since many of these are taken at lower levels within the firm, and are influenced by or are consequences of other financial, technical or market decisions taken elsewhere in the company. However, as the work of Edwards shows, factory managers often play a part in the making of strategic decisions above the level of the establishment, especially in cases where they have responsibility for the financial performance of their plants. Even where these establishments merely operate as production units, general managers can still have considerable scope to vary aspects of employee relations (with regard to employee involvement or the quantity of labour employed, for example). To treat all decisions taken at plant level as 'non-strategic' not only underestimates the influence of senior managers at this level, but also fails to appreciate the complexity of relationships between such managers and those at the corporate or divisional headquarters. To conceive of this in terms of a simple chain of authority down the managerial hierarchy is to overlook the fact that corporate managers are also involved in a search for legitimacy with their counterparts at the plant or establishment.

Within industrial relations, there have been various definitions of what is meant by strategy. Thurley and Wood, drawing upon the work of Ansoff, define strategy as 'a consistent approach over time which is *intended* to yield results in the medium and long term for a specific problem' (1983, p. 197; authors' emphasis). Gospel sees strategy much more specifically as 'the plans and policies used by management to direct work tasks; to evaluate, discipline and reward workers; and to deal with their trade unions' (1983, p. 11). More recently, Miller has defined strategic human resource management (HRM) as 'those decisions and actions which concern the management of employees at all levels in the business, and which are related to the implementation of strategies directed towards creating and sustaining competitive advantage' (1987, p. 352) Similarly, Guest, in his review of HRM, has suggested that one of the major differences between personnel and HRM is (or should be) the latter's focus on the integration of the 'people' and other functions (1987, p. 512).

Between them, these four approaches supplement the broader conceptions of strategy, and enable us to identify the key dimensions of a definition: it seems to us that to be worthy of the name 'strategy', there has to be some broad *intention* in the minds of the decision-makers at the time decisions were actually made, although every eventuality cannot possibly be fully predicted, articulated or conceived at this stage: strategy also implies some element of *proactivity* on the part of management, rather than an immediate or considered response to action initiated elsewhere; the time factor is also important in that strategy appears to relate to *long-term* rather than short-term plans for the business, those made over a period of years rather than months (although there is a temptation for individuals to define their own longer-term plans as strategic decisions, whatever the level): it also needs to be *integrative*, that is, linking various aspects of the business, rather than viewing each as a separate entity: finally, since in our view strategic decisions are not restricted to corporate headquarters alone, the *subject matter* can also vary, depending on the level at which decisions are made, and the composition of the group making them. With this attempt at clarification in mind, we can now examine whether or not it is sensible to talk of employers having strategies for the management of employee relations.

Many would argue that it is not; one of the most forceful critics is Storey who suggests that 'management scientists and Bravermanites alike have tended to attribute an exaggerated degree of rationality to managerial action. In reality, much of it is misguided, self-interested, half-hearted, short term and inchoate' (1986, p. 49). Others have similar, though perhaps not so trenchant, concerns about the meaning of management strategy, especially in industrial relations which is seen to be the province of reactivity *par excellence*; basically in how to respond to shop floor pressure, whilst at the same time maintaining production and not setting unwanted precedents (see Atkinson, 1977; Margerison, 1969). Whilst most students of labour relations would not go so far as Storey in his criticism of British management, there is plenty of support for the view that employers are lacking in strategic intent and/or the ability to sustain it over the long term. Rose and Jones, for example, note that their studies of work reorganisation schemes 'weaken rather than confirm' the notion of 'generalised and coherent strategies of control' (1985, p. 82). They go further and suggest that, of their sample, 'each case was affected by specific local contingencies and circumstances, and the broad picture that emerges is one of plant particularism (pp. 96–7).

Just because decisions are taken on the basis of the circumstances confronting the plant or the local organisation, however, it cannot be assumed that no plans or policies were made as a medium or long-term response to these factors; surely, we would expect managements to examine the environment before making decisions. Edwards, though urging caution in use of the word 'strategy', does in fact provide more clues to its nature when he argues, in relation to the engineering industry in the 1950s, that 'managers did not consciously choose to cede control to the shop floor or to make such a policy the basis for gaining workforce compliance. They *permitted* control to drift away' (1986, p. 203; our emphasis). This seems to indicate that, if nothing else, managements were aware of their (in)action, being unable in their judgement to do anything about it. Given the rather different context of the 1980s, managements are more likely to have clear goals for employee relations, although these may not always be considered cost-effective, or translate into practice, as we shall see below.

One of the principal problems in analysing complex and sensitive concepts such as management strategy is gaining access to senior managers at the time strategic decisions are actually made. In many cases, judgements have to be made on the basis of hindsight as to whether a particular sequence of events was indeed intended or considered by those who were party to the initial decision. Thus, it is obviously easier to ascribe rationality to a series of actions merely because the consequences seem to imply such an approach; in addition, the actors themselves may look back and report the process in a more logical manner than was the case at the time. Rose and Jones, amongst others, highlight the danger of teleology, of mistaking effects for a purposive process (p. 99). Thurley and Wood make a similar point, suggesting that 'it is often easy to perceive a motive and intention from an act which would surprise the actor' (1983, p. 221). Moreover, Whitaker raises an important methodological point by warning that the way in which cases are presented makes them appear to some extent as 'a smooth sequence of logical decisions taken by management representatives managing by "structured foresight"' (1986, pp. 670–1). Even R. Edwards, despite his view of mangement omnipotence, admits that management strategy 'is easier to construct in hindsight than it was to perceive in advance, and no corporate leader was convinced or even conscious of all the entries' (1979, p. 110). Clearly, we must be alert to the danger of imputing rationality with the benefit of hindsight, but this also needs to be placed in context; querying the extent to which management operates in a strategic way should not be taken to imply, conversely, that they never manage strategically.

Even authors who reject the concept of management strategy, or who are wary of its use, often present contradictory evidence. For example, Storey, having argued forcefully against the notion of strategy, then reports on his case studies on the insurance industry in the following way: 'the method of introducing new technology into these companies tends to be carefully planned and, most important of all, is conscientiously piloted in selected branches' (1986, p. 62). Whitaker, too, after urging caution in the use of the term, notes that Cadbury's decision to build a new factory away from Bournville in the 1960s was made with strategic intent, and has in fact been used as a change model in the company since that time (1986, p. 676). Indeed, he has subsequently discovered that more recent changes at Bournville have involved the same senior manager who was responsible for leading the earlier project team, having been 'implemented as part of a conscious strategy' (p. 673).

Reports by practitioners themselves also support the notion that employers do have strategies for managing labour relations, especially when they are attempting to achieve change. Wickens, for example, in explaining the decisions at Nissan and Continental Can to go for single union agreements states that

> the view in Continental and Nissan was that if we sought to be non-union, we could end up in a multi-union situation . . . attempting to be non-union would not only dissipate management energies but could end up in a situtation in which the company was not master of its own destiny. Therefore, on a rational basis, both Continental and Nissan made the decision to recognise trade unionism. (1987, pp. 129–30)

Further examples of a strategic approach to labour relations are evident from the process of 'selecting a trade union', or in the company's 'judgement' the most likely union would be the Amalgamated Engineering Union (AEU) (pp. 133, 137). Edwardes' book on the transformation of labour relations – amongst other functions – at BL is also littered with similar types of statement.

Of course, there is a danger in taking such views at face value, not least because the actors may have reinterpreted them in a more rational manner with the benefit of hindsight. Moreover, most studies of managerial work, including that of chief executives, illustrate its brevity, variety and fragmentation (Mintzberg, 1973, p. 5; Marples, 1967, p. 287), and this may well be a preferred method of working (Winkler, 1974, p. 200). Conversely, it is suggested that a longer-term view is now being taken of the management process, in which the various functions are integrated so as to achieve more coherent plans (Willman and Winch, 1985). If that is so, we need to establish whether or not they are always successfully implemented.

3.4 MODIFICATION AND RESISTANCE TO MANAGEMENT STRATEGY

One of the many criticisms levelled at Braverman, and indeed many of the earlier labour process writers, was that they neglected any consideration of how management strategy would be implemented in practice. It was assumed, along with management's apparent omnipotence more generally, that strategies, once formulated, would be converted without difficulty into practice (Wood and Kelly, 1982, p. 80). As Brown notes in his study of piecework bargaining, 'the rules that prevailed had little or no resemblance to those that had originally been laid down by management or by formal agreement' (1973, p. 85). Even if the system devised by senior management to control labour relations has been successfully implemented, it often proves difficult to maintain this over a period of time, as other priorities come to the surface (Purcell, 1979, p. 1038). However, to accept that there will be deviations from management's original plans is not to say that, in most cases, there will be no connection between the two, and that therefore such activity does not justify the title of 'strategy'. As Child notes, there are bound to be limits to the deviation of actual practice on the shop or office floor from the original strategy or policy document (1985, p. 109). We shall examine this issue from two quite separate angles; first, by analysing the manner in which other managers or supervisors may challenge, ignore or modify employee relations strategies, and secondly by considering worker resistance to management plans which may prevent their achievement in practice.

In the case of the former, Brewster and his colleagues make the distinction between espoused and operational policy which is helpful in analysing the way in which strategies are modified in practice. For them, *espoused* policy is 'a summation of the proposals, objectives and standards that top-level management hold and/or state they hold for establishing the organisation's approach to its employees' (1983, p. 63). These may or may not be committed to paper, and in some cases may be little more than broad statements about the company as a whole. *Operational* policy, on the other hand, is 'the way senior management are seen to order industrial relations priorities *vis-à-vis* those of other policies' (p. 64). It is acknowledged that this may be done subconsciously, as well as with intent, since it is a reflection of the value systems held by senior managers. It is further argued, quite rightly, that it is the operational policy which affects the way line managers operate and, one could add, the way in which employees perceive the system. A range of examples are provided from different industries (airlines, petrochemicals, and retail and distribution) which illustrate the way in which the espoused policies are ignored, amended or ordered in the face of conflicting pressures (Brewster *et al.*, 1983, pp. 65–8). According to Marsden *et al.*, industrial relations objectives are frequently those to be

> sacrificed in order to meet product market demands. This is not to deny that companies have long term objectives in the industrial relations area, but rather that strategy can be overridden by other demands, and degenerate into fire fighting. (1985, p. 35)

There are at least three separate sets of ways in which strategies may be modified or resisted by managers, in order to prevent them from being converted into practice. First, there may be opposition within management itself, either on the basis of function (for example, between personnel and production) or hierarchy (for example, between different levels of management within the same establishment or between plant and corporate HQ in a multi-plant company). The functional conflicts have been well charted elsewhere, under the banner 'who hates who?' (Lawrence and Lee, 1984, pp. 126–8). Some of these are experienced through the competing pressures of different sets of strategies/objectives, for example, when line managers decide whether to bend or break a safety rule or personnel policy (which they see as irrelevant) in order to complete a production schedule (Gill, 1974, p. 24). The willingness to challenge rules which are neither owned nor supported is even more apparent in the case of hierarchy. As Terry notes, senior managers tend to assume that supervisors will perceive management rules as legitimate and in their own interests, whereas 'such an assumption seems unjustifiable in practice' (1977, p. 80). If forced to implement policies with which they do not agree, supervisors are likely to apply these without enthusiasm, merely communicating plans and policies without putting them into context. Richbell describes the case of an espoused policy in a chemical plant, aimed at increasing the flow of information via face-to-face interaction, which failed because many line managers chose not to hold meetings at the pre-arranged times, and were not reprimanded for their inactivity (in Brewster *et al.*, 1983, p. 67). One of the most interesting cases of supervisory manipulation, indeed covert flouting, of senior management rules is reported by Armstrong *et al.*, in the case of the 'whistling forelady':

> 'about an hour after the official morning break ... the forelady cruises around whistling an odd little tune through her teeth ... without a single word, the girls flock to the lavatories ... of mornings when HE [the works director] is around, the girls do not get their extra break. (1981, p. 87)

The conspiracy is maintained as an informal custom, never brought to the attention of the senior management.

Secondly, managers and supervisors may fail to implement rules precisely so as to allow themselves discretion and leeway in their dealings with subordinates. Although custom and practice is generally seen as a means of shop floor resistance, it has become apparent that supervisors can also be active in its creation and maintenance. Terry provides a number of examples by which foremen apply rules in a more lenient fashion than was intended by their architects. The classic case was a rule which required workers to report lateness of over three minutes to their foreman who then had the authority to accept or reject any excuse; rejection meant the loss of fifteen minutes' pay. In practice, the situation was very different, and the supervisors tolerated lengthier periods of lateness, as well as a long list of 'accepted excuses'. This occurred, according to Terry, because it 'seemed to be the case that these concessions of lateness were made by the foremen to try to get cooperation from the workforce over ... issues which were unpopular with the shop floor' (1977, p. 80). Whilst the majority of reported cases have been of concessions made by managerial and supervisory staff as a trade-off for worker cooperation on other aspects of the job (Brown, 1973, pp. 98–9; Purcell, 1979, p. 1040), rules can also be applied more strictly in situations of managerial strength (Armstrong and Goodman, 1979). The application of rules can therefore be used as a control mechanism to reward, ignore or discipline selected workers. Irrespective of whether the rules are applied in a more lenient or a stricter fashion, custom and practice is created by conscious acts on the part of managers, by 'commission' as Brown terms it.

The final situation is when practices develop without managerial intent, by acts of omission rather than commission (Brown, 1973, p. 99). Supervisors may not be aware of shop floor practices which break formally defined rules since these do not explicitly or obviously challenge the system. Perhaps these emerge at a later date, being used to justify behaviour on the grounds of past precedent. They may also be unwittingly created by more senior managers during walkabouts on the shop or office floor, by virtue of their behaviour or their insistence on conformity with other conflicting rules. And, of course, workers themselves may not be aware of the extent of rule-breaking in practice although, as we see below, it is rather more likely that rules will be broken or bent by virtue of overt or covert employee resistance.

Just as managers or supervisors may modify or resist rules, so too may subordinate employees. For some writers, the workplace represents a stage for continual struggle on the part of workers, of chronic resistance to managerial actions. For example, Cressey and MacInnes (1980, p. 14) argue that workers' subjective control over the labour process enables them to use this as a 'weapon' against capital in the workplace. Conflict at work exists, according to R. Edwards, because

> the interests of workers and employers collide, and what is good for one is frequently costly for the other. Control is rendered problematic because . . . labour power is always embodied in people, who have their own interests and needs, and retain their power to resist being treated like a commodity. (1979, p. 12)

This is the reason why, according to many labour process theorists, control is *the* central problem of capitalist employers, and Braverman has been widely criticised for failing to acknowledge the role that worker resistance plays in modifying and rejecting managerial plans (see, for example, Thompson, 1983, p. 153; Wood and Kelly, 1982, p. 76).

There is a danger that resistance at work is analysed solely in terms of worker responses to employer initiatives; this does not allow for the creation of alternative rules and actions which collide with management policies. Consequently, Armstrong *et al.* (1981, p. 88) have identified two separate categories of worker resistance.

The first is employees' use of the dominant ideology to counter management plans, relying on appeals for greater efficiency, for example. Thus, if 'managerial prerogative is justified by claims to an ability to organise, it can, by the same token, be challenged when workers are convinced that the ability to organise is lacking' (p. 91). A similar point is made by Kirkbride in relation to the negotiating arena (1988, pp. 28–30). The other category is when employee arguments derive from a rejection of the dominant ideology, and are based upon quite separate principles. As Armstrong et al. note, 'they confront the assumptions and tenets of managerial ideology itself, quite systematically and over a wide range.' However, these rarely go so far as to visualise a transformed society, being confined to resistance to 'the moral interpretations of the dominant ideology' (p. 112). Most forms of industrial action, such as strikes, overtime bans and works-to-rule tend to be organised in response to managerial initiatives, as too are covert forms of sabotage which take place in secret, behind the back of management, without the perpetrators' claiming to have done them. Overt sabotage is a more direct challenge to the basis of managerial prerogative, often being celebrated by the workers who perpetrate it.

Although strikes are the most manifest form of resistance to managerial action, they are relatively uncommon in British industry. Even at the height of the so-called 'strike wave' (Smith et al., 1978), strikes accounted for only a tiny proportion of available hours at work, and their extent was small in comparison with other forms of 'lost' time (Hyman, 1972, p. 34). It is worth recalling that the average employee is on strike for considerably less than half-a-day per year, and that private sector strikes are concentrated into a few workplaces. The vast majority of workplaces do not experience a strike in any one decade, let alone a year (Marchington, 1988b, pp. 62–3). Strikes are such a source of media and employer concern precisely because they constitute a collective challenge to managerial initiatives or inaction and because they introduce another element of uncertainty into the decision-making process. In much the same manner, so do the other generally more limited forms of collective action, such as overtime bans.

Working without enthusiasm, or 'without common sense', represents for employees a much less costly, and often more immediate, form of resistance to management. Rather than explicitly challenging management plans, this type of activity can be success-ful because strict conformity to the rules cannot result in disciplin-ary action. It is designed to illustrate the unworkability of manage-ment plans and managers' incompetence in devising them in the way that they have done. Although it is difficult to quantify the extent of such action throughout the economy, there are many examples of it in practice. For example, Nichols and Armstrong describe the way in which a chemical process worker allowed a hopper to run empty, rather than use his 'initiative' to stop the process, precisely because management had banned previous prac-tices on safety grounds (1976, p. 69). In a similar vein, Analoui describes how an employee in a night-club had 'noticed' a broken pipe in a toilet, but failed to report it because he wanted to get even with the manager who had threatened to discipline him earlier; besides, he argued, 'it is not my job!' (1987, pp. 254–5). Cases such as these illustrate the imprecision of the labour con-tract, and the extent to which employers – irrespective of the state of the labour market more generally – remain dependent upon the cooperation of all employees.

Overt sabotage can represent a more dramatic form of resis-tance to managerial actions in some workplaces. Thompson de-scribes a case from the car industry where workers on the produc-tion line had traditionally exercised their initiative in choosing which doors to hang on cars coming down the track. Management devised a new rule which removed this discretion, and instructed that doors should be hung in a particular sequence to conform with the sequence of cars coming down the line:

> the result was chaos, as the workers did just what they had been told to do. Two-door cars were coming down the line with doors for four-door cars – seven inches too short . . . . Estate car doors were being smashed into position on whatever car turned up next! (1983, p. 137)

In order to make such a policy of resistance work for them, though, employees need to be collectively organised and willing to act cohesively against management, either in undertaking the sabotage or in defending other colleagues against any subsequent disciplinary action. The employees in the night-club example quoted above found it much harder to develop such an approach, given their lack of collective solidarity and their weakness in the local labour market. As Edwards and Scullion argue, in rejecting the view that workers have a toolbox of sanctions out of which to select the most appropriate form of pressure, 'sanctions are constituted through organisation, and a very developed form of organisation is required before such things as restricting the mobility of labour or withdrawing cooperation more generally can become an effective collective strategy' (1982, p. 268).

The power of employees (independently or through their trade unions) to resist management actions is dependent upon a mix of structural and behavioural factors, although it should be recognised that even the former can be influenced by both management and employee actions. Drawing upon the strategic contingencies approach of Hickson and his colleagues (1971) enables one to see that workers' power can be analysed with reference to their centrality to the production or information process, the speed with which employees can bring work to a halt, the lack of available substitutes in the labour market and the degree to which employees are able to cope with, and thus control, uncertainty in the working environment. Added on to this is workers' willingness to take action and the degree to which the most effective tactics are utilised, before and during the negotiating process (Marchington, 1975, 1982). Although this approach has been correctly criticised on a number of grounds (Kirkbride, 1985, pp. 48–9), it has also been utilised in a variety of other studies (Batstone *et al.*, 1977; Purcell *et al.*, 1978) and appears to be applied in practice (Beaumont and Leopold, 1985, pp. 15–16). The precise forms of resistance employed by workers consequently depend upon their organisation and disruptive potential, and the mix of methods used will therefore vary from one workplace or occupational group to another, as well as over time. Moreover, employers may find ways in which to reduce the disruptive potential of employees by actions such as multi-sourcing, building up stock banks, or altering the time for wage negotiations (Marchington, 1982, p. 108).

3.5 CONSENTING TO MANAGEMENT STRATEGY

In the previous section, we concentrated on the ways in which the strategies and plans made by senior managers may be amended or thwarted by their counterparts in other functions or by their more junior colleagues, and resisted by workers who were expected to comply with them. In other words, we focused upon conflicting goals and objectives, neglecting cooperative relationships, and it is to these that we now turn. As Littler and Salaman suggest, 'control must always be seen in relation to conflict, *and* in relation to the potential terrain of compromise and consensus' (1982, p. 253, emphasis in original). Conflict and consensus (along with other features of the employment relationship) are all products of particular sets of social and technical relations at work, and their extensiveness is likely to vary between workplaces and specific situations (see Edwards, 1986, p. 54). What we need to investigate are the forces which lead workers to contribute actively towards the achievement of company objectives which may, or just as likely may not, conflict with their own goals. The notion of consent, then, is central to the current discussion, this being defined by Thompson as 'self-control determined through participation in practices reproducing the capitalist labour process' (1983, p. 177). Or, to put it another way, why is it that employees often tend to work harder for their companies than they are required to do by the terms of their contract?

Burawoy was the first of the recent wave of labour process writers to treat this as an important issue, with his criticism of Braverman, and indeed Marx, for their failure to examine consent as a fundamental aspect of the capitalist labour process, comparable with conflict and coercion (1979, p. 27). He argues that 'the basis of consent lies in the organisation of activities as though they presented the worker with real choices, however narrowly confined those choices may be. It is participation in the choosing that generates consent' (p. 30). He sees the labour process as constituting a game which workers play – 'making out' in the terms of the factory in which he was employed – and he sees the game as being responsible for and generating harmony at work, rather than the converse, in which playing the game is dependent upon harmony and a broad consensus about working relationships (pp. 81–2). Furthermore, it is by 'constituting our lives as a series of games, a set of limited choices, that capitalist relations not only become objects of consent but are taken as given and immutable' (p. 93). The commitment of workers to the enterprise for which they work is further strengthened by the operation of internal labour markets and promotion devices, which foster competitive individualism, and by collective bargaining. The latter 'displaces conflict from the shop floor . . . and generates a common interest between the union and the company, based on the survival and growth of the enterprise' (pp. 114–15). This has obvious implications for the nature of unionism, as well as for management in sponsoring and assisting the development of plant-based shop floor organisation, as we have already seen in the previous chapter. Clearly, Burawoy's argument makes a number of false assumptions about the coherence of management strategies and about their problem-free translation into practice, but it does stress that workers actively cooperate in the management of the labour process, as well as contest its legitimacy. It provides for a much richer and more realistic picture of management–employee relations at work.

Perhaps the most straightforward way in which to analyse the complex nature of consent is to treat it at two levels, that of the individual job and that of the firm. In recent years, it has become more apparent to students of labour relations that even the most unskilled jobs require some tacit skills (Manwaring and Wood, 1985, p. 171), which makes the employer dependent upon the cooperation of labour; these tend to become more substantial the harder the job is to codify. For Manwaring and Wood, tacit skills refer to 'the feel and discretion which form the basis for subjectivity in even non-skilled work and are vital to efficient performance in all work situations' (p. 177). As Storey notes, 'the absolute removal of subordinates' initiative would render them . . . frequently immovable and inactive, and even more frequently operating inefficiently' (1983, pp. 12–13). Often, what appear from the outside to be unskilled jobs rely to a considerable extent on operator knowledge and dexterity built up over a lengthy period of time. In more complicated work, especially that of a one-off nature, tacit skills become even more central to the achievement of a high quality job, consequently increasing the operator's value to the employer.

The work of chemical plant operators has always been difficult to categorise on the skill continuum, with some writers (for example, Braverman) arguing that computer control has led to deskilling, whilst others (for example, Blauner (1964)) seeing it as the route to more skilful and less alienated work. Recent research by Buchanan provides support for the Blauner thesis, albeit in less evangelical terms, when he notes

> operators had to understand the process, the product, the equipment and the nature of the computer controls. They used their experience, judgement and intuition to *override* the computer controls when they knew they were not functioning correctly . . . . The computer could not effectively control the process without skilled human intervention. (1986, p. 71, our emphasis)

And further, they 'used their knowledge of the plant to maintain continuous production in circumstances where the computer controls would *automatically* shut the plant down' (p. 76, our emphasis). Moreover, the users of computer technology develop an understanding and tacit feel which 'their managers and supervisors who do not operate the equipment cannot have' (p. 76). These provide concrete examples of the way in which workers, rather than seeking to use their power to extract greater concessions from management, actually assist employers to undertake the production process more efficiently. Moreover, they used their ability to keep production going when they could, conversely, have allowed it to grind to a halt.

The obvious question is why workers should do this, especially when there is often unlikely to be any tangible material reward for action beyond the call of duty? As we have seen above, such a cooperative stance on the part of workers cannot be taken for granted, as the studies by Nichols and Armstrong (1976) show in relation to chemical workers, and Beynon (1973) illustrates at Ford on the assembly line. For Knights, at least part of the answer can be found in a closer examination of identity relations at work. He argues that, 'even though claiming only to work for money, workers frequently go beyond the responsibilities of their job description, make up for management mistakes . . . and commit themselves to "clearing up" backlogs of work.' They do this via the generation of a counter ideology which 'elevates the practical over the theoretical, manual over mental labour, and "working to live" over "living to work". The latter of each of these antinomies they associate with managerial positions' (1987, p. 29). In other words, manual workers especially (though not exclusively, as Sturdy (1987) shows in relation to office staff) regard themselves as more expert than managers precisely because of their specific knowledge of concrete tasks and systems. In the process, they offer a greater amount of labour than they are formally required to do, and so contribute to the achievement of organisational goals to which they themselves may not be consciously committed. To understand this further, we need to examine consent at the level of the firm.

On this theme, one question which has been posed in a number of surveys (Goldthorpe *et al.*, 1968; Wedderburn and Crompton, 1972; Cousins and Brown, 1975) requires employees to choose whether their firm is more like a football team (because teamwork means success and is to everyone's advantage) or whether teamwork is impossible (because people are really on opposite sides). In each case, a relatively high proportion of employees endorsed the football team image, ranging from 67 per cent in the Goldthorpe car worker study through to 79 per cent in the Cousins and Brown shipbuilding case. This is not to suggest that such views represent a positive endorsement of all aspects of capitalist social relations, and a rejection of industrial action should this seem appropriate. Indeed, in the car worker study, employees went on strike soon after the report was published (no connection between the two events!). Ramsay is critical of the simplistic nature of these 'firm and football team questions', and he argues that workers are responding with a vision of what work ought to be like rather than with an assessment of what it is really like (1975, p. 397). On redesigning the question to add a third possibility, he found that the greatest proportion of respondents chose the option 'a firm is like a football team, but only because people have to work together to get things done. Very few chose the 'pure' football team answer, which identified similarity of interests in the major features of the firm. The commitment of employees to their organisations is often highly calculative, 'a pragmatic acceptance by employees who accept that one way or another the current relation has to be lived with' (Ramsay, 1975, p. 399).

In material terms, though, it is not altogether surprising that employees should have an interest in the survival and prosperity of the companies for whom they work, as well as in their own individual position, since there are obviously links between the two. Non-managerial employees often build up a considerable length of service with employers, particularly at one site within a company, and they are often resentful of managers who are drafted in to 'sort out' the plant (Marchington, 1982, p. 60). As Littler and Salaman put it, 'while having opposed interests, workers and employers have shared interests: in the success of their products, in competitive advantage, ultimately in the success of "their" firm' (1984, p. 65). Cressey and MacInnes note a similar tendency (1980, p. 15). It is rare for workers totally to reject major elements of the dominant ideology – in fact, at one level, there is much they can find to support in it – and many therefore assume 'helper' functions, and assist management to respond to what are often seen as 'impersonal market forces', beyond the control of senior management (Armstrong *et al.*, 1981, p. 83). Of course, this is not to portray the labour process as a haven of consent, but to stress the possibilities for and limits of both cooperation and conflict at work (Manwaring and Wood 1985, p. 191). Given changes to the British economy since 1980, it is probable that many employees who continue to work in the private sector (especially in manufacturing) see their own personal fortunes to be even more closely tied in with the success of their current employer. Insecurity in the local labour market may be a much more potent force for changed attitudes than any vague notion of an enterprise culture.

3.6 CONCLUSION

Although many writers use the term 'management strategy' with regularity, it is rare for the concept to be 'unpacked' and examined in terms of its constituent parts. In this chapter, we have sought to undertake this task in order to analyse the term in a more careful manner. In particular, we feel that there is a need to differentiate between the formulation of strategy and its implementation, as well as between resistance to management actions and consent with and commitment to the goals of the enterprise. To describe strategies without assessing whether or not these operate on the shop or office floor is to provide a partial picture of the concept, as, too, is any investigation of resistance to managerial goals without a parallel treatment of consent. Ultimately, management strategy can neither be assumed nor rejected on *a priori* grounds, but needs to subjected to empirical analysis in specific cases.

Managements clearly vary in their strategic foresight, and in their approach to employee relations. We shall now turn our attention in Chapter 4 to a consideration of how and why management styles may vary between workplaces.

4 · MANAGEMENT STYLE AND PRODUCT MARKET COMPETITION

4.1 INTRODUCTION

The last decade has seen a number of studies analysing the styles employers use for the management of employee relations, and in particular in examining the variations in style which are apparent between and within different companies. This growing research focus in industrial relations stems from Fox's paper for the Donovan Commission, and the subsequent criticism and refinement of the unitary–pluralistic distinction by a number of writers. Within the labour process field, Friedman's differentiation between responsible autonomy and direct control strategies has provided the most useful extension to Braverman's analysis of management control, even though it has also attracted some criticism. On a practical level, interest in management style has been stimulated by the recent debate about 'macho' management, and its use in the British context as a response to greater competitive pressures and slacker labour markets; we have already reviewed this literature in Chapter 2, indicating its shortcomings, so it is unnecessary to repeat those arguments here (see Batstone, 1984; Mackay, 1986; Edwards, 1987; Marchington, 1988a). If nothing else, the debate has at least directed attention to how and why differences occur in the way employers choose to manage the labour process (Poole, 1986b).

One again, we shall proceed on the basis of a series of questions which help to focus our attention on the principal issues relating to management style. In particular:

- How do styles of managing employee relations vary between different workplaces and companies, as well as over periods of time?
- What effect do different product market circumstances have upon the styles used by employers to manage employee relations?
- To what extent are senior managers free to choose appropriate styles for the management of employee relations, or are these determined by the (product market) circumstances in which each company operates?

4.2 TYPOLOGIES OF MANAGEMENT STYLE

In his Research Paper for the Donovan Commission, Fox outlined two contrasting frames of reference (unitary and pluralistic) which embody the main selective influences employed by managers, and which cause them to supplement, omit and structure what they notice (1966, p. 2). The unitary frame of reference conceives of the enterprise in terms of a team with one source of authority and one focus of loyalty. All members of the team are assumed to work to the best of their ability, accept their place in the hierarchy, and follow the appointed leader. From the pluralistic frame of reference, on the other hand, the organisation is seen to contain many separate and competitive interests, and it is seen as management's function to balance these competing demands on resources. Rival sources of leadership are to be expected in the company, and cannot be unified, liquidated or integrated totally into or out of the system (Fox, 1966, p. 4). There are three basic differences between these two frames of reference; in relation to management's acceptance and recognition of unions, their views about management prerogatives and employee participation, and in the perceived legitimacy of and reactions to conflict at work (Marchington, 1982, pp. 38–47).

Fox himself developed this approach further in 1974 (pp. 297–313) to encompass six different patterns of management–employee relations, based largely on the unitary–pluralistic distinction. In this schema, the patterns resulted from a combination of unitary and pluralistic frames of reference held by the different parties; thus, the 'traditional' pattern occurred when managers and employees both held unitary frames of reference, the 'sophisticated modern' pattern was an amalgam of pluralist perspectives, 'sophisticated paternalism' (unlikely in Fox's view) was a combination of pluralist employers and unitary employees, 'classical conflict' and 'continuous challenge' were variants of unitary employers and pluralist employees. The final pattern, 'standard modern', was the result of ambivalent frames of reference within both management and worker groups; this could occur because of splits within the managerial hierarchy, for example, or as a result of experience, with individual managers' frames of reference varying from one event to another or over time.

The Fox categorisation has provided the basis for recent industrial relations literature on management styles, most of which has emanated from John Purcell and his colleagues. Purcell and Sisson identified five ideal-typical styles of industrial relations management (1983). The first of these is the traditional, which is much the same as Fox's traditionalist pattern, being characterised by forceful opposition to trade unions and an overtly exploitative approach to the management of people at work. Their sophisticated paternalist style is quite different from that of Fox in that managements still exhibit strong elements of unitarist frames of reference, despite their concern for employee development; typical examples are companies such as IBM or Marks and Spencer. Although most of the enterprises in this category do not recognise unions, their approach to management is substantially different from the traditionalists. They do not 'take it for granted that their employees accept the company's objectives or automatically legitimise management decision-making; they spend considerable time and resources in ensuring that their employees have the *right* approach' (1983, p. 114; our emphasis). In other words, this group spans the unitary–pluralistic distinction, exhibiting elements of both in their management styles. Purcell and Sisson's third style – the sophisticated moderns – is similar to that of Fox insofar as there is a congruence of pluralist frames of reference, but very different in that Fox portrayed this as the most unstable of any of the patterns. The authors sub-divide this category further, by distinguishing between the consultative and constitutional styles of management; the former recognise unions, but are keen on informality and an integrative approach to employee relations (ICI is the most-quoted example); the latter operate by a strict codification of all collective agreements, almost a statute law model, according to Purcell and Sisson, in which peace is maintained by a respect for the other side's disruptive potential (Ford is the example quoted, although recent attempts by that company to introduce employee involvement may now make it inappropriate). Unlike the Fox pattern, these two styles (and the sophisticated paternalist) are seen as stable, uniform and consistent across the enterprise, as well as over time (p. 116). The final category is the standard modern, or opportunist, in which the approach to employee relations is seen to vary between establishments and over time, depending upon the circumstances confronting the organisation/establishment (GEC is an oft-quoted example here).

In more recent publications, Purcell has refined the styles approach in a number of ways. First, he has articulated a more precise definition of 'style' which excludes pragmatic, reactive responses to labour problems, but implies 'the existence of a distinctive set of guiding principles, written or otherwise, which set parameters to and signposts for management action in the way employees are treated and particular events handled' (1987, p. 535). Style has to be seen as ubiquitous and continuous, not resting upon the whims of a few senior managers in one location (p. 546). Furthermore, the analysis of styles is not really about outcomes, he argues, but about the originating philosophies and policies which influence action (p. 534), and about links with business policy (p. 547). In other words, management style is conceptualised as akin to culture, something which guides strategies, rather than the attempted application of strategy at the point of production. This definition seems unduly restrictive since it effectively excludes the opportunistic style; it is also confusing in that it tends to conflate strategy with culture and style.

Purcell's second refinement is to differentiate between management's attitudes and policies toward employees on an *individual* and a *collective* basis. Individualism is the extent to which employees are treated as a resource, rather than a commodity at work, and this relates to factors such as advancement, fulfilment and opportunity for self-expression (Purcell and Gray, 1986, p. 213; Purcell, 1987, p. 536). A half-way house between the two extremes of resource and commodity status for labour is paternalism (1987, p. 538). Collectivism is defined as 'the recognition by management of the collective interests of groups of employees in the decision-making process' (1986, p. 213; this needs to incorporate not only the structures for employee participation and collective bargaining, but also the approach of management towards these institutions. It is crucial to examine 'the degree of legitimacy afforded to the collective by management, and thereby the extent to which it is accepted or opposed' (1987, p. 539). The collectivist dimension therefore spans the range from unitary to cooperative, with adversarial collectivism in the middle. In his original article, Purcell saw these two dimensions as cross-cutting, but in his later paper he argues that both can develop at the same time; consequently, the two dimensions are presented in graph form (see 1986, p. 213; 1987, p. 541). This new representation renders the typology more dynamic, making allowance for companies which alter their styles along both dimensions at the same time; it is rather less certain, however, that there have been any conceptual changes to the model between the two articles.

Within the labour process tradition, there have been a number of critics of Braverman's assumption that management strategy is equivalent to Taylorism, the latter being the only approach observable under capitalism. R. Edwards (1979) produced a threefold categorisation of strategy – simple, technical and bureaucratic control – which illustrated variation not only over time, but also between different parts of the economy. This distinction has been criticised by Lazonick for its historical inaccuracies (1983, pp. 131), whilst Gospel has questioned its relevance to the British context, given the history of strong trade unionism in this country (1983, p. 12).

The work of Friedman offers more scope. It is based on three industry-area case studies, the most comprehensive of which is on the car industry in the Coventry area. He proposes, amongst other things, that there are two major types of strategy which top managers use in order to exercise authority over labour; responsible autonomy (RA) and direct control (DC) (1977, p. 78). Responsible autonomy 'attempts to harness the adaptability of labour power by giving workers leeway and encouraging them to adapt to changing situations in a manner beneficial to the firm. To do this, top managers give workers status, authority and responsibility.' Direct control, conversely, 'tries to limit the scope for labour power to vary, by coercive threats, close supervision and minimising individual workers responsibility. [This] tries to limit its particularly harmful effects and treats workers as though they were machines.' Whilst the latter tendency was clearly articulated by Braverman, Friedman argues that conditions are not always appropriate for management to adopt such an approach. Thus, direct control over the work process may be loosened as 'part of strategy for maintaining or augmenting managerial control over productive activity as a whole (pp. 84–5). There are obvious similarities between this idea and Flanders' suggestion that managements needed to 'share control in order to regain control' (1975, p. 197). Friedman provides support for his dichotomy with examples of shifts between DC and RA over time, and also within and between firms at the same time; for example, skilled workers in the early nineteenth century were subject to RA approaches, whilst their unskilled counterparts felt the force of DC strategies (pp. 88–9). In Friedman's view, neither strategy is possible as an ultimate ideal, since both are based upon fundamental contradictions: thus, RA can never totally remove the problem of managing labour because it does not remove alienation, but merely softens its operation. Moreover, its continued success is reliant upon good fortunes in the product market. Similarly, DC is also regarded as impossible in its pure form because workers cannot be closely supervised at all times and all work (no matter how unskilled) contains some elements of subjectivity. Furthermore, the extreme subdivision of labour may increase its disruptive potential as well as reducing flexibility (pp. 106–8). The attraction of Friedman's argument, aside from its simplicity, is its sensitivity to the connections between management strategies and (product and labour) market conditions, as well as inherent dynamism; we shall return to this later in the chapter.

Of course, this is not to accept Friedman's argument without qualification. In common with many labour process writers, there is an assumption that employers are generally successful in their application of strategies, not only in pushing these down the managerial hierarchy, but in putting them into effect. In addition, there have been criticisms that the approach is too simple, since it collapses the wide range of approaches into just two (Wood and

Kelly, 1982, pp. 84–5), and that it fails to consider whether both approaches may be pursued at the same time with the same group of workers (Wood and Kelly, 1982, p. 84; Edwards, 1986, pp. 38–9). For Edwards, this is a particularly serious shortcoming; he argues that

> typologies of management strategy are flawed. The main reason is that they posit one mode of gaining workers' compliance within each distinct strategy. Firms' employment policies are in fact likely to be more complex than such categorisations suggest, embracing several different ways of gaining compliance. (p. 55)

A further objection raised by Wood and Kelly, and also Edwards, is that RA is developed in response to worker resistance, whereas it could well have its origins in management alone; this could be the case whereby RA develops in sectors with weak or non-existent unionism (Wood and Kelly, 1982, p. 75).

Friedman himself outlines a number of other criticisms of the model in a more recent article in *Capital and Class* (1986, pp. 97–124), accepting these as stimuli to develop his approach yet further; the simplicity of the distinction is defended, quite rightly in our view, because it represents 'the fundamental tension between the need to gain cooperation from those who do the work, and the need to force them to do things they do not wish to do' in order to achieve employer goals (p. 121). Principally, he suggests improvements to the RA/DC model which ought to make it easier to specify the relation between strategies and concrete practices. This he does by distinguishing various categories of activities which are required in all labour processes, of which labour market relations is clearly one (p. 105). Others could then be added as appropriate for each labour process. Other criticisms he is less willing to accept; in particular, bearing in mind the observations of Edwards outlined above, he argues that any coincidence of supposedly incongruent strategies (that is, RA and DC at the same time) will reflect variations within organisations by level or function, caused in part at least by time-lags between the formulation of strategy and its implementation in practice (pp. 116–17). Furthermore, he implies that analysts need to examine the underlying motives of managerial initiatives, since what may appear to be RA (or DC) on the surface might have been introduced with quite different intentions; he cites the attempt by Chrysler to develop participation in 1975 as such an example (pp. 113–14). Whilst there may have been an incongruity in this particular case, and possibly others, there is no reason equally to assume that this is inevitable. Moreover, the conceptualisation of RA and DC as opposite ends of a continuum implies a clarity in management initiatives, a coherence in management organisation, and an omnipotence in management activity which cannot be taken for granted, as we saw in Chapter 3.

Whilst each of the previous authors has presented some form of typology for differentiating between management approaches to employee relations, Edwards argues conversely that there are fundamental problems with the notion of typology itself (1986, p. 2). There are a number of reasons for this, all of which are connected, and some of which we have already dealt with above and in the previous chapter; firms will use a range of techniques to persuade employees to work; activity may be the result of *ad hoc* adjustments and not grand strategy; the actions of employees can have a substantial effect upon patterns of control in the workplace; external influences can prevent some forms of control, and encourage others (pp. 2–3). In other words, he suggests that 'the structure of control should be seen as the result, and a potentially unstable one, of past interactions between employers and workers, in the context of specific external influences' (p. 3). A more profitable way to conceive of patterns of control in the workplace, he suggests, is to differentiate between *detailed* and *general* control; the former is concerned with the details of work tasks, such as the allocation of overtime or the application of discipline, whilst the latter refers to 'the accommodation of workers to the overall aims of the enterprise' (p. 6). This allows for the appearance of supposedly contradictory practices (such as quality circles and strict time-keeping rules) in the same workplace at the same time. However, having argued against typologies, Edwards later proposes his own version – termed 'heuristic devices' – which, he argues, is produced from the challenges made by workers, their approach and organisation, rather than the actions of employers (pp. 226–36). It appears that he has merely substituted the actions of one actor for another in attempting to differentiate between workplaces. Whilst accepting that management cannot be seen in isolation from other influences, particularly product and labour markets, it seems to us that any analysis of management would be seriously limited if no attempt were made to compare and contrast their approaches and activities.

Product markets and employee relations

Although it is clearly valuable to try and describe different styles for the management of people at work, it is also crucial to identify reasons for those differences. Purcell and Sisson (1983, pp. 116–17) argue that the state of the product market within which the company operates, and the role played by the founder of the enterprise are the two key factors which influence the style adopted by the organisation. They provide a number of examples of the latter (such as Ford, Mond (ICI), or Watson (IBM)) to support their case, but they also illustrate the limited value of this factor in relation to conglomerate companies which have a multiplicity of styles and lack a strong corporate influence from the centre. Friedman also stresses the influence of the product market on management style, but in addition he points to the power of organised labour, via resistance, to effect changes in style and strategy (1977).

Other factors can also be related to management style; in particular, technology, size of establishment or enterprise and ownership can also be added to product markets, organisational emergency and development, and labour force character and organisation to form a list of potential influencing factors. For example, it is often argued that management style can vary between establishments, depending upon the numbers employed, and most of the indices of union orginsation illustrate clearly the differences between smaller and larger places of work. The sector in which workers are employed can also be a source of difference, as is evident from the more recent history of employee relations in the public service sector as managers in these organisations find themselves under increasing pressure to cut costs and maintain quality at the same time. Similar points could also be made about technology. For a fuller discussion of all these factors, see Marchington (1982). However, there is a danger that such approaches are implicitly deterministic, since they search for exogenous factors which will explain why styles vary between workplaces. As we shall see in the next section, these factors are often partly a product of managerial choice, whether this is in relation to technology, plant size or whatever.

For the purpose of this book, we shall concentrate on the interaction of the product market and management style for three reasons. First, both Purcell and his colleagues, and Friedman, suggest that the character of the product market is an important influence on management style, although in neither of these approaches is there much explicit discussion of how these two factors interact in specific workplaces. Secondly, most industrial relations commentators have recently stressed the influence of a much changed competitive environment for the way in which management operates with regard to labour, and suggest that somehow it is more important than other factors. And thirdly, whilst there has been an increased emphasis on the product market, this has not been developed in a way which allows for a more explicit theorisation of the links between markets and the management of employee relations. Often this has been little more than a ritual genuflection to the force of the political and economic environment in causing adjustments to management style. For example, it is assumed that a chapter delineating the macro changes will be sufficient to place the rest of the textbook or research report in context, and that employee relations practice is necessarily adjusted in line with these contingent circumstances (see, for example, Brewster and Connock, 1985; Edwards, 1987). The link between the two is not theorised or developed, and there is no attempt to integrate employee relations practice and market conditions in the context of specific workplaces. This kind of approach leaves unanswered the key question of why individual companies in specific industries, faced by apparently similar environmental conditions, adopt quite different approaches to the management of labour. It also overlooks the fact that senior managers may be able to influence the market, as well as merely respond to it, and that even in highly competitive conditions there is some room for managerial choice and manoeuvre. In other words, it must be recalled that product market conditions do not determine management style, even though more junior managers may feel that this is the case, and such a perspective may serve as a convenient façade behind which managements may hide. Unfortunately, much of the literature takes the line of product market determinism, probably because labour relations issues are so often downstream from corporate decisions. We shall return to a discussion of choice and determinism after we have reviewed the material which does attempt to examine employee relations in the context of the product market.

Those studies which have attempted to analyse the links between product markets and employee relations broadly take one of three forms. First, there have been in-depth analyses of specific establishments, companies or industries at a particular point in time, which describe the key features of the product market – often amongst other factors – and explicitly or implicitly link this to employee relations. Not surprisingly, the most comprehensive accounts have been in situations where the organisation operates in fiercely competitive conditions, and for which the product market consequently represents a critical uncertainty for management decision-making.

One of the clearest accounts of the competitive environment can be found in Goodman *et al.*'s book on the footwear industry. In this, they argue that any description of the product market must not just be for background material, but should 'relate the contexts and the characteristics of the industry to specific *issues* which confront the actors' (1977, p. 31, emphasis in original). The key features of the market are its segmented but highly competitive nature, the fact that it suffers from seasonal and cyclical variations, the declining market share held by British manufacturers, and the influence of fashion and appearance which leads to diversity in output (p. 37). This uncertain and volatile market environment has led to considerable worker flexibility and adaptability, patterns of short-time working, and also stable relationships between bargainers so as to protect wage standards (p. 38). Throughout all of their account, it is the pressure of the market which comes across, and the lack of realistic choice for managers whose success is seen to be dependent on market fortunes. Most of the firms are small and there are few barriers to entry into the market. This leads the owner-directors to be preoccupied with survival, which 'tended to mean that their concern was to get orders which depended on designing the "right" shoe and delivering it on time at a competitive price' (p. 153). Of course, their perceived lack of choice may also have something to do with the lack of professional management expertise, especially in the small companies. In the larger firms, the market is also highly uncertain, although this is mitigated to some extent by greater control over retail outlets and by national advertising (p. 176). The finished product is highly visible in the market place, and employees are made to feel aware of the 'power' of the market over their lives, especially since there are a number of regional centres for the industry (p. 50).

A similar picture emerges in the kitchen furniture company studied by Marchington and Loveridge; they report on the fashion orientation, intense competition, and considerable variation in demand, not just on a seasonal basis but also with rather less predictability from one week to the next (1983, pp. 75–7). There is little stability in the market, and firms' market share varies greatly as new firms enter and older ones are replaced regularly; for example, in 1976 (when the research was undertaken) the top ten firms held about 70 per cent of the market, with the smallest 75 per cent of firms having just 10 per cent of the market between them. However, half of the 'top ten' had entered this league for the first time that particular year (Marchington, 1980, p. 26). Once again, this competitive environment led to a management obsession with the market and the 'need' for flexibility, speed of response, change and survival. Production plans were continually updated, and small orders were often rushed through ahead of the queue so as to satisfy a particular 'high prestige' customer. On occasions, new designs were produced in order to meet an exhibition deadline, only for more junior management to find technical problems with the production process (1983, p. 78). As we have already observed, in this situation, management rationalised their failure to involve employees by referring to the demands of the product market.

Another industry exhibiting many of the same features as footwear and furniture is clothing. Rainnie describes how the major retailers, such as Marks and Spencer, are able to exert considerable pressure on the clothing companies, since the industry is characterised by intense competition between producers, ease of entry and exit in the market, fashion changes, and demand fluctuations (1984, p. 153). The producers have an ambivalent relationship with the retailers since they want security and the opportunity to schedule long production runs, but at the same time recognise the dangers of attachment to one major retailer, especially if the latter raises its quality standards or expects quicker delivery (p. 149). Producers are willing to comply with the retailers for fear of losing out on a place in the high street stores. Further support for this view comes from the research of Truman and Keating who argue, in a somewhat deterministic manner, that 'the market for clothing at any one time determines not only the quantity of articles to be produced but also the *way* in which they are produced' (1988, p. 22; our emphasis).

Within the food industry, Purcell and Gray have contrasted management styles in two different divisions of the same large company. One of these served the 'branded' market, and it was concluded that high market share and profitability gave this division a degree of leeway to pursue a consultative style of management; for example, the decision to close a particular operation could be implemented over a three-year period given the company's position. In the other division, which served the 'own label' market, the situation was quite different: a competitive market

> with the customers both able and willing to play one supplier off against another in terms of price, delivery performance and quality .... In these circumstances, the dominant concern of top management was cost control, meeting customer requirements with flexible production systems and working arrangements. There was a firm belief in the managerial prerogative. (1986, p. 217)

According to the authors, the most powerful influences on management style were 'the nature of the product markets served, the division's position in these markets, and the historical tradition of the originating companies' (p. 216). In earlier work by Purcell, the product market is also identified as a key influence in a number of industries; for example, in a company supplying braking equipment to the vehicle industry, dependence on a small number of customers led to rapid and unilaterally made decisions in response to sudden changes in, and even cancellations of, orders (1981, pp. 93–5).

Each of these cases illustrates the effect of the product market on employee relations, and paints a picture of employers reacting to factors which are felt to be outside or beyond their control. At plant level, there is often little doubt in the managers' minds that the market exercises a disproportionate influence over the way in which issues are handled. Even senior managers at each establishment were rarely, if ever, in a position to take a proactive stance in relation to the market, either because of some features in the latter which made individual companies relatively powerless in the face of the market as a whole, or because strategic decisions were taken at higher levels within the enterprise.

Unfortunately, little has been written about the relationship between the market and employee relations in less competitive conditions, or in situations where individual companies have greater power over the market, largely because in such circumstances the market is a source of little uncertainty. For example, Knights and Collinson suggest that it is difficult to generalise from Burawoy's work at Allied owing to the secure product market enjoyed by the plant which supplied other parts of the corporation. In these circumstances, they argue, consent is more easily achieved than in situations characterised by uncertainty (1985, p. 205).

In this regard, the chemical industry offers an interesting example. Typically, the industry has experienced a general pattern of growth, although it has been subject to some degree of cyclical variation in demand, largely because different parts of the industry feed into different market segments; for example, rubber and plastics are tied in with the fortunes of the car industry, whilst fertilisers and pesticides depend upon agriculture (Pettigrew, 1985, p. 59). The market for goods tends to be international in nature, and each of these is supplied by a small number of major producers, most of which are multinationals. Thus, in contradistinction to the clothing market, the producers are relatively powerful in relation to the customers. Chemicals, of whatever form, is a costly market to get into, and barriers to entry are significant, given the cost of plant and equipment (Pettigrew, pp. 56–7). In addition, the major companies do not confine their operations to one segment of the market, but compete across the range, and this, too, has the effect of cushioning any downturn in individual segments; thus, for example, different parts of ICI have been profitable at different times in the company's history, to the extent that senior management has seen fit to provide individual plants with some degree of protection against short-term difficulties. Moreover, the industry is also characterised by a much longer lead-time between order and delivery, between planning and sale, than is the case in the more fashion-oriented industries described above; for example, it is typical to start construction on new plant and equipment years in advance of production. In Blauner's view, this leads to workers feeling far more secure in their employment than employees in most other industries. Individual plants do not hire and fire as consumer demand rises and dips. The number of workers necessary to operate and maintain the equipment has already been reduced to the minimum. The core labour force in an automated technology plant therefore has an unusually high degree of job security. (1964, p. 128)

As we shall see from the case studies analysed in subsequent chapters, this did not prevent management in the chemical company from reporting a more competitive environment, although its degree and form clearly varies from one industry to another.

As well as analyses of companies or industries at a particular point in time, there are also studies which examine changes in the management of the labour process in the context of longer-run historical adjustments in product market conditions; these constitute the second group of studies. For example, Fox relates the role of industry-wide collective bargaining in footwear to the highly competitive market, and argues that employers saw its value in terms of market regulation and industrial peace (1974, p. 305). However, he notes that as employers began to feel constrained by market pressures, they sought cost reductions by minimising the discretionary content in work and threatened earnings and job security (pp. 307–8). Gospel also puts considerable emphasis on the product market to explain changes in management approaches to labour, although he is less explicit than Fox about its effects; he notes, almost in passing, that intense international competition increases pressure to reduce costs, and that subcontracting has been used to deal with situations of high product demand (1983, pp. 7–8).

Friedman provides one of the most explicit treatments of the link between product markets and employee relations, via his distinction between responsible autonomy and direct control. The former is more likely to occur during periods of growth and a lower severity of competition since 'top managers will be tempted to placate worker demands' (1984, p. 189). Conversely, in a declining market, overhung with the threat of redundancies, 'the basis of responsible autonomy (employment security) will be undermined', thus provoking a move toward direct control (p. 189). Friedman finds that this association fits well with the observed strategies of car firms, especially those based in and around Coventry, for the majority of this century, although the move back to direct control in the 1950s is rather later than he would have predicted (pp. 190–5). The period since 1980 also presents a problem for this analysis, since it would have been expected, on the basis of fiercely competitive conditions in the vehicle market and a fall in demand for British cars in the early part of the decade, that employers would have pursued strong direct control strategies. Although this may have been the case in certain companies, notably British Leyland, the period has also been characterised by attempts to increase employee involvement, as a way of securing greater commitment to work and to corporate goals; in this respect, the moves by Ford away from explicit direct control approaches is highly relevant, although these policies have been more successful in the United States than in Britain (Werther, 1985). For Friedman, the roots of responsible autonomy are to be found in worker resistance and the power to force management to loosen control. Consequently, he overlooks the possibility that managements may find responsible autonomy strategies attractive at times when labour is relatively weak, and that they may take a more proactive stance in their attempts to generate worker consent. Alternatively, of course, it may be argued that the current fashion for internal labour markets and employee development does not constitute responsible autonomy at all, having no more than a superficial resemblance to the 'real' thing.

Kelly adopts a quite different approach from the above authors in his critique of the labour process debate. He argues that we need to

> consider the *full circuit* of industrial capital as the starting point for analyses of changes in the division of labour: purchase of labour power; extraction of surplus value within the labour process; realisation of surplus value within product markets. (1985, p. 32, emphasis in original)

It is possible for there to be contradictions in this circuit, and it is the disarticulations between these stages which help us to understand why changes occur in the labour process. If job redesign is a management response to worker resistance, we should have expected it to fall away during the 1980s; however, intensified product market competition provides 'an even greater incentive for the use of job redesign as one way of resolving product market–labour process contradictions' (p. 45). This approach seems to reflect events in the 1980s rather more accurately, as we shall see below.

The third type of research relating product market conditions to management practice is that which has examined a particular industry or company over a period of time in the last decade. Much of this reports on changes in employee relations following a 'shock' or major readjustment in the product market. For example, Batstone *et al.* illustrate the way in which patterns of employee relations in British Telecom underwent a major change with the moves to a 'market-driven' strategy following liberalisation of the network in the early 1980s. Prior to this, the authors note, there was a high degree of consensus between management and unions about modernisation, with both parties willing to bolster the position of the other. Given the protected monopoly position of the company, there was little perceived need to adopt a confrontational stance in order to push through changes (1984, pp. 141–2). A shock to the market position led to a quite different management approach to the unions, and a more negative assessment of their role. Thus, management wished to see a union which would assist them in the process of achieving change, but instead 'felt the unions acted as a distorting lens, and spoke of mischievous and slanted information' (pp. 145–6). Consequently, management increasingly turned to direct communication with employees, with the effect that the unions saw their role being undermined by the back door. Cappelli shows how a similar event – deregulation of the entire US airline industry – led to significant adjustments in employee relations. He describes how different carriers arrived at different solutions, depending upon their existing position within the market, as well as on other features such as the size of their fleet, current schedules and so on (1985, p. 321). He reminds us, quite rightly, that

> while industry-wide competitive pressures are certainly a driving force behind changes in labour relations, they do not have a uniform influence . . . . Carriers react to the competitive environment in a variety of ways, and it is their *response* to that environment which is the most important *determinant* of labour relations. (p. 336; our emphasis)

In his view, diversity is best explained by 'the different business strategies carriers use to address competitive markets' (p. 336).

The way in which changes in market conditions impact on the management of employee relations also figures prominently in a number of case studies analysed by Purcell (1981). He reports that the threat by a major customer to withdraw a key order if quality did not improve acted as a stimulus to reform industrial relations in a previously conflict-ridden plant. In this case, the role of corporate management (from the parent company in the United States) was central to the process of achieving change, with the assertion that 'this was the last chance for the plant' (1981, p. 210). Although the plant was saved on this occasion, events in the following year revealed 'how precarious the market was for crossbar exchange equipment', and the decision to close the factory was taken at European HQ, that is, outside the control of British management (pp. 220–1). A quite different set of circumstances, in this case the expansion of the white goods market, also illustrates the interplay of market and management in another of the case studies described by Purcell. Corporate Headquarters had reached the conclusion that a new factory was needed to build more washing machines. Group management visited the British plant and told the stewards 'in a carefully prepared presentation lasting a number of days that either industrial relations were to be improved dramatically through cooperation with management on flexibility, productivity and maximum efficiency, or the new plant would go to France (a rival bidder)' (p. 173). No-one at the plant knew whether or not group management was bluffing, but the threat was seen as real enough by both unions and local management. Although the new plant was eventually built in Britain, subsequent events once again showed the 'almost intolerable' pressures that the market can place on industrial relations (p. 182). In the end, the company took unilateral action in response to the next product market crisis but, as Purcell correctly points out, this form of action is not _determined_ by the market. He notes:

> to suggest that product market pressures _forced_ a change in management's handling of industrial relations is too simple. It implies there was no choice when in fact a lengthy and often bitter debate took place between senior managers. (p. 187, our emphasis)

Even if managements are not in a position to choose the market in which the company operates, they still have some discretion in choosing how to react to the market in terms of handling employee relations, and in the language they use in describing their product market to employees.

Another shock to the system, this time the introduction of radials on to the US tyre market, provided the focus for Kochan *et al.* in their seminal piece on strategic choice and industrial relations. They recognise that markets vary between different industries, and that consequently so can the role of strategic choice: the latter can only occur 'where the parties have discretion over their decisions, that is where environmental constraints do not severely curtail the parties' choice of alternatives' (1984, p. 21). Product market change can be either gradual (as in the case of the shift to smaller cars in the United States) or abrupt (as in the case of deregulation or the introduction of new products on to the market). In any event, the subsequent increase in competitive pressures 'forces firms to make decisions that can have far-reaching effects' (p. 24). In the tyre industry, each of the major companies chose a different competitive strategy, with different consequences for the management of labour; Goodyear chose to compete across all markets, and opened up new non-union plants in the South so as to reduce costs; Firestone decided to consolidate by closing certain lines, but remained in the market and generated competition between the different plants; Goodrich moved out of the tyre market altogether, and maintained good relations with its employees via a policy of diversification; Uniroyal attempted a rapid cost-cutting exercise, closed three of its five plants, and encountered concerted union opposition in the process (pp. 34–6). What this makes clear, however, is the interaction between the product market and employee relations, and the key role played by senior managers in this process, Kochan *et al.* stress that

> a complex interaction occurs between a more demanding competitive environment and the shaping of key business decisions. This interaction also produces options and diversity in industrial relations. Thus, a more complete explanation of the recent changes in industrial relations requires consideration of variables that capture these interactions as well as the traditional environmental factors included in the industrial relations systems framework. (1984, pp. 34–5)

In other words, the market can be both an influence *on* the management process, especially in the short term, but can also be influenced *by* management decisions about choice of market segment.

There have been two recent attempts to theorise more explicitly on the links between markets and industrial relations management, but both suffer from a number of shortcomings. First, Thurley and Wood outline a matrix which sets out a number of hypothetical relations between business strategy and industrial relations strategy, and in each case the appropriate conditions which correspond to these strategies (1983, pp. 205–8). They identify seven possible ideal types which cover a wide range of different sorts of business, and then describe the broad nature of industrial relations relevant to each case. Some of these examples enhance our understanding, but most are too vague and ill-defined to allow for any development of general principles. For example, the public service organisation with a monopoly market is likely to recognise unions and promote industrial democracy, whereas the new firm trying to break into markets will rely heavily on product innovation, and will try to avoid unions, develop skills and demand considerable flexibility. In other cases, there is no information about product markets, or it is idiosyncratic and tangential. The use of set categories (such as multinational company) rather than factors (such as market predictability) makes the model very static, and appears to imply that all multinationals (department stores, key private and public companies, etc.) have enough similarities to be classed together. It is difficult to see how this model could be usefully adapted to increase our understanding of the interplay between markets and employee relations management.

The second approach, by Thomason (1984, pp. 575–91), has the advantage of using generalisable factors. The author develops work by the Boston Consulting Group to propose a two-dimensional model of associations between the product market and employee relations; he differentiates between movements in the overall market and the size of the individual market share held by the company, in order to describe four patterns of industrial relations management. Thus, the 'wildcat' undertaking has a low share of a rising market, would be short of cash, and in need of flexibility and versatility; consequently, the 'indicated' industrial relations strategy would tend towards autocracy and union avoidance. The 'star', with a high share of a growing market, has as its principal goal the achievement of order, and this means that trade unions can be recognised (or avoided) so long as they assist management to attain its objective. The 'cash cow' has a high share of a stagnant or falling market, and its major aim is to reduce costs (including those of labour) as well as to increase the amount of flexibility inherent within the enterprise. Finally, the 'dog', with a small share of a declining market, is likely to confront many industrial relations problems, as the twin pressures of the market and cash shortages increase the likelihood of conflict and coercive methods of control.

Whilst this approach appears more fruitful than the Thurley and Wood typology, it is overtly deterministic in nature. It implies that particular industrial relations management strategies are 'congruent' with current market position, thus implying that there is no room for choice on the part of senior management. Thomason is alert to this criticism, arguing that 'these are no more than broad indications of possible congruencies between the approach to the market and the approach to ordering industrial relations' (p. 578). However, as we shall see below, he remains firmly within the contingency perspective in assuming that deviations from this 'fit' are due to managerial failures to recognise or mobilise support for 'desirable adjustments' (p. 579), one part of which may be trade union or employee resistance. There are also other limitations to this approach, not the least of which is the lack of empirical evidence against which to test the model, either in its more deterministic form or in its softer version whereby deviations are allowed. Nevertheless, it does offer a framework which, if nothing else, is useful in refining our understanding of the product market; we shall return to this in a later chapter.

Determinism versus choice

Broadly, there are four ways in which the relationship between product markets and employee relations could be explained, which between them take in notions of determinism and choice (Astley and Van de Ven, 1983). At one extreme is the idea that the state of the product market largely determines the nature of management style in employee relations, with managers acting as mere cyphers, operating in accordance with the economic 'rules' of the market place. This 'task contingency' approach aims to 'identify those organisational designs which will be efficient for given contextual situations' (Child, 1977, pp. 217–18). Given conditions of relative uncertainty, it is assumed that management style is contingent upon the context in which the organisation operates. As Child notes, according to this approach, the contingencies are 'relevant and variable parameters for which allowance and adjustment in management practice ... have to be made' (p. 217). In other words, management practice should explicity and unambiguously follow from the position of the organisation in its environment (Lawrence and Lorsch, 1969, p. 186).

There are a number of problems with this deterministic perspective, not the least being its failure to provide conclusive evidence that it works in practice (Child, 1977, p. 226; Miller, 1987, pp. 3–7). Moreover, it gives insufficient emphasis to the role of political processes within organisations, since decision-making appears to be regarded solely as a matter of management accommodating to operational contingencies to achieve the best possible fit with the environment (Child, 1973, p. 240). The organisation is reified, and treated as an entity in itself, thus amplifying the deterministic nature of task contingency approaches yet further (Wood, 1979, p. 354).

An awareness of these defects led to the development of a second and more realistic version of contingency theory, dubbed by Child, the 'political contingency' perspective (1977, p. 218). This takes account of the fact that power is important within organisations, and that senior managers have the ability to influence decision-making in ways which do not conform to the 'best fit' with contextual conditions. Within this perspective, managerial choice is severely constrained though not specified by environmental influences, and it opens up

> the possibility of more than one feasible organisational response to the same task environmental stimulus .... The chances are that the task environment constrains the choice of organisational design; but it does not constrain it to just one possibility. (Khandawalla, 1977, pp. 248–9)

It introduces the idea of managerial preferences, of acceptable and unacceptable alternatives, and the processes by which decisions are made in organisations. This approach would suggest that managerial style can be adapted in a number of ways to take account of the nature of the product market, its exact configuration being dependent on the power exerted by individual managers within the enterprise to mould this in accordance with their own objectives.

Despite the fact that this represents an advance on the earlier approach, it does not challenge the fundamental basis on which contingency theory operates. Thus, rather than determining action, the environment is seen as limiting the number of feasible options which confront senior managers; rather than allowing for senior managers to have some influence over the environment, their creativity is only exercised in response to situational stimuli, influenced by their perceptions of the environment; rather than viewing the link between management and the environment as potentially a two-way relationship, it is seen as unidirectional. Although there is recognition of the political nature of decision-making, it only tends to appear at a later stage of the process in terms of choosing between alternatives, as 'part of the problem of application' (Wood, 1979, p. 342). Moreover, as Child notes, it still does not allow for the opportunities presented to organisational decision-makers to select their environment or product market niche, or even to influence the external conditions themselves. Consequently, it overlooks the fact that 'some degree of environmental selection is open to most organisations, and some degree of environmental manipulation is open to most large organisations' (1972, p. 4).

This leads directly on to considerations of strategic choice, the third point on the determinism-autonomy continuum, for which the relationship between external and internal factors is rather more complex. On the one hand, managerial choice is constrained by the environment within which the company operates, especially in the short run and at lower levels in the managerial hierarchy (MacDonald, 1985, p. 532). Presumably, this is why the majority of managers perceive there to be so little choice in their dealings with employees, conceiving of the market or other external factors as largely determining management practice. On the other hand, however, senior managers – especially though not exclusively – have a considerable amount of room for manoeuvre, and their decisions also determine to some extent the environment within which the organisation operates; as we have already seen, choices can be made about the kinds of market in which the company will compete (Kochan *et al.*, 1984, pp. 32–4), the location of its operations (Whitaker, 1986, pp. 661–2), the size of each

establishment (Child, 1977, p. 222), the type of employee recruited (Peach, 1983, p. 18), and to some extent the type of
technology employed (Kelly, 1985, pp. 37–8). Consequently, any
analysis of organisation and environment must 'recognise the
exercise of choice by organisational decision-makers . . . their decisions as to where the organisation's operations shall be located,
the clientèle it shall serve, or the types of employee it shall recruit,
determine the limits to its environment' (Child, 1972, p. 10). Thus,
according to Child, 'strategic choice is the critical variable in a
theory of organisations' (1972, p. 15).

Nonetheless, care has to be taken to not merely replace one
determinant by another, to substitute choice for determinism, in
our attempt to analyse links between factors such as the product
market and employee relations. Just as it is inaccurate in the vast
majority of situations to imply that management action is determined by the market, so it is equally misleading to view the market
as under the control of management, as a factor to be manipulated
at will. Choice should be viewed as both a cause and a
consequence of environmental influences (Hrebiniak and Joyce,
1985, p. 337); that is, managements have some influence over the
kind of markets in which they choose to operate, and in some cases
over the structure of that market itself, as well as having some
choice over the way in which they respond to environmental
pressures. Or, to put it another way, we need to be much more
aware of the processes by which decisions are made in organisations, and rather more sensitive to the character of the environment, in order to analyse the linkage in a more realistic and
comprehensive manner.

The final way in which we can theorise about links between the
product market and the management of employee relations is via
the concept of legitimisation; in this case, managements use
information about the state of the market in order to justify to
employees the decision they wish to make (or have taken),
whereas in fact they may well have several options from which to
choose. In their attempts to persuade individuals to comply with
instructions, managers clearly make choices about how much
information to give to employees, as well as how and when (if at
all) to release it. Preferences can often be legitimised by reference
to the external environment, which suggests that there is no
alternative to the prescribed course of action. Wilkinson's study of

technical change illustrates this well; arguments about efficiency can serve as 'scientific glosses which conceal or obscure the political considerations' (1983, p. 84); furthermore, 'efficiency can be used as an ideological tool which legitimates social and political choices' (p. 86). In a similar vein, Ackroyd and his colleagues, in their review of the influence of Japan on British employment relations, suggest that one form this may take is 'mediated Japanisation'. By this they mean 'the practice of using an appeal to Japanese efficiency as a way of legitimating the introduction of indigenous changes that are seen as necessary or desirable' (1988, p. 15). This tactic has also been observed by Marchington and Loveridge (1983, p. 82) in their studies of employee participation, whereby senior management attempted to legitimise its use of authority through superior knowledge of the environment. In short, the environment can provide a valuable source of legitimacy for managerial decision-making, irrespective of its impact in real terms.

4.3 CONCLUSIONS

In this chapter, our principal aim has been to appraise critically a variety of studies which examine differences in managerial approaches to employee relations, and attempt to tie this in to a greater appreciation of the product market environment within which companies operate. The major advantages of the models put forward by Freidman and Purcell are their simplicity and generalisability, so we shall evaluate these against the evidence from our case studies. We also focused more explicitly on the product market since this appears to be a prime source of managerial and employee concern, and arguably constitutes a major constraint or opportunity for companies at the current time. We feel that there have been two major shortcomings of the studies which have examined employee relations in its product market context. One is the implicit assumption that product markets largely determine managerial activity, a view which clearly ignores the potential influence which senior managers may have over the market, as well as the uses to which the spectre of market pressures can be put in legitimising managerial actions to employees. The second of these shortcomings is the difficulty of generalising from descriptions of individual product markets in a way which allows for comparability between different industries or companies; it may prove beneficial to be able to rank markets according to their competitiveness, since this would at least represent an advance on the typical reference to a 'more competitive' product market environment. Since our case study companies come from quite different industries, the hope is that we can contribute something to this debate. We shall now turn to an examination of the four cases, commencing with the chemical company.

PART II

EMPLOYEE RELATIONS IN PRACTICE

5 · ICHEM: ON THE PATH TO HRM

5.1 INTRODUCTION

Ichem is situated on a large industrial estate, just a few miles from the centre of a northern city, and industrial chemicals have been manufactured on the site since the later 1930s. Ichem is part of a large European-owned multinational, Multichem, which has interests throughout the whole of the chemical industry, though not outside it. Within the United Kingdom, Multichem employs about 7,000 people in a number of different divisions (and many more overseas), Ichem being a single-site division with the full range of management functions, including sales, represented at the establishment. Although it is company policy to allow divisional – in this case, site – autonomy, there is interaction with the centre about personnel matters, such as pay determination, and in the last few years there has been a rather more explicit attempt to increase quality awareness throughout the company.

Of all the companies in our study, Ichem has the most investment-oriented approach for managing employee relations. Following the 'turnaround' project and the 'New Deal' in the early 1980s (which is discussed below), clocking has been abolished for manual workers, conditions have been progressively harmonised, pay levels have increased substantially, information is regularly disclosed to all employees, and management has sought to develop teamwork principles on the chemical plants. At the same time, the unions have become less central to employee relations within the factory, partly because of management's attitude to the convenor, but also as a result of the increased emphasis on direct communications with the workforce. Of course, this style of management is facilitated by the relatively favourable product market conditions within which Ichem operates, although it should also be noted that the initiatives outlined above were first planned in the more difficult trading circumstances of the 1970s.

5.2 WORK ORGANISATION

Ichem now employs approximately 580 people, a little less than half the number who worked at the site through the 1970s. Numbers employed were halved as part of Ichem's 'reconstruction to profit' programme in 1980, although the run-down in personnel actually took place over a four-year period, principally through voluntary means and early retirement. The cutbacks were planned on a *pro rata* basis across the plant, and on the same day that the announcement was made to the workforce, half the Divisional Board members went. With all other groups, it proved possible to find sufficient volunteers or early retirees – hardly surprising, given the scale of payments offered to tempt employees to leave. The numbers employed fell consistently in the early 1980s, stabilising in 1983 at around 550. Towards the end of the research period, numbers began to rise again as market prospects continued to look sound. Although the intention was for 'equal misery', the shop floor staff have taken a bigger share of the reduction, and the ratio of manual:non-manual workers has shifted from 50:50 at the beginning of the 1980s to nearer 40:60 by 1987. The personnel department was heavily involved in managing the run-down in numbers, providing advice on the offer, engaging in extensive counselling of redundant employees, inviting alternative employers on to the site to hold recruitment interviews, and generally trying to make the dislocation as painless as possible. In the event, the reduction in people employed took place without any industrial action, an outcome which satisfied management, especially since the site had experienced a spate of strikes in the 1970s.

The manual workforce is almost entirely made up of men, although there are substantial numbers of women in the administrative, clerical and laboratory functions. Labour turnover at the site tends to be negligible – one or two people per year, and there are large numbers of staff who have built up lengthy periods of service with Ichem, the average being well over twelve years. The age profile of the manual workers is tipped toward older employees, despite the workforce reductions and early retirements in the early 1980s. Absenteeism, which was running at 12 per cent in the late 1970s, has fallen progressively throughout the 1980s, stabilising at a little over 4 per cent since 1985; personnel management are particularly pleased about this since they feel it vindicates the harmonised sickness policy, whereby all employees receive full pay from the first day of absence.

There are three separate manufacturing plants on site, two of which are technologically advanced, utilising the latest computer systems introduced over the course of the 1980s. All production areas operate continuously on the continental four-shift pattern, so even though there are approximately one hundred operators on production, only twenty or so are employed in total on the three plants at any point in time. The Personnel Manager joked with us that this handful of workers 'kept' the rest of the division, in so doing acknowledging Ichem's dependence on these operators, and perhaps providing a clue to its employee relations policies. Chemical process workers, though conventionally regarded as semi-skilled, undertake a wide range of tasks varying from the most technologically advanced to the heaviest and most mundane of labouring activities. On all but the most technically advanced of the plants at Ichem, there is provision for manual interventions to the process, which on occasions requires 'hands-on' work in dirty physical surroundings. One of the newest computerised plants offers operators the least opportunity to exercise control over the process, even though the operators were involved in the planning stages and management was keen on the operators' having some feel for the product. All the process operators have been trained up by the company to City and Guilds standards (qualified chemical operator), so it is inevitable that these workers feel some frustration with the tasks they undertake.

One of the aims of the New Deal, which followed 'reconstruction to profit' and the turnaround programme, was to increase flexibility by 'radically altering the job content, responsibility, environment, status and payment' of the staff represented by the manual stewards to the extent that 'all employees will extend their job content to all aspects of the function within which they operate.' However, it was also recognised within the New Deal agreement that some individuals would experience difficulty in completing all the tasks on the plants, and it was made clear that these workers would continue to receive the same rate of pay as other process operators. A further feature of the New Deal was that flexibility should eventually become operational between as well as within plants, initially between similar processes, but ultimately across the whole site. Whilst supervisors are responsible for notifying the process operators of the workload, it is up to them how to organise the work within the constraints allowed by the chemical reactions. It is common for the teams to be flexible within the plants, largely because they prefer to run the job in this way. Operators feel that rotating tasks helps to alleviate boredom, keeps them up-to-date on all aspects of the work, and satisfies their own desire for some variety and control over the process. Comments from all interviewees provided examples of this. On the most automated of the plants, one of the operators stressed that

> the three of us do anything on the plant. As well as operating the computer, we go around the plant checking valves and pumps for leakages, and also drumming-off. It [the last of these] is a simple job, and it makes a nice change.

As well as enhancing variety and job control, however, team-working also provides the group with an informal disciplinary function, since it becomes their responsibility for ensuring that the job gets done, rather than waiting for instructions from supervision at each stage of the process.

Although flexibility within plants is now a normal feature of the labour process at Ichem, mobility between plants is only just developing, largely because management did not push for this in the early days of the deal. Towards the end of our research programme, movement had started to occur between the plants, since management had encountered problems in securing adequate cover at times of holiday and leave entitlement, as well as during training courses. Again, initial indications were that the employees involved found this relatively attractive, as it provided them with further variety in their day-to-day operations.

The engineering function is centrally organised, providing a series of services to the site as a whole. There are twenty-one mechanical craftsmen, sixteen for instrument/electrical, and fourteen for a variety of more specific operations required at the factory, such as rigging and scaffolding, and pipe-fitting and welding. All are employed on days, but there is a call-out system for night-time emergencies. Following the negotiation of the New Deal, there have been some moves towards greater flexibility between the various trades at the factory, although it is specified that the craftsmen will not become multi-trade. According to the agreement

> craft personnel will operate as a flexible trade group at basic skills level, whilst continuing to specialise in their own fields of competence. For at least 85 per cent of a craftsman's time it is envisaged that he will be working within his own trade group.

Most of the agreement relates to an easing of demarcations at the edges of the individual trades – for example, fitters doing welding work in emergencies, or turners maintaining their own machines. Some parts of the agreement allow for the complete integration of two trades (such as between riggers and scaffolders for example), whereas others indicate that demarcations shall be strictly adhered to because of the serious safety implications of fires in chemical works (such as that governing heavy electrical work for example). Again, as with the process workers, the skilled personnel at Ichem appeared to accept the flexibility provisions within the New Deal, and in some cases went further, especially on the night shift.

The other areas in which manual (or semi-manual) employment is concentrated are the warehouse (with eighteen staff), locker room, and the ancillary services, which includes catering and security. The latter is the line management responsibility of the Personnel Manager, again a key feature of Multichem's policy of ensuring that the personnel function maintains an awareness of general management issues and also a credibility with line managers. The catering services are provided in-house, and in recent years have been at the forefront of ideas for healthy eating campaigns, a part of the overall commitment of management at the factory to health and fitness. Unlike some other employers, management at Multichem had not chosen to subcontract these functions out to other companies, preferring to retain the services in-house, since they could maintain better control over quality. The warehouse employees are on a two-shift system, and from interviews with staff from within the area it was apparent that they were also fairly flexible between different tasks. However, new demarcations were emerging in line with the preferences of the individuals within the department, such that some employees undertake sampling work in addition to their more traditional duties and some enjoy driving stacker trucks more than others.

5.3 THE MARKET ENVIRONMENT

Across the three plants at the establishment, Ichem produces two sets of products, with one of these (the principal product for the past fifty years) accounting for over 80 per cent of the company's sales. Most of these are sold overseas, and Ichem is one of a handful of international companies which compete in this market; within Multichem, it is the only site which produces this particular product range. Sales are generally to the industrial, rather than the domestic, market, and in recent years demand has increased, since the product is used in improving safety at work. Indeed, it enjoys a good reputation in the field as a high quality product, for which reliability is more important than price. As the patent on this range will run out in the next few years, Ichem is anticipating greater competition in the 1990s from companies in Japan and the United States. Significantly, the Personnel Manager is convinced that high-quality products and service are the key to continuing success in the future, a factor which to a large extent explains the company's commitment both to product and operator quality.

The other product is a recent addition to the company's range and this has found a primary market in Third World and developing countries. The investment in this new computerised plant is intended to secure the company's prosperity well into the next century, although in terms of numbers employed it represents a minor part of the total workforce. Ichem has devoted considerable energy to generating new orders for this range, and has used the services of manual workers in demonstrating the product, and in commissioning new applications overseas. This policy has been successfully used by Ichem for a number of reasons: it gives manual employees some variety in their work; it utilises their knowledge of the product; it demonstrates to customers that the company employs high-quality workers on the manufacture of the product; it gives employees a clearer understanding of the end-product of their efforts, so making them more aware of customer specifications, and in recognition of their services it even provides them with a perk, since the company gives a 'free' holiday to the worker and his or her family.

Whilst competitive forces appear uppermost in the minds of management, even in the personnel function (which is often criticised in Britain for its neglect of business matters), competition is not as cut-throat or intense as in the other companies we have investigated; as we shall see, orders do not vary from day to day as in Multistores, or seasonally as at Foodpack. Though similar to Typeng in depending on a few large contracts, with a long time-lag between order and delivery, the market as a whole has not experienced the declining fortunes and massive insecurities which have faced the heavy engineering industry, nor is the market characterised by one-off orders. Indeed, there is evidence that the few large companies in the world which compete in these markets are especially sensitive to the instability created by customers switching orders from one supplier to another. During 1987, a large order which had typically been divided between Ichem and one of its American rivals was given solely to Ichem. Meeting the demand required virtually all of the plant's productive capacity; production in this kind of chemical plant can to some extent be adjusted by opening or closing valves, rather than increasing the number of direct workers or productive units, which would not be feasible in the short-run in any event. However, rather than delight in this 'gain', Ichem had liaised with its American counterpart, intending to subcontract a proportion of the order in the expectation of reciprocity, should the positions be reversed in subsequent years. Although this example indicates the way in which Ichem attempts to manage its product market rather than merely respond to its vagaries, the company is also heavily dependent on exchange rate fluctuations since so many sales (74 per cent) are overseas.

Ichem's case illustrates perfectly the danger in accepting managerial assessments alone of increased competitive pressures. Whilst the environment does seem much tougher to management, compared with previous times, the market is very different from that experienced by the other companies in our sample. There is only a handful of suppliers in the market, and quality is seen as an essential component of the purchaser's decision to buy, probably rather more so than price. The time-lag between order and delivery is such that plans can be made with a longer time-frame than is the case for many employers. Demand can be balanced out over the course of the year to create relatively stable production schedules, and in any event deviations in production do not lead to widely differing employment needs. Consequently, it is easier for the company to commit itself to job security than in most other industries. Close relationships can be – and are – built up with customers, who are likely to require repeat orders on a regular basis, once again demonstrating the importance of quality in the manufacturing environment.

5.4 MANAGEMENT STRATEGY AND STYLE

Multichem has been characterised as a forward-thinking employer, open and dynamic in its style and approach to the management of people, according to the author of a book on the company's history and development. It reorganised its activities in the late 1960s following an American consultancy report on the future of the business; even at that time, corporate messages emphasised security of employment and positive employment policies. In 1971, this found expression in Multichem's corporate principles, and each of the divisions/establishments adapts these to suit their own circumstances. In reality, all that happens is that the division/establishment amends information relating to the nomenclature of the site, referring to Ichem rather than Dyeco or wherever else. We did, in fact, manage to conduct interviews at a number of Multichem subsidiaries throughout the United Kingdom and the name of the site was the only detail which varied between them. The booklet of corporate principles is an expression of the needs of the business, but also of its obligations to the community, the environment, customers, employees and shareholders. The section on employees occupies most space in the booklet, and in this there is stress on teamwork, internal labour markets, participation and communication, training and welfare. In particular, the booklet states:

- We will strive to create an atmosphere conducive at all levels to the effective teamwork which is of great importance for the success of the company.

- Promotions will be made as far as possible from within the company.
- We will encourage participation in decision-making within the scope of an employee's responsibilities.
- We will ensure that each employee receives all relevant information necessary for the performance of duties and for an understanding of how these relate to the company as a whole.
- We will progressively provide for the possibility of developing the potential of employees by means of training, education, job rotation and performance appraisal.
- We treat employees fairly and with dignity, and provide for safe and healthy working conditions, as well as schemes designed to afford protection to the employee and his family in case of sickness, old age or death.

Generally, documents such as these are often more notable in their breach rather than their observance, but at Ichem it appears to have formed a key part of management's approach to employee relations. In the mid-1980s, following reconstruction and the 'New Deal', when senior management started to plan for the 1990s, they commenced from the standpoint of the corporate principles. The Managing Director of Ichem also has a seat on the UK Board and he has been a keen proponent of these principles, both at division-al and company level; for example, he has been a leading light in local attempts to encourage inward investment into the region, and he has been instrumental in building up links with the com-munity. In addition, he is renowned for his walkabouts, whereby he spends whole mornings or afternoons wandering around the plant talking with people about the job and social matters. Moreover, he always eats lunch in the staff canteen (single dining area, harmonised conditions), and really does seem to ensure that he mixes with different people each day. Of course, this can all be seen as nothing more than enlightened human relations, but his highly personal approach to management was generally com-mented upon favourably by employees.

In addition to the corporate principles, which encourage some convergence between the different sites and divisions, Group Resources provides a range of central services in the areas of management education and training, staff development, and per-sonnel services. In management development, for example, a central training programme is provided at three levels; for junior and middle management, for those with senior management potential who are likely to be promoted within five years and, finally, for those suitable for imminent Board level appointments. Training managers from the different divisions meet regularly with the Director of Management Education and Development to monitor progress and discuss future action. In a similar vein, the Staff Development group has the brief to provide a stream of suitable candidates for higher management positions, and the practice of rotation and movement between divisions has become more typical throughout the 1980s; for example, the personnel directors of several other divisions within Multichem had in the past occupied personnel positions at Ichem, as, too, had the Group (UK-wide) Management Education and Development Director. Contact between the sites is extensive, both on an informal and a more regular formalised basis, and the members of the personnel function at Ichem were well acquainted with their colleagues at different establishments. A Personnel Policy manual is held at Group HQ, itemising common terms and conditions across the sites, but in many areas this does little more than to specify guidelines rather than rigidly impose practices. For example, on employee involvement, the policy manual merely lays down broad generalities about the objectives of EI, and how these tie in with corporate principles, the actual practices being left to individual divisions. As we discovered from research at other sites within Multichem, employee involvement takes quite different forms in these separate establishments.

Quality is an area in which, at first sight, the influence of the centre appears to be more significant, although even here Group personnel seem to nudge and cajole rather than seek to impose a Multichem directive. Senior management within the company as a whole views high quality products and customer service as an ideal in the more competitive environment, this interest stemming from a marketing analysis at the European HQ in the early 1980s. Consequently, all divisions were obliged to monitor progress and record their achievements, so that in the 1986 Employee Reports for the UK company, again freely available to all staff, quality featured as a key component of the reports from most of the divisions. For a number of these, the mechanism chosen for improving quality was Total Quality Management (TQM), and this new venture was introduced by the same group of consultants in several of the cases, though not all. At Ichem, conversely, there was less of a change, principally because the company had already initiated quality improvements at the time of the 'New Deal'. In the event, Ichem merely sought to formalise and reinforce previous practice rather than embarking on a new programme. 'Getting it right first time' was chosen as the motto, and all employees at the factory were due to go on a refresher course during the latter part of 1988. The booklet which accompanied the publication of the quality campaign made it clear that this was no new-fangled venture, but was an extension of the programme which had been operating since the early 1980s. The booklet noted that

> The success of these measures is evidenced in our performance since then. To maintain this high level of achievement requires the pursuit of quality and excellence. We have been building on this change of culture and style .... In this way we have ensured continuity.

In other words, as with many other initiatives within Multichem, Ichem had been at the forefront of change.

To gain the impression from this that there is a one-way influence from the Group to the divisions is to misinterpret the nature of the relationship, and to assign too much power to the centre. In some instances, as with the quality campaign, individual divisions are ahead of the field. In others, it is clear that employee relations practices suitable for one division are not appropriate for others; for example some divisions do not recognise trade unions whereas others have a *de facto* closed shop. Moreover, the small number of personnel at Group level makes it difficult, if not impossible, to impose measures on individual divisions, as, too, does the dependence of Group personnel on their colleagues at the factories for ideas and information. It is more accurate to view the relationship as relatively equal, whereby ideas emerge from the regular discussions between the centre and the divisions. As the Personnel Manager at Ichem put it, when describing the Group Personnel Service Manager, 'he is our kind of man, he's all right, he knows what it is all about'; the search for legitimacy is clearly a two-way process.

On occasions, the centre has attempted to take a more directive role. At the beginning of the 1986 pay negotiations, pressure was placed on the individual divisions to hold down basic wage increases, apparently because of a commitment by the Managing Director to a plea from the CBI. However, this was bound to cause problems in Multichem because the sites have different settlement dates, workers are in a range of different unions or are non-union members, and profitability and performance vary significantly between the divisions. Nonetheless, the hope was that manual workers' pay settlements would be at about the same level. While this caused great consternation with the local negotiators, they followed this line, although there was plenty of room for one-off site bonuses dependent on performance. Not surprisingly, the senior stewards at the main unionised sites soon became aware of standard offers across the company and, as we shall see below, made attempts to organise an inter-site response.

In the event, the pay negotiations were all concluded without industrial action taking place – although it was threatened – principally because each site could offer sizeable bonus payments if performance had been good. In the case of Ichem, a mandate for industrial action was not supported and bonus for the year averaged over £1,000 per employee. At the meetings of the Group Personnel Committee soon after the conclusion of all the negotiations, the review made it clear that this was a dangerous approach for a company committed, in theory at least, to devolved collective bargaining. By the following year, there was a reversion to previous practice, and although there were again similarities across Multichem in the final settlements on base rates, the pressure from the centre had dissipated. On pay, as with a number of other benefits, Ichem tends to offer some of the most favourable conditions within the Group.

Much of this stems from the massive adjustments in 1980–4, following the 'turnaround' project, which ultimately resulted in the 'New Deal'. Along with the halving in numbers employed, there was also a rationalisation of plant capacity to just three major production units, all of which were updated with considerable investment in new technology, and the disposal of large amounts of land which used to belong to the company. For those employees remaining at the site, pay levels were increased, job security was enhanced, terms and conditions were dramatically improved, and workforce flexibility and teamwork became more central to manual work at the factory. In addition to the revitalised and common canteen arrangements, extra sports and welfare facilities have been provided, the most recent being a gymnasium which is available for workers at all times of the day and night, and has proved especially attractive to shift workers. Shop floor operatives have also been encouraged to enrol on courses, and Ichem now reckons that on average each employee receives over seven days training per year, on and off-site, this applying equally to manual workers and office and laboratory staff.

Two of the most significant elements of the New Deal, especially to the manual workers who remained at Ichem, were the Security of Employment Agreement (SEA), concluded in 1982, and the simplification of the payment system. The general principle which underlies the SEA is an 'aim to provide continuing employment for all employees, and to increase individual security as their length of service with the division increases.' Furthermore,

> both the division and the unions confirm their commitment to the principle of minimising in the spirit of cooperation and in accordance with good industrial relations practice the human, social and industrial problems relating to redundancy, and by discussion, consultation and negotiation, to ensure as far as practicable job security for employees.

Since these deals were signed, continued good fortune in the market place has ensured that practical management commitment to these objectives has not been tested, so it is impossible to judge how concrete these assurances would be in the event of a downturn. However, manning levels are so low on any individual plant that, save for the closure of a complete operation, it is unlikely that Ichem could manage with fewer production workers than it currently employs.

The pay system for manual workers now comprises just three grades, one of which is a common craft rate, one for all process operators and personnel in the warehouse and associated areas, and one for the ancillary staff, such as those in the canteen and the locker room. Before the New Deal, there had been a range of different pay grades, and several more levels of supervision, including the position of chargehand. Nowadays, although the skilled employees are on a higher base rate than the process operators, the latter tend to earn more because they receive shift and weekend disturbance allowances. The ancillary workers are paid rather less than both these groups of employees, a fact that reflects the service nature of their role, and their marginality to the production process. All employees, however, receive an annual site-wide bonus payment, which is dependent upon the performance of the division, thus helping to reinforce the commitment of Ichem employees to the future of the plant, at least in financial terms. As we shall see below, all employees receive a considerable amount of information about the performance of the factory/ division on a regular quarterly basis, so they tend to be fairly well aware of current and future prospects.

Ichem has a very distinctive management style, more 'progressive' than the rest of Multichem's UK outlets according to the Group personnel department, although not necessarily appropriate for the needs of other divisions. The style can best be described as 'responsible autonomy', following Friedman, and it owes much to the charismatic personalities of the Managing Director and his personnel colleague on the Board. Although this progressive style was tried before the New Deal, it was not until the aftermath of the trauma surrounding the turnaround that it found more explicit expression within the company. It is based upon a notion of employee relations which puts primacy upon the reduction of direct supervisory control over employees and the encouragement of responsibility and discretion in work.

One of the first pieces of the old industrial relations to be removed in the early 1980s was clocking. Management took away the clock, relying instead upon individual operatives to control their own timekeeping and only intervening in the event of a regular pattern of lateness or an abuse of the privilege. According to the Personnel Director, 'the majority of the manual workforce always came in early prior to the change, so the abolition of clocking was hardly a big deal anyway. All we did was to recognise this and start treating people as adults.' For the few who are poor timekeepers supervisors are expected to take immediate remedial action through counselling, but if there is no improvement harsher measures are taken through the disciplinary procedure. In other words, self-control is rewarded whilst 'offenders' are punished, and supervisors are encouraged to become managers of their teams rather than slavishly interpreting company rule-books and standard procedures in pure quantitative terms. In much the same manner, blue collar workers were encouraged to take greater responsibility for the organisation of their own work, for developing rules to allow for rotation betwen tasks on the team, and for making initial decisions about the services required in the event of a breakdown. The role of chargehand was abolished, and the operatives were 'paid to be their own chargehands'. The whole climate of employee relations is superficially very similar to the styles celebrated in books such as Peters and Waterman's *In Search of Excellence*. But the commitment to an open and assertive style goes much deeper than this, and quite a number of the managers, especially in personnel, have worked their way up from the shop floor, having also played an active role in the union. The Personnel Manager has worked his way up from the shop floor, and has a practical and emotional attachment to operator control over the work process, recalling the days when he used to baulk at incompetent instructions. As he told us, 'The operators know the job. They have loads of experience and they are highly competent. The supervisor only gets in their way, they want to control their own work.' All the managers with whom we spoke supported this view, referring to greater openness and discretions in management style.

The manual workers we interviewed certainly appeared to approve of this new approach, although they did recognise it was hard as well as open. According to one of the process operators, 'It used to be very strict here. It's still firm, but much more open and friendly, everyone is on first name terms, even the Managing Director.' Some referred to the positive advantages which had arisen out of the reduction in the number of layers of management (now down to four), whilst others pointed to the substantial fringe benefits such as social facilities, paternity leave, etc. which had been gained since the time of the New Deal for those fortunate enough to have retained jobs at Ichem. Underpinning all this, of course, were the higher levels of pay and the feeling that employment was now much more secure for those who worked at the factory. Although the stewards made no attempt to deny the substantive gains which had been achieved in recent years, their view was rather more guarded. As we shall see below, the unions are now less central to activities at Ichem, and the stewards saw the move towards an individualistic approach to employee relations as having potentially disastrous consequences for their future activity. One of the senior stewards summed up his concerns in the following way

Management style has changed for the better if you're an ordinary employee, but not if you're a steward. The unions are taking a hammering, and the stewards are worried about losing their authority. Everything is so good in the company here now and the membership accept it, but where will it be in five or ten years' time? We'll have to start the union all over again.

This seems an appropriate point at which to examine the system of collective bargaining and union organisation at Ichem in more detail.

5.5 COLLECTIVE BARGAINING AND UNION ORGANISATION

Employees at Ichem are categorised for administrative purposes into four separate bargaining units, although not all these groups enjoy collective representation rights. The senior managers are in their own bargaining unit, but this seems something of a misnomer, given that salaries are individually negotiated and unions are not recognised for this small section of the workforce (the top twenty-five managers on the site). Chemists, engineers and personnel officers are part of the next bargaining unit, for which a union (MSF) is recognised, but only for individual representation in the event of grievance or disciplinary matters. Union density for this unit is less than fifty per cent. The other two bargaining units do have negotiating rights, and these form the bulk of union membership at Ichem; clerical, secretarial, technical, laboratory, and supervisory staff are the core of the white collar group who have been unionised into MSF, and union density is currently at about sixty-five per cent for these employees. The manual workers form the final and the largest unit on site, with only a handful of people not in the appropriate union. The skilled workers are in the AEU (forty-four members) or the EETPU (seven members), whilst the process operators and ancillary workers (warehouse and canteen) are all in the TGWU; the latter has almost 200 members on site. Union membership is actively encouraged by management, a check-off system is operated, and stewards are allowed access to new starters to persuade them of the merits of joining the union.

There are ten shop stewards in the manual workers' bargaining unit, who together form the joint shop stewards committee (JSSC) at Ichem. Three of these represent the craft employees, thus making the constituencies for this group very small. Four stewards cover the process operators (one for each shift), and there is one each for the warehouse and the remainder of the ancillary workforce. The final steward is the convenor, who does not have a specific constituency to represent. Although he has been full-time on union duties at periods in the past, notably at the time of the New Deal, he is no longer; as we shall see below, this is a source of some resentment on the part of the stewards, which causes them to query the depth of management's supposed commitment to the principle of unionism at Ichem.

The New Deal seemed to indicate that the unions would play a key part in the future of the company, stating that

> the role filled by representatives will be developed in order that they can contribute to the effectiveness of the agreement and to the benefit of their members. This development will take the form of closer contact with local management and supervision, more joint involvement in anticipating and heading off potential problems, and a more frequent contact with the senior management team.

During and immediately after the New Deal, the convenor was heavily involved in discussions with management to the extent that he operated as a full-time union representative. At that time, management found him extremely valuable, and it was acknowledged by all sides that he made a significant contribution to the new industrial relations on site. Following the conclusion of these negotiations, though continuing in the role of convenor, he was put back as a process operator. This meant that he reverted to working shifts and was consequently less able to meet with all sections of the manual workforce on the site.

Management legitimised this action on a number of grounds, but principally that the smaller size of manual union membership (now fewer than 250) no longer made it economic or useful for them to continue with a full-time union representative on site. Underlying this was also some suspicion about the motives of the convenor, whom management viewed as a politically-inspired person more interested in a career within the union than in the future of Ichem as a manufacturing site. In addition, they were dubious about the strength of his links with the shop floor, and about his ability to represent their interests effectively. During our research period, the Personnel Manager repeatedly made reference to the convenor's isolation on the shop floor and to the fact that he seemed to have no friends amongst the membership. Thus, on both numerical and pragmatic grounds, management felt that the removal of full-time status was a justifiable move.

Whilst the stewards could see some logic in the numbers argument, they felt that management had done the convenor a disservice, and interpreted the action as an assault upon the position of the union *per se* rather than an adjustment to the new situation. This feeling has been reinforced by subsequent events, which have tended to marginalise the convenor even more, and have resulted in acrimony in recent negotiations. Rather than greater frequency of contact between themselves and the senior management team, the stewards reckon this has reduced since the time of the New Deal. Following their monthly JSSC meeting, the convenor contacts management with a series of concerns. The person with whom they used to communicate was the Personnel Manager, but now it is a personnel officer with special responsibilities for their bargaining unit. This means that access to the top is restricted, and that management is slow in responding to their concerns, that they are 'talking with the monkey rather than the organ grinder', to adapt the well-used phrase. As we shall see below, their only direct and regular contact with the senior management team, and in this case with the Managing Director plus most of his Board, is by means of the Quarterly Review, and they feel that this degree of interaction is insufficient. Furthermore, the more senior stewards with whom we spoke also indicated that they were finding it more difficult to get time off to attend to union business. As one of the craft stewards noted,

> I thought we had a good balance in management–union relations, but they have started to watch us, and ask us why we want to go to a meeting. I am an experienced, realistic and responsible shop steward. I should know what is reasonable and I do. It annoys me that I have to justify my actions.

Other stewards supported this general perception of a more difficult climate, and referred to 'an edge from both sides at the moment'.

Two of the most recent sets of pay negotiations perhaps provide the clearest clue to the nature of management–union, as opposed to management–employee, relations at Ichem, and to the role of the unions at the factory and throughout Multichem at large. As we have already seen, the 1986 pay negotiations were particularly difficult at Ichem. There were recriminations all round, with counter claims about the willingness of both parties to break with sound negotiating conventions; management accused the stewards of not communicating the offer in sufficient detail to their members, as part of their (the stewards') attempt to justify calls for industrial action at Ichem and to mobilise support for an inter-site initiative throughout the company as a whole. The stewards complained that certain managers leaked selective information to the shop floor, and that at the end of the meeting which concluded the negotiations, a senior manager 'read out a bollocking and then left giving us no chance to come back.' Employees whom we interviewed also recognised the conflicts which surfaced at these negotiations, but saw them in terms of a personality clash between the Personnel Director and the convenor. Whatever the interpretation, however, collective relationships at the site could not be characterised as especially good!

It was also apparent, however, that there were rifts within the steward body, and that the convenor was tolerated by the other stewards, rather than being actively supported by them. In their view, as committed union members, an attack on the convenor was automatically translated into union victimisation, but they, too, were prepared to do deals without him if this could be arranged. Prior to the 1988 negotiations, the convenor requested time-off to join a union delegation to an Eastern European country, at a time which happened to coincide with the wage negotiating period. Management agreed to his request, but reminded him of the clash; he had already talked with the rest of the steward body about this, and they were willing to continue negotiations in his absence. As soon as he had departed, the rest of the stewards approached management, asking for immediate negotiations and a settlement before his return. This was achieved, to the satisfaction of the management, the other stewards and the workforce. The standing of the convenor with his colleagues from other sites was hardly any better, as was demonstrated in the 1986 negotiations, and this does not seem to have improved since then, according to our union contacts elsewhere in Multichem. They attribute the failure to develop a company-wide stance on pay directly to him, since they felt his incentive for inter-site combination was personally motivated, rather than offering strategic benefits to the workers across Multichem as a whole.

5.6 EMPLOYEE INVOLVEMENT

Of all the companies in our study, Ichem has the least extensive set of formal institutions for employee involvement, Apart from the Quarterly Review, EI tends to be practised by informal means and by a degree of operator control over the process through teamwork. There are no grand schemes for team briefing, nor are there quality circles, manufacturing cells or customer care committees. Communications meetings do occur in some areas, but this is at the discretion of the supervisor concerned, and it is not subject to formal monitoring by the personnel department. Indeed, the major emphasis at Ichem was on the necessity for systems to evolve within their own context, and an abhorrence of 'imported' techniques or expensive contracts with management consultants, whereby solutions are bought off the peg. More than any other site in our research, at Ichem there was a firm belief that organic regeneration was superior to transplanted organs.

The pinnacle of the system, at least in status terms, is the Quarterly Review. This was introduced as part of the New Deal, and consists of a series of meetings every three months, starting with the Managing Director and finishing with the shop floor. The Managing Director himself was the driving force behind this approach, which he sees as the embodiment of his commitment to open management and increased employee awareness about the state of the business. The purpose of the meetings is to transmit information to all employees about the performance of the division, and about future prospects. Although we were given access to most things at Ichem, we were not allowed to attend a Quarterly Review because it was felt that this could damage confidentiality and create a dangerous precedent for other visitors; this meeting was for Ichem employees and outsiders were not welcome.

Every quarter, as part of the formal monitoring process, all managers are required to write progress reports on their departments. These are then sent to the personnel department for compilation into a single script, which goes to the Managing Director for his approval. In line with a published schedule, every three months the Managing Director makes two detailed presentations on the same day, both with exactly the same material – according to the personnel department; in the morning, he speaks to senior managers and in the afternoon to the employee representatives, with both sessions lasting up to two hours. All participants are also provided with a script of the presentation, apart from the confidential material, which is retained. During the following week, all the senior managers brief the staff for about one hour, this being organised to coincide with shift and production requirements. Once again, a summary sheet is distributed to all employees for reinforcement. Questions are encouraged, and each quarter all these are noted and compiled by a senior manager before being shown to the Managing Director; typically, this would total some seventy or eighty questions. Those which cannot be answered immediately are put on an action list for reply as soon as possible. Though there are some similarities between this system and team briefing, namely in the regular dissemination of information from the top to the bottom of the hierarchy, there are also some fundamental differences. Individuals are not always briefed by their immediate boss, and, indeed, a recent initiative has been to encourage presentations from senior managers from other departments (line or staff) precisely because it can lead to a wider awareness of business matters. Other differences relate to the length of the presentations, their regularity, the handouts, and the number of levels involved in the cascade down the management chain.

The content of a Quarterly Review typically consists of the following components:

- Sales relative to plan and to previous year, broken down into individual businesses within the site, and between home and overseas markets. Costs of inputs. Raw materials targets for the next quarter. Major customers.
- New technology, new building work and product development.
- Logistics, warehouse and transport.
- Safety issues such as recent records, and awards from the

British Safety Council, Royal Society for the Prevention of Accidents, Chemical Industries Association. Environmental protection.
- Quality assurance.
- Public relations.
- Medical issues, such as health and anti-smoking campaigns, blood screening, breast examination facilities.
- Personnel statistics, leavers and starters, training programmes.
- Added value as a percentage of turnover, and in relation to the price of raw materials and revenue costs.
- Outlook for the forthcoming year.

In the Quarterly Reviews in the latter half of 1987, two messages were central to the meetings and they both reflected more deep-rooted concerns within the company. First, the notion of quality pervaded all aspects of the presentations, according to the participants, with emphasis on 'efficient service to the customer.' Secondly, the Reviews stressed the importance of 'teamworking' and 'people management', issues which again were central to the training initiative throughout Ichem. Following a review of the format for the system, senior management have also made it 'snappier' and have increased their use of visual aids in the presentations. Initial responses seemed favourable to this shift in direction as well.

The stewards appeared to value this forum, largely because they receive detailed information direct from the Managing Director, and they are able to ask him questions about this if necessary. One of the senior stewards felt that management was 'very open, they don't try to hide anything from us, and there is plenty of opportunity for us to ask questions. The Managing Director seems a very genuine bloke.' However, the stewards were also fully aware that the information which they received illustrated management's interpretation of events, tending to support decisions which had already been made or were about to be taken. 'They tell us that the competitors are at the door when they want to keep costs down', said another of the senior stewards, but equally 'the information which we get is pretty useful for the wage negotiations.' Even the steward who was most critical of arrangements, was still highly committed to the system and Ichem because, he said, 'I want the company to succeed, not because I'm a capitalist but because it's my bread and butter.' The managers also found it a useful way in which to ensure regular communications with staff, and also to expose people in their own departments to thinking from other functions within management.

The manual workers we interviewed seemed to value the Quarterly Review as well, and they even had suggestions on how to improve the meetings. They were all keen to receive confidential information from senior management, since this was felt to illustrate their, i.e. management's, interest in the workers and encourage them to be part of the firm, as one of the craftsmen put it. Another commented that 'some of the information is bordering on the release of commercial secrets. But the lads are responsible, conscious of the company's position and their own future.' Most of them felt the presentations could be made more interesting and appropriate for the staff, especially in relation to performance figures, and one expressed an interest in where the company's products ended up, that is, their ultimate use. What struck us, though, about Ichem were the generally positive attitudes to the company, perhaps a position born out of relief at continued employment after the turnaround project, but reinforced by the buoyant product market circumstances which have confronted the company in the last few years.

Aside from the Quarterly Review, there are no other formal systems for employee involvement, such as a JCC or quality circles. Nevertheless, there are informal mechanisms for communicating with employees and these have evolved in certain parts of the factory. In the process areas and the warehouse, communication takes place on an informal basis with frequent discussions between the supervisors and the manual workers when the need arises. In the engineering area, amongst the instrument and electrical employees, a more formalised arrangement has emerged under the auspices of the electrical foreman. He has arranged a meeting approximately once a month in order to brief employees about the progress of work through their area, to remind them of specific issues – for example, safety, following an accident to a contractor – and to ask for their suggestions to resolve problems. Although not all employees can always be present, meetings are arranged at times when the majority can attend and do so. However, his enthusiasm for these meetings was not shared by all the staff; as one of them said, 'If the foreman's getting too much flack, he just closes the meeting down . . . we're asked our views, but nothing ever happens.' Obviously, EI is far from perfect.

5.7 CONCLUSION

As we mentioned in the introduction to this chapter, Ichem has gone a long way to reforming its employee relations since the turnaround project of the early 1980s. The style of management which is practised has certain similarities to HRM, especially in the contribution of the personnel department to strategic decisions and the shift towards an individualistic, investment-centred approach to employee relations. The position of the unions in the factory has become more marginal, partly owing to personality conflicts between the convenor and management, but also because it is difficult to conceive of a clear and effective role for unionism in the current climate. Since management has taken the initiative in communicating direct to employees, since substantive benefits have improved considerably over the course of the decade, and since the product market allows management some degree of latitude in choosing how to organise employee relations, the union appears less central to its members. However, it is somewhat harder to determine whether this would be sustained should market conditions change dramatically.

6 · FOODPACK: COMMUNICATING FOR CHANGE

6.1 INTRODUCTION

The Foodpack site is located on an industrial estate several miles south of a large Northern city, where the company has manufactured the principal product for well over fifty years. The independent company which started operations was taken over in the 1930s, and it is now part of a large multinational divisionalised company, which has extensive interests in a wide range of foodstuffs, including baking, cereals, cakes and condiments. The company as a whole employs over 30,000 people around the world, with the vast majority of these in the United Kingdom. Foodpack manufactures its products in accordance with a divisional schedule, so no marketing or selling function exists at the site. However, it is the only plant within the company which makes this specific range of goods.

The plant is of interest to employee relations specialists for a number of reasons; although fewer than 200 people are employed at the site, five separate unions are recognised for bargaining purposes, an unusual feature, perhaps, given current interest in single-union agreements. Nevertheless, there is a three-year, no-strike deal in operation at the factory with the largest union. In addition, management at the plant has embarked on a series of initiatives to improve communications with the shop floor workers, and this more direct approach appears to have found favour with these employees. Because of these developments, themselves the result of a greater preoccupation with quality and market awareness, the unions have come to occupy a more marginal position within the framework of factory-level employee relations.

6.2 WORK ORGANISATION

Foodpack employs the smallest number of people of any of the establishments involved in our study. Unlike Ichem or Typeng, it had not suffered a dramatic decline in employment levels over the course of the 1980s, and numbers had varied between a high of 235 in 1983 to a low of 174 in 1987. Two rounds of redundancies took place in the mid-1980s, one following the reorganisation of distribution arrangements within the division, and the other caused by the introduction of new machinery with lower labour requirement. The early part of the decade had seen growth, and so, too, had the final year of our research (1988); this led one of the stewards to tell us that employees now felt more secure following 'a big phase of change, costing jobs. Now it's steadying down. The factory has become more modern and more viable.' Certainly, all the employees we interviewed were optimistic about the future.

Direct employees, that is, those involved in production itself, comprised about 60 per cent of the total during the whole period, with skilled manual and non-manual employees making up the rest. The gender composition of the workforce, especially the direct workers, had undergone quite significant changes during the course of the 1980s, although this was in the opposite direction to trends in the labour market more generally. Whilst there were twice as many women as men employed on direct work until 1983, over the next five years this distribution altered, so that by 1986 there were more men than women on this category of work. Well over 90 per cent of the workforce are full-timers, and again this pattern has been maintained throughout the decade. What makes this even more interesting is the fact that Foodpack's sister plant, from another division but just half a mile down the road, employs substantial numbers of part-timers (70 per cent of all production workers) because, in the words of the Personnel Manger, of the 'considerable economic advantages' they offer to management. Foodpack recruits an extra fifteen workers on a temporary basis annually between September and December in order to cope with increased production requirements in the run-up to Christmas, but if possible the same people are re-employed each year. There is little labour turnover at the site, partly because of the lack of alternative work in the area, but also as a consequence of the network of family ties within the plant; indeed, amongst manual workers, the average length of service at Foodpack is well over ten years. Absenteeism varied between 4 per cent and 10 per cent over the couse of the decade, with a somewhat higher rate among direct workers as compared with indirect workers.

The flow of work through the factory commences with receipt of raw materials – the majority of which are purchased from outside the group – and terminates in the warehouse. Most of the ingredients, especially the bulkier ones, are delivered daily, some being purchased annually before being stored in dehydrated form in an outside warehouse. In between, there are two principal parts to the workflow; first, the manufacturing process, which can also be conveniently subdivided into two parts, the first of which is baking (also incorporating mixing, spreading and drying). This operation is highly mechanised, although the machinery is far from new, having been bought in the 1950s. The second stage of the manufacturing process is milling, sieving and blending, which is also highly automated, using computer controls for weighing and 'pumping' materials from one part of the operation to the next. These two operations, both currently male preserves, are worked on a three-shift basis. On any one shift, the team comprises just four people, one of whom is supervisor and one is a 'floater' who is available to assist in the event of any sudden emergencies. There is a considerable element of functional flexibility between workers on these operations, as workers rotate tasks, usually on an hourly basis, and clean ovens, other equipment, and the surrounding work area at the end of a production run. Indeed, an agreement signed in 1981 requires employees to perform work outside their normal job provided it is within their capability, and this certainly appears to be upheld within these teams. Moreover, this group of employees is also numerically flexible in that they work longer hours for several months each year, so as to maintain baking and blending on a six-day basis in accordance with production schedules. In addition, they report for work on Sundays during the peak periods in order to clean and set up the operation for the forthcoming week. Because of this, earnings can increase dramatically in the months before Christmas. Although there is substantial horizontal flexibility between the process workers, this does not extend to maintenance of their own equipment; that remains a skilled job undertaken by the engineers.

The other principal stage in the workflow is packaging. There are nine lines in all, six of which pack products made on site, with the remainder packing products for other plants within the division. This is the most labour-intensive part of the factory (with about one hundred people employed in total) and, although it is still a female-dominated area, a significant minority of young men now work on the packing lines. Some of these lines are operated on a days-only basis, with an extra twilight shift for the peak three-month period, although the majority of the packers are employed on a two-shift basis (6 a.m. to 2 p.m.; 2 p.m. to 10 p.m.).

On the packing lines, operatives rotate on a prearranged basis, usually by the hour or the day, in order to suit their own particular needs as a group; this is not a management-led initiative but, according to the packers themselves, one which has resulted from their desire to inject some variety into their work in an attempt to 'kill the boredom' associated with the repetitive tasks they undertake. A more recent development which has been introduced by management (the Quality Control Manger) is to extend the jobs of packers to incorporate inspection tasks as well. This involves check-weighing of the packs, and testing to ensure that the product is not contaminated with any foreign bodies, such as metal. Management sees this as a valuable way in which to increase employee awareness of the importance of product quality, and, once again, packers did seem to have received this message. The shop floor operatives we interviewed were all keen on the variety which greater flexibility/job rotation had created for them at work, and were especially supportive of movements within work teams. There was also some flexibility between different packing operations; as one of the packers commented, 'There's a lot of flexibility here. You could work anywhere in the factory. I, mostly work on X [a particular product line] but we move if there is no work there.' Functional flexibility did not appear to be a contentious issue at Foodpack, as workers either rotated between tasks on the line because it suited their own, rather limited, preferences, or moved between teams in accordance with management instructions. Flexibility within a team is relatively easy to appreciate, given that employees on most of the packing lines receive the same rate of pay, and are therefore not undertaking tasks beyond their job 'slot'. In order to achieve flexibility between operations, basically from the simple to the more complex packing lines, which involves work from another job slot, management pays the higher rate for the time the employee works on the alternative line. Conversely if a packer moves to a simpler line, the pay rate is protected.

In addition to the manufacture and packing of products, there is also an engineering function, comprising eleven fitters, who deal with heavier engineering work, such as pump or gearbox repair, and electricians, and eleven mechanics, responsible for maintenance of the packaging machines. The different trades work a variety of shift arrangements, the fitters being available on a twenty-four hour basis. There is a strict and carefully controlled demarcation between the work of the fitters and the packaging engineers, as well as an intense rivalry, and each group is paid a separate rate. The latter regard the work of the former as cruder than their own ('He's like a car mechanic, no good for television sets'), whereas the fitters reckon their own skills to be much broader than those of the packaging engineers ('We do everything which isn't attached to the machines. Anything required making, we make'). Indeed, one of the fitters we interviewed had spent the previous few weeks making a piece of equipment for the factory of which he was justifiably proud. The electricians viewed their own jobs as different from the others, although one of the older hands felt that this demarcation was breaking down with the influx of new and younger labour into the works; however, he also pointed out that there had been no pressure from management to increase functional flexibility between the crafts, a stance later confirmed by the Personnel Manager. Any tolerance shown by the craft workers towards horizontal flexibility certainly did not extend to the softening of vertical demarcations, which would allow production workers to undertake their own maintenance.

6.3 THE MARKET ENVIRONMENT

Foodpack competes in a mature market, especially in relation to its principal products, for which it is the brand leader, having a fifty per cent share of the UK market. In recent years, the company has developed a new set of flavours within this range in order to respond to consumer preference for more specialised versions of the product. According to one of the senior managers on site, this diversification has enabled the company to maintain competitive advantage over its rivals, and at the same time 'educate' the public into using the principal product more regularly over the course of the year. In addition, Foodpack has also taken over the packing operations for a number of products made elsewhere within the division, and at the end of our research, management was commissioning a totally new line to manufacture a quite different range of goods. The introduction of new specialities of the branded product, plus the venture into new products altogether, have given employees greater faith in the future viability of the plant.

Although the market is quantitatively mature, there have also been substantial changes in its character, especially in relation to customer profile. Over the course of the 1980s, the major retailers have increasingly sought to pressure the manufacturers into producing 'own-label' lines for them, a process exacerbated by the increasingly severe competition within the retail sector itself. For their part, the manufacturers feel that they cannot afford not to have a presence in at least one of the major multiples, and senior management at divisional level within the parent company has been keen to negotiate deals with the retailers, partly because it feels there is little choice if the plant is to remain viable into the next decade. The retailers have used their power to pare down the profit margins of the manufacturers, and have also sought to impose stringent quality and hygiene standards on them. This has clearly had a significant impact upon Foodpack's operations, even though as a matter of corporate policy, the company as a whole is committed to supporting its own brands 'though nothing like to the extent of Kelloggs in advertising Corn Flakes'.

The most dramatic effect of this change in customer profile is in relation to quality, not just of the finished product but also of the raw materials and the manufacturing environment within which production takes place. One of the most recent appointments has been that of the Quality Control Manager, brought in with the brief of updating a 'backward' technical system and extending the quality function beyond its original principal role of check-weighing. His feeling was that 'people in this factory needed to be made aware of quality. They thought that because they had made the product for so long it must be all right. They had become complacent and blinkered.' In recent years, Foodpack has received visits from the major retail outlets, during which time external inspectors conduct a thorough appraisal of existing methods and conditions. One well-known retailer in particular is renowned for the extent of its inspections, and for examining nooks and crannies where no-one had previously looked! As we shall see below, in the section on employee involvement, the weekly news bulletin generally carries items advising employees in advance about impending visits from big customers. Although these inspections had the specific objective of examining 'own-label' lines, management had used them to legitimise its aim of upgrading quality and hygiene standards throughout the factory as a whole.

The other significant feature of the market is its highly seasonal character, with major peaks in demand at Christmas and Easter, and severe troughs in the early spring and the summer; for example, production is five or six times higher in October than it is in May. Whilst it would obviously be possible to iron out some of these dramatic fluctuations in output, the divisional head office is unwilling to countenance such a move because of the high storage costs it would involve. As we have already seen, Foodpack management copes with this by recruiting a small number of temporary workers for the packing lines, and by the provision of a twilight shift for the three months up to Christmas. During this time, permanent employees also work considerably longer hours, and weekend overtime becomes a normal feature of the job, to the extent that some employees are able to increase their weekly pay by up to fifty per cent over this period. Again, as we shall see below, it is difficult to maintain the continuity of team briefing during the peak periods because of the more immediate pressures of production schedules. But at least the seasonality in demand is predictable, and Foodpack managers know the rough order of these peaks and troughs in advance. It also means that the nature of work undertaken can vary over the course of the year, and that there can be a concentration on cleaning after the Christmas rush.

6.4 MANAGEMENT STRATEGY AND STYLE

The corporation as a whole comprises seven divisions, each of which is responsible for a sizeable range of products or part of the world. Given the diversity of markets within which the company operates, the range of technologies employed, and its presence in the United States, and Australia and the Far East (which themselves constitute separate divisions), the key locus for strategic decisions is at divisional – rather than corporate – level. For example, production schedules are set by divisional management, products are marketed and sold by staff operating across the division as a whole, and longer-term employee relations initiatives emanate from senior management in the personnel function at that level. The division within which Foodpack is located has recently revised its corporate plan, largely due to the impact of the Managing Director appointed in the early 1980s, and personnel considerations have found expression within this. The divisional Personnel Director himself acknowledged that human resource issues, whilst important in the formulation of the plan, would always remain downstream from marketing and production demands. Two of the principal strategic tasks undertaken in the divisional personnel function over the last few years have been an evaluation of relocating certain production units to other parts of the United Kingdom, and an assessment of potential union reactions to a possible rationalisation of the distribution network. Both these activities had their roots in external factors, notably decisions by some of the large retail outlets to take control of their own transport operations via backwards vertical integration.

Given the substantial differences in employee relations conditions and climate between the sites, there is also a considerable element of plant autonomy and decentralisation within the division. Patterns of unionisation vary from one site to another, partly a result of local circumstances but also because of the acquisition of new companies and product lines; in all there are approximately thirty different bargaining units within the division. Historically, Foodpack has operated its own management and personnel systems with minimal interference from the division, precisely because the success of its products in the market place has generated a degree of complacency. As we shall see below, this tended to produce a relatively *ad hoc*, reactive and informal system for the management of employee relations. More recently, however, the impact of the superstores, through 'own-brand' products and heightened quality awareness, has combined with a more proactive stance from the divisional personnel function to decrease plant autonomy. Certain activities are now organised from divisional level, of which management selection and development are probably the most significant, since they cover all the senior managerial personnel at the Foodpack site. Equally, the Personnel Director now has a team of specialists working with him at divisional level which includes employee relations, training and development, and recruitment and personnel systems. In addition, there are formal meetings between the site personnel managers and the divisional staff two or three times each year, and contact on other occasions as appropriate. However, despite a much increased influence from the division, there are clearly limits to this, principally because personnel managers at plant level need to tailor their plans to the general objectives of the factory and the local labour market context.

At divisional level, it is felt that the informal approach favoured by the Managing Director has set the tone for management style throughout the division. This is reflected in the corporate philosopy he introduced in mid-1985, whose 'defined set of values, culture and philosophy' has provided the foundation for the division's internally resourced management development programme. The corporate philosophy regarding management style can be summarised in the following way:

- The relaxation of formality on the sites, and introduction of first name terms with all irrespective of status.
- Creative management.
- The practice of openness and frankness, especially with superordinates.
- Fairness, firmness and integrity in management.
- An acceptance that people are bound to make mistakes at some time.
- Prompt attention to requests up or down the hierarchy.
- Delegation as far down the line as possible.

The new management style is also reflected in the large number of recent appointments at divisional and site level of young and energetic managers who are committed to these principles and their operation. Indeed, it would be only a slight exaggeration to see these changes as a 'palace revolution' in the division. The approach certainly appears to have been internalised by many of the senior managers at site level; the Personnel Manager at Foodpack remarked that 'so far as he [the Divisional Managing

Director] is concerned, it is not just a piece of paper, and he acts upon it. It is a break with the past and will take time to find acceptance.' The site Personnel Manager is one of the most committed enthusiasts for this shift in emphasis, besides having an interest in fashionable employee relations techniques used in other companies. He is particularly dismissive of the general standard of British management, largely for its failure to get 'out and about on the shop floor'. The clarity of his views, and the vigour with which he conveys them to others, seemed to make a favourable impression on those around him, including the senior steward. Soon after we completed our research, he was promoted to take over responsibility for a number of sites throughout the division, although he also retained a strategic presence at Foodpack. Other senior appointments made during 1986 and 1987 included the Production Manager and the Quality Control Manager, as well as new Personnel Officer, all of whom came from outside the division or the company as a whole. One of the new appointments spoke of this grouping as 'the new boys' club', and it was clear that many of the most recent initiatives, for example, team briefing, regular newsletters, quality awareness and healthy eating campaigns, had emanated from this set of managers. However, the previous Factory Manager was still in place, and it was widely acknowledged that he had been highly instrumental in facilitating these appointments, negotiating money from the division for improvements to the plant, and giving the 'new boys' room for manoeuvre. He delegated much of the task of running the operation to his management team, concentrating on links with the division, so his presence was not particularly common on the shop floor. Overall, our contacts at both divisional level and at the plant felt that a new management style was emerging, one which was more proactive, open and organismic, rather than reactive, hierarchical and mechanistic.

As we saw in Chapter 3, however, the fact that senior management feels that there has been a change in style is no guarantee that it will be recognised elsewhere in the plant, or that it will be accepted by other managers and shop floor workers. The supervisors we interviewed had identified changes in management style in recent years, and commonly referred to a more open atmosphere and less of the 'big whip'. More information seemed to reach them now, a situation they approved of, and which, they felt, was largely owed to the new personalities on site. Another foreman also remarked about the significance of the changes, but he saw this in the context of a more quiescent workforce; he said, 'There's very little need for disciplinary action at this site . . . we have little trouble from the unions. It is very open and getting more so.' He continued, 'I used to learn more from my shop steward than through management channels. Now anything that's being brought in is discussed, consulted first.' The implications of this for the relative position of stewards and supervisors are something to which we shall return in the next section.

The shop stewards also recognised this shift to a more open management style, interpreting it as a move towards greater cooperation, and a reduction in adversarial relations. The former senior steward (who retired from this position in 1986 on ill-health grounds, but had remained a steward) felt that management used to be much more ruthless, but that the situation had improved since many of the old guard had retired. He remarked, 'We always used to suspect a hidden motive – not so much now. It's a lot easier.' The shop stewards' implicit acceptance of managerial pre-rogatives is very evident from their statements about the way change is introduced, some of which would not have been out of place in an Industrial Society booklet! For example, 'If people are informed in advance, it takes away the sting, the shock of change', or 'I like the way that managers are now more open because good communications lead to greater motivation at work.' The new senior steward's only reservation about this more open approach was that some line managers were not always effective at com-municating; that is, she was more concerned about the social skills or competence of managers to communicate effectively than she was about the fact that increased direct communications might marginalise the union within the workplace.

None of the manual workers we interviewed was overtly critical of the new approach either, and, indeed, most welcomed the more open management style. Some of this was defined in terms of improved welfare and social facilities, whereas other respondents made more explicit reference to the process by which routine management was carried out. The most succinct description of this came from one of the packers who told us, 'Managers here are very friendly. They talk *to* you, not *down to* you.' But it should also be recalled that openness is not synonymous with a lack of management control – quite the contrary, in fact. Whilst management had sought to increase cooperation by the greater disclosure of information to employees, this was contingent upon a responsible attitude from the workforce. Management was acknowledged to be stricter about timekeeping and general discipline, but also to apply these standards in a consistent manner which for that reason proved more acceptable to the mass of manual workers. This is not to say that there is complete and deep-rooted unanimity at Foodpack; we were told of management 'bloomers', and disagreement with specific decisions, but the underlying emphasis was either implicitly or explicitly positive about recent changes. One of the fitters referred to the professionalism and openness of management, its willingness to listen to grievances, and its concern for product quality, the latter especially being an objective with which he thoroughly agreed.

The flexibility and commitment of staff is further illustrated by an incident which occurred towards the end of our time at the company. Foodpack had ventured into a new product market within the food sector, and management had agreed a delivery date for this new product with the sole customer, a major retail outlet. There had been a series of commissioning problems with the new line, both at the manufacturing stage and with the packing operations, and the company became concerned that the delivery dates would not be met. Indeed, on the Friday afternoon that the first delivery was due to take place, it became obvious that the target would not be met unless extra labour was drafted on to the packing line. Management consequently appealed to the shop floor workers in mid-afternoon to seek a number of volunteers to assist with the final push and stay at the factory until the job was complete. The fact that management had no difficulty in securing sufficient support for this extra work clearly tells us something about the attitude of the staff towards their employment.

The point is further reinforced by the results gained from a questionnaire analysis, undertaken by sandwich students from a local polytechnic, which compared employee attitudes between 1986 and 1988. Whilst problems clearly remained, the results did indicate an improvement in relations at Foodpack; for example, in response to a question about whether the plant was viewed as a better or worse place at which to work than it was twelve months ago, over seventy-five per cent of employees felt it to be better, compared with an even split two years before. In terms of their general attitudes towards work and the company, although job security still ranked as their most important concern – not by much, however – respondents also displayed a greater commitment to the company and a feeling that their jobs were now more interesting than had previously been the case.

It would appear, therefore, that changes in management style have percolated down to the manual workers at Foodpack. To a large extent, this also represents a strategic shift, emanating from initiatives by key individuals at divisional level, with support from the Factory Manager at Foodpack itself. The trend towards greater centralisation of 'employee relations thinking' will probably continue into the future, since it is a longer-term aim of the Divisional Personnel Director. Common management development programmes represent one route to achieving this, and so, too, does greater coordination of personnel activities across the sites, not necessarily in terms of common conditions and settlements, but more in relation to the broad parameters of negotiations and communications. However, there is still an overwhelming recognition that any shift towards centralisation has to be tempered because of the specific product and labour market environments within which individual plants operate.

6.5 COLLECTIVE BARGAINING AND UNION ORGANISATION

Despite the relatively small size of the factory, there are five separate unions recognised for bargaining purposes, and a total of thirteen shop stewards is allowed within the agreement. By far the largest union on site (representing the ninety-seven direct production workers) is the GMBATU, which has a post-entry union membership agreement with Foodpack; neither side has pressed for a ballot following the legislative changes in the 1982 Employment Act. These employees are represented by seven stewards, including the senior steward. The other unions have much lower membership levels at the company; the AEU covers the eighteen fitters (maintenance and packaging), and the EETPU has just four members. A *de facto* closed shop also operates for both these groups, and each has one steward on site. The white collar employees are in MATSA and SATA, with the former having approximately twice as many members, although neither union is able to claim more than about half the potential membership; each union has two representatives on site. All the unions, even those representing the white collar workers, have a long history at Foodpack.

The most significant aspect of recent negotiations was the conclusion of a three-year pay deal in 1985, which contained provision for a 'no-strike' deal and pendulum arbitration. Management at the plant had been keen to achieve such an agreement, following a number of years in which industrial relations went through a 'turbulent phase', although the company did manage to avoid any major strike action. In the early 1980s, senior management was able to buy out overtime guarantees, and a commitment to flexible working was also achieved. Nevertheless, the next few years were characterised by a series of leapfrogging claims, which, whilst not always successful, did take up a considerable amount of management time and energy.

In order to assist in the securing of major capital investment at the site, management and the GMBATU agreed to a three-year deal for the settlement of wages and the avoidance of disputes. Within the agreement, both parties accept the need for continuity of production, and the fact that the sustained growth and development of the business is dependent upon cooperation of all employees on site. The first five stages of the disputes procedure are fairly typical, allowing for hearings by more senior management and union representatives, culminating in a meeting between the Factory Manager, the Personnel Manager, a full-time officer of the union, and other trade union representatives as appropriate. Strict time limits govern each stage of this procedure. The sixth and final stage allows for a range of options to avoid dispute; one of these is pendulum arbitration, for which the written terms of reference are to be agreed in advance and the decision is binding on both the parties. Thus, as with most of the so-called 'no-strike' agreements, the major deviation from conventional procedures lies in the lack of mention of strikes, rather than in their explicit prohibition. Arbitration has been used twice during the three years, and seems to have resulted in a satisfactory outcome for both parties. Whilst the Personnel Manager feels the deal has been expensive, at between six and seven-and-a-half per cent per annum, plus an extra day's holiday and additional shift payments, he is also keen on a similar agreement for the next three years. In his view, 'It has de-hassled the meetings between stewards and management. There's no need for posturing and game playing. It's allowed us to get into other areas.' The Production Manager felt that the deal had bought industrial peace for three years.

Surprisingly perhaps, the implicit no-strike deal did not appear controversial to the union representatives either. According to the former senior steward, the union had always gone through procedure at Foodpack prior to the new agreement, and had been willing to accept arbitration in the event of a failure to agree. He added that 'if members went ahead with action, they'd be on their own.' For him, the only real effect of the new deal was that his members were given more money! Despite our questioning them about the deal, the shop floor operatives did not regard the agreement as extraordinary either, their only opinion being that the plant was now a better place at which to work. This lack of reaction to the new deal is probably easier to understand in the context of the considerable indifference shown by members towards their unions; typical among their comments were the following: 'It's a good thing to have a union, but it doesn't play a big part here', or 'I usually keep clear of the union', or 'I don't have much to do with the union unless we are talking about the pay rise.' One man from the baking department lamented the fact that the union was 'not as strong as it used to be. It seems as though the fight has gone', but this view did not seem to be typical of the shop floor as a whole. Even amongst the craft workers, there was little evidence of more militant attitudes, and indeed the senior EETPU steward only remained the representative because 'no other bugger will do it'. The only interviewee to suggest a link between the three-year deal and the lack of union militancy was a foreman, who noted that 'friction has eased off in the last few years . . . the deal has taken a lot of the bullets away.'

If the role of the stewards has been reduced by the negotiation of a three-year deal, their day-to-day relations with management have also undergone some adjustments as well. Prior to the arrival of the new Production Manager, the stewards had met twice a month on a formal basis, once with the previous manager, and once on their own. The new appointee was dismayed to discover that the corridor was 'overrun with a constant stream of stewards beating a path to the door of the personnel department', and that they often knew rather more about company affairs than did the supervisors. He determined to alter the balance, by using team briefing to ensure that managers were able to compete with the unions' communications role, but he did not want to alienate the stewards, so he continued with the system of meetings on a monthly basis. Ostensibly, these were designed as an open forum, for either party to say what it wanted to the other off the record, but they also served the underlying purpose of pressurising the foremen to give information to the shop floor before the stewards could do so. At these meetings, the Production Manager provided the stewards with information about a wide range of matters, including production and sales forecasts, new trade deals, and other developments in the division as a whole. He also highlighted forthcoming initiatives, such as a review of communications, training plans, and the impending renegotiation of the three-year deal. He was quite adamant though, that this meeting was not for negotiating purposes, but for the trading of views, and in particular for him to convey his thoughts to the stewards – in a sense, a structuring of expectations.

Both the Personnel Manager and the Production Manager are fully aware of the effect of this approach on the position of the unions at Foodpack. At different times during our contact with the company, each of them had told us that the need to negotiate had been reduced in recent years. The Personnel Manager put it like this: 'It's pushing negotiations down to consultation, and consultation down to communication. You need only do the last two if you do it right because ultimately there's only one best way of running the business.' The implication of this is that the unions will become progressively more marginal to the administration of employee relations, given that their role in the negotiating process and their centrality to the membership is reduced. Nevertheless, the Personnel Manager remained insistent that his perspective still left considerable space for union activity within the plant. For him, the union would remain important because continuous pressure keeps management on its toes, and because of its representational role within the workplace. He argued, 'the unions are necessary because every now and then we get it wrong ... we ignore stewards at our peril. They still have a huge potential influence over the workforce.' Moreover, he vigorously rejected our view that management was marginalising the activity of the unions in the plant; as at Ichem, the Foodpack Personnel Manager felt that we had misinterpreted their reduced willingness to do business with the senior steward as an assault on the principle of unionism *per se*. Unlike the state of affairs at Ichem, however, this was not a matter linked to the political motivations of the convenor, but concerned her overall lack of ability. Whatever the interpretation, though, it is clear that the collective arena now occupies a much less central place within the system of employee relations at Foodpack.

6.6 EMPLOYEE INVOLVEMENT

In a recent annual report of the parent company, employee involvement formed a major part of the section on its review of employment; one of the objectives of the Group was 'progressive employment policies, not only for reasons of social responsibility, but also to secure the willing commitment of employees at all levels to the objectives of the business.' Communication and consultation were singled out as of major importance, particularly 'at a time when the pace of change, commercial and technological, has accelerated beyond anything imaginable to a previous generation.' The specific mechanisms used extensively within the company were cited as work group briefings, video presentations, and employee attitude surveys, the latter having been a regular feature of EI activity since the early 1970s. However, the fact that companies report their commitment to employee involvement does not necessarily mean this is actually implemented or positively pursued within individual factories.

At Foodpack, the move to more extensive EI is a recent phenomenon, directly brought about by the commitment of the new régime (at divisional and plant level) to improve communications as part of a wider conception of human resource management. Although there had been a previous attempt to introduce briefing at Foodpack, this had soon collapsed, and when we first visited the site in early 1986, there was no regular or site-wide coordination of EI. By the end of our research period, team briefing and a weekly newsletter had been introduced, and improved communications had become central to the management approach. The initial impetus at site level for this came with the appointment of the new Personnel Manager, who had most recently been employed at the company's sister plant, but had previous experience with another firm in the food industry. In both his former jobs, he had found direct communications to be a valuable technique, and he was keen to introduce team briefing into Foodpack. In order to gain the support of the Factory Manager for change, he needed evidence to back up his views. This came from two sources; first, the most recent company-wide attitude survey had suggested that there were communication problems at the site, and that Foodpack was faring much worse than other plants in the division. Secondly, he persuaded a placement student to follow up this study and tailor questions to local circumstances. Put together, these revealed that communications operated almost exclusively via the grapevine, a network enhanced by the large number of family ties and long periods of service characteristic of the site. Supervisors were found to play only a minor part in communications, and rather less than the shop stewards. The Factory Manager agreed to provide the time and resources to improve communications, one part of which was the creation of a new training facility on site. The Personnel Manager wrote a training manual on team briefing for the supervisors, and he also invited a number of speakers to the factory to give presentations to the supervisors; these included managers from companies elsewhere which had experience of introducing team briefing – for example, Jaguar – , an academic with a knowledge of Japan, and sessions from the Manpower Services Commission, as it then was, on skills development. This programme was designed to heighten interest in and awareness of briefing, before the launch in early 1987.

Although the ground had been well prepared, the Personnel Manager was under no illusion that team briefing offered a panacea for all the company's ills, and he was sensitive to its potential pitfalls. At the time of the launch, he said, 'People can soon realise that they're being brought together and told a lot of crap. Also, they may develop into bitching sessions.' He felt that allowance also needed to be made for the recipients of the message: 'You have got to remember that this audience is not used to receiving information. But it is equally important not to talk down to the shop floor, only to talk in relevant language.' He knew that changes would not take place instantaneously. 'It takes six months before people see that you're for real, and the benefits take a year to eighteen months to feed through.' He saw team briefing as a method for stimulating employee commitment and removing barriers to motivation: 'People in their natural state are motivated. It's just that management are good at putting up barriers, and team briefing can help to remove these.'

The system itself was designed to operate broadly in accordance with the traditional and well-known principles espoused by the Industrial Society, and information would be directed down the management chain, following the monthly brief by the Factory Manager to his subordinates. This group would then be responsible for briefing the first line managers within five days, and the message would reach the shop floor within ten days, rather longer than the time envisaged by the Industrial Society. However, the usual 70/30 split between local and central, in this case, site-wide, information was to apply. The new Production Manager took up his appointment soon after the launch, and he, too, was fully committed to its development, having had experience of briefing in another division within the Group. He saw it as a way to re-establish the position of supervisors in the communications chain, get this group together, and 'bring them on board'. As we shall see later, he also envisaged this as a way of reducing the influence of the stewards.

Towards the end of our research at Foodpack, we conducted a more detailed examination of how team briefing had developed during its first nine months, and this supplemented a management review of initial progress. Put together, these suggested that the programme had not gone strictly according to plan, but had evolved 'biologically rather than procedurally', in the words of the Personnel Manager. There had been some concern that too little information emanated from the Factory Manager, and there were some doubts about the quality of the presentations by the supervisors. The Personnel Manager decided that another course of training would therefore be in order, and that supervisors would be encouraged to use alternative techniques, such as videos, for presenting the information. However, he was also fully committed to the notion that the system should evolve, rather than being strictly defined and imposed from above, so that 'people will own it and not be turned off.'

The users of the system, both briefers and the briefed, varied in their assessment, with the packing operators exhibiting greatest interest in and satisfaction with developments so far. One of them noted,

> We like to know exactly what is going on. When you get it off the shop floor, it's been twisted. Things have been done as a result of our suggestions . . . like health and safety, and housekeeping in the plant.

Another said, 'We get to hear about visits from big customers. Then we have to clean the shop floor!' Yet another felt it had reduced a lot of the 'us and them; managers and workers are the same people now, they're much more approachable.' In terms of the content of the briefs, all the packers confirmed that much of the presentation was related to plant or company-wide affairs, such as the sales performance of the different brands, new products, share movements or profits. Clearly, therefore, team briefing seems to have had a direct, if minor, effect on activity and also on attitudes to the company. The briefer of this group was less convinced about the value of some of his sessions, relating this to the abilities and interests of the staff involved. He said, somewhat condescendingly, 'If it directly involves the people then they want to listen. If it's about company policy, shares, corporate growth, etc. then they are not interested. They don't really understand it, although this affects them indirectly.' Nevertheless, he felt that it was a worthwhile exercise, and was committed to its continuation, even though there were a number of teething problems with the system, especially in terms of the type of information which was communicated. He saw the system as crucial in ensuring that the management message reached the shop floor, thus reducing the impact of 'distortions' via the grapevine.

Other departments, such as baking and engineering, were less convinced about the value of the sessions. The bakers' foremen address their groups every month, but this 'gets squeezed in when there is a breakdown or at any other convenient moment, such as when we change commodities'. Because of the continuous nature of the process, and the extensive shift arrangements for this group of operators, it was not always possible for these supervisors to attend their brief by the Production Manager. One of these also indicated the difficulty he faced in trying to interest his staff, since much of the information is about 'market performance, management changes, company acquisitions, not just about Foodpack. That kind of information interests some, but not others . . . nine out of ten here are only interested if it affects their pockets.' But he also acknowledged that team briefing was beginning to have an effect on attitudes, since they now have a better idea of 'what they are doing, and why they are doing it. Conversation is now on a higher level.' One of the bakers remained sceptical about the whole exercise, commenting that

> It's of no interest to me what the Managing Director is doing, whether he is moving, or whether he has got a new car, unless it affects my job. The general feeling on the shift is much the same.

The engineers were also dubious about the benefits of more information of the type they had been given, and one of them described his feelings in this way: 'Whilst it gives you more interest in what is going on, I'm not dying to know. I'm not won over myself. I haven't bought shares or anything, though I might do when I've got a bit of money.' Proponents of new realism and an enterprise culture would do well to recognise that such a calculative orientation to work is not unusual on the shop floor.

There are always likely to be problems in maintaining team briefing in an environment where workloads are highly variable over the course of the year, particularly during the peak periods when continuity of production is paramount. At Foodpack, whilst it was relatively easy to sustain the briefing operation during the slacker periods, it became much more difficult during the run-up to Christmas, when all machines are working at full speed. Indeed, since one of the principal aims of team briefing is to increase employee awareness of the commercial context within which the company operates, it would make little sense to stop the line at peak times merely to remind people that they should be working extra hard to meet deadlines! In choosing between production and briefing, the former easily achieved primacy in the Christmas rush, and many interviewees believed that the exercise had been dropped altogether, being replaced by the weekly news bulletin. In fact, it had not, and regular briefs recommenced soon after Christmas, but the seeds of doubt had been sown. Moreover, it seemed strange to us that employees had not been made sufficiently aware of the temporary suspension of briefing, considering that this would appear to be precisely the kind of information most suited to the exercise.

The weekly news bulletin was instituted by the Production

Manager within several months of his arrival, and this was posted on notice-boards all over the factory. Unlike information on most notice-boards, this particular one-page document was enthusiastically received and widely read. It had expanded in format since its inception, and by the end of 1987 it had grown to include information about visits from customers, production schedules, new product tests, and statistics on absenteeism rates in different departments. It also included the number and names of new starters, progress on filling vacancies, and even the movements of senior managers. The Production Manager also used the news bulletin to record his appreciation of previous results by individual departments – for example, 'some amazing results last week, well done lads!' – as well as reminders that performance has to be maintained, as in the message, 'Been going quite well, and must continue if we are going to meet the trade'. Information about possible developments also featured, for example. 'If this happens, we may move the shrinkwrap back.' He was convinced that measures such as this produced benefits in terms of commitment and involvement, and that the provision of information prevented unnecessary difficulties at later junctures. As an example he cited a case from his previous job where a machine had lain idle for eighteen months before it was used, precisely because managers had not communicated in advance. It should also be noted that the news bulletin was not the only contact which shop floor operatives had with him, since he made a point of 'walking the factory' for the first hour or so every morning. His presence was clear for all to see.

For the Production Manager, these mechanisms for direct communication with the shop floor had clearly had an effect on the position of worker representatives within the factory. He said, 'team briefing is not intended to undermine the unions ... but', he added with a smile, 'it does.' He felt that the stewards saw this as a challenge, but he need not have worried because our interviews suggested quite the opposite. The ex-senior steward could see no objection to team briefing in principle, since 'the more informed we are the better it is. It saves us a hell of a lot of work because it's management's job to communicate.' His criticisms of briefings related to the ability of the briefers, or the type of information which was briefed, rather than any more sinister intent on the part of management. The most adversarial/opportunistic comment from the stewards concerning briefing or the newsletter was that the information might be 'handy for negotiations, since it tells us how the factory and the group is doing'. In general, the new methods were much appreciated, even though it appeared to us that the stewards could well be acquiescing in their own emasculation.

The workforce as a whole displayed a similar view; as we have already mentioned, the attitude survey which had first been carried out in 1986 was repeated in 1988, and the results indicated that the recent initiatives had been well received. Whereas forty per cent of the workforce had felt management had not communicated very much to them in 1986, only sixteen per cent felt this in 1988; whilst only four per cent had said that they received a lot of information at the time of the first survey, this had increased to twenty-two per cent by the second. The newsletter was now seen as the most effective form of communication, whereas two years before it had been the grapevine. Similarly, the relative positions of supervisors and shop stewards in the communications chain had also altered, with the former now being seen as much more central. Moreover, respondents also considered team briefing to be their most preferred method for receipt of information in the future. The effect of the recent changes to the communications system has therefore been quite significant, at least in terms of its impact on the employees themselves.

6.7 CONCLUSIONS

Whereas management at Ichem had gone some way towards an HRM approach to employee relations, those at Foodpack had rather further to go. A series of new appointments at divisional and plant level had produced a range of initiatives aimed at reforming the system, and the factory had certainly seen a number of important changes during the latter half of the 1980s, namely team briefing, regular newsletters, quality campaigns, and a three-year, no-strike deal. For the most part, shop floor employees at Foodpack seemed to value all of these changes, regarding them as symptomatic of a more open and professional approach to employee relations. At the same time, it was our view that the unions were becoming increasingly marginal within the factory, subordinated to the demands of the product market.

7 · MULTISTORES: COOPERATING WITH CUSTOMER CARE

7.1 INTRODUCTION

Multistores is one of the leading supermarket chains in the country, operating in well over one hundred different locations in Britain. The company moved into the superstore market in the early 1960s and, like many in the field, is still growing, having opened twenty new stores during the period of our research. The company as a whole employs well over 30,000 people; in contrast to the employees in the other companies in our study, many of the staff are part-timers and the size of the workforce has been steadily increasing during the course of the 1980s. Multistores is also the most overtly centralised of our research locations, largely owing to the similarity of operations at each store, the type of products sold, and the kind of staff recruited; we shall see later, though, that there still remain variations between the stores.

Within the retail sector, Multistores is relatively unusual in having a union recognition agreement with the GMBATU, and in actively supporting union membership at the stores. At the same time, however, management has placed increasing emphasis on direct communications with the shop floor (via team briefing) and on customer care campaigns, as manifested in a range of competitions aimed at improving service within the stores. More broadly, following a business review in the mid-1980s, the company is in the process of introducing a new management ethos, with a more explicit focus on the development and importance of employees; after all, unlike the case in the majority of organisations, shop floor workers at Multistores are the principal point of contact with the customer, much closer to them than management.

7.2 WORK ORGANISATION

Within Multistores, we concentrated our research on two sites, each of which reflected a different stage in the company's development; the first of these, Grimsight, is an inner city store which was opened in the late 1970s, and services a multiracial, generally low-income group of customers, although it does attract a small proportion of middle-class shoppers. By contrast, the Smalltown store is located on the fringes of another large Northern city; this was opened in the mid-1980s, and is a much brighter and more up-market operation. Grimsight employs 265 people, whereas Smalltown is slightly bigger at 329. Employment numbers have remained stable at both sites, following the initial bulge associated with the opening of a new store, whereby temporaries are taken on to deal with 'excessive' customer flow during the early months of trading; at the Smalltown store, the General Manager lamented the fact that the company was still seen locally as a 'hire and fire' employer, a reputation it has struggled to overcome since that time.

The vast majority of staff employed at the two sites, as throughout the company as a whole, are female and part-time. Using Grimsight as the example, seventy-four per cent of the staff there are on part-time contracts, and a similar proportion are also women; only fourteen per cent of the women employed at the store are full-time, and this figure includes the managerial staff. Conversely, only a small proportion of the men work other than full-time, although as at Foodpack this figure is on the increase, as young men are now more willing to take part-time jobs in what has traditionally been termed 'women's work'. The whole industry is characterised by high rates of labour turnover, and Multistores is no exception at just under fifty per cent per annum across the company; Grimsight has the dubious privilege of having one of the higher rates, with turnover in 1986 running at fifty-five per cent. Many of those who leave do so soon after taking up employment, but equally some employees have worked at the stores since they opened. It should also be noted that high rates of turnover are not restricted to shop floor staff, but also characterise those in managerial positions. Some of these managerial moves result from the growth of the company, reflecting a policy which requires 'experienced' staff to commission new store openings, but much also arises from competition within the retail trade for high quality management; indeed at Grimsight, the General Manager, one of his three Departmental Managers, and the Personnel Manager had all been recruited from other companies in the sector. Unlike turnover rates, those for absence tend to be low. For example at Smalltown they are as low as three per cent, a figure which many manufacturing sites would find extremely acceptable. A further significant feature of the labour force is its youth, partly amongst the shop floor workers but more noticeable within the ranks of management.

For the industry as a whole, which is characterised by low pay when compared with the national average, Multistores is one of the top payers, athough some ten per cent below the market leader. Within the company, there are eight separate pay grades, each of which incorporates an 'appointment' and an 'established' rate in order to encourage staff to remain with the company; some of these, such as those for bakers and butchers, also have a career ladder within them, but this does not apply to the majority of jobs. The differential between the highest and the lowest paid employees covered by the GMBATU is approximately twenty-five per cent, with staff such as butchers at the top, and shop assistants and cleaners at the bottom. The sole deviation from national rates is the payment of a London allowance.

Within each store, the largest numbers of staff are employed on checkout and other sales floor activities; at Grimsight, the checkout operators account for seventy-six of the 265 employees, and these are primarily female part-timers working an average of twenty hours per week. Sales floor operations can be further subdivided into fresh food, grocery and non-food, and all these are again areas of female predominance, with the vast majority of staff working part-time; at Smalltown, for example, just six of the fifty-three food hall assistants were full-time. The non-food operations, i.e. clothing and footwear, electrical and houseware, and do-it-yourself, employ fewer people than the food hall – about twenty in each store – but approximately half of these are fulltimers. Behind the scenes, there are a number of other operations which are typically the male preserve at these stores. The largest is the warehouse which at Smalltown should employ sixteen staff, but owing to turnover problems had only a little over half this number at the time of our interviews. These workers are responsible for the receipt, checking and storage of goods, in readiness for use on the sales floor. Two further areas, the bakery and meat departments, require qualified staff, and recently the company has been training its own recruits, since it has encountered problems in buying in qualified personnel. Both these departments employ relatively small numbers of people, for example, twelve in the bakery and ten butchers at the Smalltown store. Whilst these employees have some contact with the customers, it is no more than two or three times each day. The management structure in the stores tends to follow a standard format, with three departmental heads (fresh food, grocery and non-food), personnel, customer services, office and security managers all reporting to the General Manager. One of the departmental heads typically acts as the deputy to this person, and it is usual for these managers to move around the different departments, as well as the stores, in order to gain experience for eventual promotion.

Workforce flexibility does not appear to be an issue in this environment for a number of reasons. First, the contract of employment specifically allows management the right to redirect staff to other work in the event of changing patterns of demand during the day, i.e. 'employees will assist in other areas as and when required.' In both the stores, staff spent most of their working hours on the task for which they were employed, but did undertake other work as necessary. For instance, checkout operators would fill shelves, or move to the customer service desk or the cigarette kiosk, if work was slack and there was extra pressure on these departments. This was facilitated by the nature of the pay agreement, as the work they would undertake was either on the same rate or at a lower point on the scale. Secondly, rotation and flexibility tended to suit the needs of the staff themselves, since it introduced an element of variety into their work, and provided them with an opportunity to utilise their skills in other areas of the store or department. It was typical for staff to rotate between jobs in line with their own particular preferences. In the bakery, for example, employees shifted from the ovens to the mixing operations on a daily or weekly rota. As one of them put it to us, 'The rota stops you cracking up, doing the same thing all the time. On the oven, all you have to do is watch the thermometer.' Even so, the tradesmen (butchers and bakers) still found their jobs to be de-skilled in relation to the nature of work which they would have been doing had they remained in smaller and more specialised shops. Thirdly, the climate within the stores rendered flexibility a normal part of the job, partly through the lack of adversarial traditions in the industry and the company, but also because managers themselves helped out in the event of a sudden surge in demand, or if the store was understaffed. At the Smalltown store, for example, the Personel Manager worked on a checkout during part of one Bank Holiday, and this was not an unusual event.

Staff were also numerically flexible in terms of the hours worked at the store. We have already mentioned that the vast majority of employees were on part-time contracts, but other staff also worked unsocial hours. For instance, the bakers started work at different times, depending upon the day of the week, but nevertheless it was always very early in the morning, between 3 a.m. and 5 a.m. In addition, at both Smalltown and Grimsight, they also tended to work at least eight hours overtime each week. A number of staff in the meat department also started work early each day in order to ensure that products were prepared in time for the opening of the shop. Of course, stores are open on Saturdays and for late-night shoppers, both of which arrangements are still relatively unusual for many parts of the private and public sector, and Bank Holiday opening was also introduced in 1988.

7.3 THE MARKET ENVIRONMENT

The range of products sold by Multistores can be categorised under the three headings already used in relation to the organisation of the stores: grocery, fresh foods and non-food. The grocery market is mature, with no scope for significant future growth, and this has become increasingly competitive as the major superstores fight for new locations before the expected market saturation in the early 1990s. The fresh foods market has undergone substantial changes during the course of the last decade, because of increasingly health conscious customers, and the premium placed upon quality of produce, rather than price alone. As part of its competitive strategy, in common with other major food retailers, Multistores has moved into the province of 'own label' products, thus enabling the company to increase its control over quality; we have already seen the other side of this relationship at Foodpack. The emphasis on quality, rather than price, was often reiterated during our time at Multistores, as was a quote from the Managing Director likening competition in the business to that confronting the regular or repeat passenger about to embark on a flight across the Atlantic: since all the airlines provide the same type of aeroplane – Jumbo jets – choice is made on the basis of the quality of customer service offered during the flight. Notwithstanding the accuracy of this observation, it does indicate the kind of market within which Multistores is now keen to operate, and the distance it has travelled from the days when the company was renowned for its 'cheap and cheerful' image. Multistores has also been keen to exploit the growing non-food market in recent years, as this offers the possibility of providing a more complete service to customers, and persuading them that the store can fulfil all their shopping needs.

In general terms, therefore, there has been overall market growth during the 1980s, but, at the same time, an increase in competition between the major retailers for a share of this market. Multistores has been opening up new superstores in different parts of the country, as well as revamping its original shops in order to increase available floor space, develop the range of goods on offer, and update the image of the company as a whole. Greater control over suppliers is now seen as a crucial component of competitive advantage, as, too, is the provision of more customer facilities such as a cafeteria, hairdressing, and in some cases petrol and garage services. Multistores recognises, according to one of its senior managers, that it will never become market leader, but is nonetheless keen to maintain a presence in the top four or five in the sector.

This philosophy has significant implications for employee relations, particularly with regard to the quality of service provided and, therefore, the recruitment and training of staff employed. The company, like many others in the retail and finance sectors more generally, has introduced a series of campaigns aimed at customer care on either an individual basis ('employee of the month'), or collectively ('store of the year'), both of which we shall describe in more detail in the section on employee involvement. At the same time, Multistores is attempting to improve its induction training, an activity which takes up considerable time and effort, in view of the high levels of labour turnover in the company. The group at which this is most clearly directly aimed consists of those employees who are in regular contact with customers, the staff on the sales floor and checkouts. Herein lies an important contradiction, however, which has not been considered in the supposed distinction between core and peripheral workers. The employees who are closest to the customer are those with the lowest rates of pay, the least status and generally the smallest number of hours worked – hardly the key, long-serving, committed core workers deemed to be central to the enterprise, but more likely the numerically flexible workers whose head count is adjusted in line with customer demand.

Demand for goods and services varies considerably, yet largely predictably, over the course of the day and the week, thus providing the context within which different types of part-time labour is considered essential. There are peaks at lunch-time and early evening during the week, whereas mornings are traditionally the quietest periods. Similarly, demand increases during the course of the week, with Monday and Tuesday the least pressurised. Saturday shopping has always been extensive, and stores have started to open on Bank Holidays as well. The use of schoolchildren and college students for Saturday working has also been a regular feature of the retail industry for many years, and in Multistores this pool of labour now appears to operate as an extended internal labour market, a source of recruits for permanent positions in the future. It should not be overlooked, though, that the provision of part-time work also offers attractive options to many employees, who may prefer this mode of working, since it can fit in with other domestic or family responsibilities, such as child care. Although perhaps reflective of the limited expectations held by many employees, especially women with children, it was a point made repeatedly by the individuals with whom we talked at both stores.

The customer profile at Multistores is significantly different from that encountered at all of our other research sites, being reflected in the very large number of sales made, and consequently the lack of power of any individual customer *vis-à-vis* the company. Nevertheless, Multistores was at pains to point out to its employees the importance of each customer, and the link between market success and employment stability; posters displayed around the stores indicate this quite graphically. For example, 'A smile or thank you costs nothing', or 'Think customer first and they will think Multistores first'. One full poster ran as follows:

Satisfied customers who keep coming back again and again strengthen sales and jobs!

Our success and security depend upon *every* employee supporting the sales effort through *personal interest* and *good workmanship*.

CUSTOMERS make pay days possible.

Of course, there were also differences in customer profile between Grimsight and Smalltown, which have an effect upon the average size of purchase per customer, the range of stock held, and even the distribution of employment at each store. In particular, given the more up-market location of the Smalltown store, the bakery and meat departments there were much larger than at Grimsight, and the type of products sold also varied.

7.4 MANAGEMENT STRATEGY AND STYLE

Multistores is by far the most centralised of the four companies involved in our research, not only in terms of organisation structure and systems, but also in its employee relations. Policy matters are determined at the head office, and all goods are ordered centrally in accordance with a Stock and Order Sheet specifying a list of approved suppliers. Wage budgets are set as a percentage of sales, and any store which overspends on labour is not allowed to recruit more staff until the ratio is re-established. Similarly, pay rates are determined centrally according to a structure negotiated at corporate level with GMBATU, and this includes details such as a standard deduction for employees who are late for work. In other words, at least in terms of formal mechanisms, general managers have very little discretion at their disposal for operating or employment decisions.

This high degree of centralisation is rationalised by senior management on a number of grounds; according to one of the head office managers, 'The biggest argument for centralisation is having over 100 units, but this needs to be seen in the context of significant similarities between the establishments. Economies of scale become important in several areas, such as advertising and marketing, and purchasing and ordering of stocks. In addition, Multistores is keen to project a standard corporate image, so that customers can correctly anticipate that each store will offer a similar range of products. From a management viewpoint, centralisation also offers advantages for wage-bargaining, since it prevents the possibility of the union's playing off one unit against another in order to increase pay levels. Even organisation structures and numbers of union representatives allowed at store level are determined at corporate level in accordance with various blueprints, thus enabling more effective control to be maintained over store performance on the basis of inter-store comparisons.

The link between the centre and the stores is achieved largely through a regional structure, which incorporates, amongst other functions, general and personnel management. There are approximately ten stores in each region. The regional controllers (general managers) are in regular contact with store managers via visits and meetings, as well as in assessing which establishments should win the mantle of 'store of the year'. During our time at Smalltown, the Regional Manager was a regular visitor to the site, and on one occasion he even called the Personnel Manager away from a stores council, the monthly consultative meeting, to gather information about the employment situation in the store. The Regional Personnel Manager (RPM) also plays an important part in this link, through visiting the stores every two weeks or so and through meetings for store personnel managers, which were held every couple of months. The regularity with which the RPMs visit sites is rather greater than at any of the other cases in our study, especially in comparison with Ichem, where visits to the factory were irregular. The RPM's role in Multistores is partly to resolve more serious problems, but also to maintain company standards and train personnel practitioners at store level. Accordingly, they appear to have a much higher status in the eyes of the local personnel people than was the case elsewhere. At the bi-monthly meetings, the store personnel managers are briefed on company-wide concerns or initiatives, such as how to operate a new computer system for wages, methods for reducing labour turnover, employment law cases, as well as the putting forward of issues of local concern. In addition, a key task for the RPM is training the new store personnel managers and organising their development by rotation around the stores. Despite this obvious status difference, the relationship between these two levels of manager seemed to be close and informal.

In the mid-1980s, the company conducted a wide-ranging business review, from which it was concluded that a new and more progressive management style was needed in Multistores. It was recognised that the business was going through a 'period in the doldrums. We were becoming complacent and needed to break out', one of the senior managers told us. A variety of changes were made to the business, including the introduction of a new corporate image and the development of a five-year business plan with the overall strategic objective to be 'the best in the market'. The notion of a new management ethos was central to these ideas, and more explicit emphasis was put on the 'people' component in management development programmes, that is, not just employees, but also customers. By the end of our research period, most of the senior managers – those at General Store Manager and above – had been through the new scheme. In addition, it is now company policy to provide all new starters with a handbook, incorporating the new motto on the front, and in which the Managing Director writes of his belief that 'our staff are our most important asset and we will do everything to help you enjoy working with us.' The attempt to be more open, progressive and developmental in relation to employees is a view which found considerable support throughout the echelons of senior management. The corporate Employee Relations Manager with whom we talked saw this as a shift to human resource management, and as closely associated with business strategy via the customer care campaign. To be successful, it was implied, required well-trained and motivated staff, which in turn demanded that managers supply them with relevant and meaningful information. As another of the senior managers put it, 'We needed to develop a more positive and open management style, away from the old autocratic approach which doesn't work well.' At corporate level, it was understood that the company needed to become more professional in every respect, but particularly in its approach to the management of human resources. However, it was also felt that the welfare aspect of personnel, so crucial to the earlier conceptions of the role, should not be jettisoned in favour of this changed emphasis.

We were also keen to discover whether this attempt to modernise management style had percolated down to store level, and, in particular, whether employees on the sales floor or in the ancillary departments had noticed any shift in the way in which they were managed on a daily basis. The Store Personnel Manager at Grimsight, who had worked in personnel for another company in the retail sector before joining the company in 1987, felt that the concern with 'pounds, shillings and pence' was still explicit within Multistores. The union branch secretary with responsibility for the Smalltown store was highly sceptical about the depth and nature of the 'fair weather philosophy', as he saw it. At the end of the day, 'employees always lose out to profit . . . although the company is spending a lot of money on the customer care campaign, if you treat employees right then customer care follows.' Many of the employees we interviewed had noticed a change of style in recent years, with a shift from autocratic management to a more participative approach. One of the women on the sales floor contrasted styles in the following way:

> When I started [five years ago] the managers were always on your back, moaning all the time, doing their fruit over the smallest thing, rude as well . . . the new Manager is easy-going, a good laugh, not on your back every five minutes, she's good.

Others also noted a 'softer' style in recent years, combined with more communications and, at Grimsight in particular, a stress on informality.

However, as at the other sites in this study, a more open approach and greater informality has not been at the expense of a tough stance towards disciplinary matters, and in ensuring that work is completed on time and to the correct standards. For example, the Staff Handbook specifies uniform deductions for lateness on an agreed scale, as well as the action to be taken against persistent offenders. Equally, employees referred to the firmer style adopted by managers when they themselves were under pressure, although, again, such approaches are not considered to be illegitimate in any way: 'If all the work has been done, they are easy-going. They get a bit tougher if they are under pressure. Just like the other places I've worked, they're all right.' In other words, despite some evidence that employees in the stores have noticed changes in management style in recent years, the distinctions are much murkier and less clear-cut than those suggested by senior managers; the changes also fail to generate quite the same level of excitement among individuals on the shop floor.

For those employees who had worked in more than one store, or who had 'outlived' more than one general store manager, the GSM was felt to have a key influence on management style. At Smalltown, the approach was more formalised and overtly hierarchical than the informal and friendly climate at Grimsight; at the latter, the GSM personally knew a large number of the staff, regularly came on to the shop floor, and saw the senior steward most days on an informal basis. This is helped by the fact that the staff canteen is on the same corridor as all the management offices, and a good deal of business appears to take place in the canteen itself. The same physical characteristics apply to the Smalltown store, but the GSM is regarded as an elusive figure with whom the staff rarely dealt except in the more formal circumstances of the stores council. Another indicator of this difference is the willingness of the two GSMs to disclose business information; at Smalltown, figures on store performance were not released for fear that they might fall into the hands of competitors, whereas at Grimsight, the weekly results were displayed on a board adjacent to the reception area in a form which clearly indicated the sales of each department in relation to the previous week's results. Evidence from employees at the two stores gave further support to this difference in climate and, as we have already noted, despite the centralised nature of the systems within Multistores, differences are noticeable between the stores, not just in relation to management style. For example, the exact mix of employees varies between the stores, as does the amount of overtime worked, and the ratio of part-timers to full-time employees. Provided the GSM remains within budget, there remains some discretion in the way that this money is utilised. In much the same way, attempts to amend the style of management within the company are also mediated by the approach adopted by the GSM.

7.5 COLLECTIVE BARGAINING AND UNION ORGANISATION

Multistores is one of the few retail companies to have developed a positive relationship with a trade union, in this case the GMBATU (or GMB), with links going back to the late 1960s, a period of rapid store growth and somewhat greater union confidence. The decision to recognise the GMB came after a six-month assessment by management of the potential advantages and disadvantages of a union-free environment. Senior management concluded that unionisation had much to offer the expanding business, not least because it would help to achieve unity and centralisation of employee relations. A single union deal also made sense to management, since this would prevent other unions from securing a foothold in this growing, and extremely ripe, sector of the economy and, clearly, the GMB was hardly likely to refuse the offer, as it involved a sizeable increase in membership. Management preferred the GMB to other unions, partly because it was already recognised in another division within the company, but also because senior management felt that on practical and ideological grounds it had more to offer than the alternatives. The GMB was thought to be politically middle-of-the-road, and a union with which Multistores felt it could do business. Accordingly, a sole recognition agreement was signed, with provision for compulsory union membership in defined circumstances, that is, where more than sixty per cent of employees are in the union; at both the stores we studied, this provision was applied, and it seems to be implicit within the company's terms and conditions. Since the late 1960s, the agreement has been updated, but not drastically modified by subsequent events. There is nothing particularly unusual about the agreement, and it covers the standard items, such as the extent of recognition, check-off, grievance and disputes procedures, equal opportunities, health and safety and the allocation of shop stewards, as well as agreed time-off provisions.

Despite the relevant clauses in the 1982 Employment Act, Multistores chose not to ballot employees about continuing with compulsory union membership. Instead, the company and the union reached agreement that any employee who wished to leave the union could do so, although very few have chosen this route. For its part, the company reiterated its commitment to union membership by inserting a section in the Staff Handbook which positively supports the work of the union, and advises new starters that they will be *required* to join within four weeks of commencing employment. Furthermore, at Grimsight and Smalltown, the senior steward is invited to the induction programme for new starters in order to identify the benefits of becoming a union member, gaining support from the Personnel Manager if necessary.

Relations between Multistores and the GMB continue to follow a largely cooperative, rather than adversarial, pattern, and both the union officials and the head office management with whom we spoke felt that the relationship was generally good. For its part, the union had been able to increase membership considerably and had achieved a number of substantive gains for its members in Multistores. Typical of these were reductions in the length of the working week, higher rates of youth pay, and improved pay and conditions, plus a range of procedural adjustments to maintain fairness and consistency. The company had also been greatly assisted by the union in terms of the order which it provided to employee relations and also in other ways which derived from the union's extensive political links. As one senior manager put it, 'It's a win–win situation. It does a good job for us and for them since they get more members.' This positive relationship is further exemplified by the fact that the union invites a senior manager from Multistores to address its national conference, and by the more recent agreement to provide joint management–union training courses for shop stewards, in addition to those sponsored by the TUC. The union branch secretary who covered the Smalltown store, in addition to a number of others in the same region, described his relationship with management as 'first class', and regularly visited the sites to deal with issues informally, besides those directed through the grievance procedure.

The national agreement lays down a formula for the number of stewards to be allowed at each store, depending on its size (square feet of floor-space). Some of the largest stores in the company are allowed up to seven shop stewards, but both Grimsight and Smalltown had an allocation of four; during various parts of our research period, the actual number of stewards dropped below this in both stores, and at Smalltown, the union encountered difficulty in generating enough interest from the members to maintain sufficient representation. Although steward constituencies are defined on the basis of department, in both cases, non-food; warehouse; checkouts and offices; and grocery and fresh food, in reality the union is generally willing to accept representation from wherever it is offered.

This problem appears to owe more to membership indifference

than to any management hostility at local level. Almost without exception, union members expressed little interest in, or commitment to, the union; a typical comment was 'I'm a member, but I don't get involved unless I have to.' Stewards were called upon in the event of a disciplinary hearing, but aside from this the union played virtually no part in the life of the store for most of these workers. An instrumental/insurance orientation pervaded their attitudes to union membership, a notion summed up by references to the union as 'them' rather than 'us'. A minority of our interviewees were more overtly critical about their 'enforced' membership of the union, but for the most part union membership did not generate any great interest or hostility among Multistores' employees. The highly centralised nature of union–management relations in the company, particularly over pay and conditions, clearly gives the union little chance to win improvements in individual stores. If anything, managers seem to be keener on the union than are the members, valuing the stewards as a means of resolving issues in the store, as a lubricant to good employee relations, and as a point of informal contact with shop floor opinion. However, there are also limits to this collaborative relationship, as we shall see below, for the constitution of the stores council specifically prevents the stewards from occupying all the seats on this committee. When combined with other mechanisms for direct employee involvement, this tends to place the union in a more marginal role than the national agreement might otherwise imply.

Furthermore, the stewards themselves lack extensive experience of unionism, partly because of the nature of the industry, the agreement, and the workforce, but also because of the relative 'youth' of each store. This is particularly apparent at the Small-town site which, at the time of our research, had only been open for three years. In addition, the senior steward, who is young and new to the industry, had only taken up office during 1987 when the previous incumbent left the compny. He was appalled by the apathy of the membership, and this had encouraged him to take on the senior steward's role; during the few months that he had been senior steward, he had already attended a union course, managed to persuade another person to fill a vacant steward's position, and had secured the agreement of the Personnel Manager to institute a regular fortnightly meeting with the stewards. The enormity of his task was made clear to us by one of his non-steward colleagues on the stores council, who still thought that the position of senior steward was vacant, three months after it had been filled! Union commitment appeared somewhat stronger at Grimsight, but even here the senior steward (who had considerably more experience) was concerned about the apathy of the membership, and about the difficulties she encountered in persuading people to stand for office. In short, the union's role in the store is constrained to a large extent by the members themselves and also by the national agreement.

7.6 EMPLOYEE INVOLVEMENT

Within Multistores a number of different mechanisms exist for employee involvement, each of which reflects distinct stages in the development of the company. The stores councils have their origins in the initial agreements between the company and the GMB, although these committees have also undergone a change of name from 'works committee'. More recent initiatives are concerned with direct communication through team briefing and employee involvement through customer care committees. All three of these techniques operate in the Smalltown and Grimsight stores, although, as we shall see, none of them quite measures up to conventional expectations. We also need to be aware that the context within which employee involvement has been introduced puts a premium on the development of employee commitment, the creation of positive attitudes to change, and an awareness of competitive circumstances, rather than viewing EI as a mechanism to channel and contain discontent. We can now analyse each of the techniques in turn, commencing with the stores councils.

The constitution of the stores councils was laid down in the original procedure agreement recognising the GMB, although at that time they were known as works committees. The original aims of the councils were to provide a system of consultation at work-place level which would enable representatives to 'discuss and where possible resolve those problems affecting the working environment'. Their role was to provide a channel of communication between employees and management. According to the national agreement, the council should comprise the following: the General

Store Manager as Chair, with other management nominations as appropriate, including the provision of secretarial support; two safety representatives; the shop stewards in the store, including one of this number as Vice-Chair; and three other employees elected by ballot. Meetings are scheduled on a monthly basis, on a predetermined date, the only specified agenda item being health and safety, but with time for a wide range of issues to be discussed. Minutes are to be approved by the Chair and Vice-Chair, and posted around the store, in addition to being sent to council members, the Regional Personnel Manager, the Employee Relations Manager at head office, and the appropriate union official. There is no provision for consultative machinery above the level of the store.

If the councils we observed are typical, and there is no reason to suppose they are not, they do not appear to operate in accordance with this blueprint. Most of the Multistores' employees whom we interviewed, including the Personnel Manager at Smalltown who was secretary to the Council at her store, did not know about the constitution. Meetings at Smalltown were held monthly, but the business seemed to reflect local interests, rather than complying with national agreements. At Grimsight, the stores council rarely met during 1987, partly as a result of a personnel vacancy over the first part of the year, but also because of the GSM's preference for informality. The composition of the Smalltown council, which we were able to attend on several occasions, deviated from the Agreement because there were insufficient stewards in the store; in fact, the non-steward representatives tended to be rather more vociferous than were the stewards. The passage of minutes up the hierarchy did take place, but the Employee Relations Manager at corporate level rarely read these in any detail. On the contrary, for him, the principal purpose of the exercise was 'a discipline to ensure that they're happening, rather than to read them . . . there has to be something which sticks out like a sore thumb before a memo is despatched.' The RPM who covered the Grimsight store reckoned that she would normally monitor the activity of the stores council quite carefully in order to ensure that meetings were held, although she acknowledged that the Grimsight store had suffered special problems over the recent past. Neither of these managers seemed concerned that the councils did not conform to that laid down in the agreement, and another senior manager emphasised that non-stewards occupied a crucial role on these bodies precisely because the company did not want to become dependent upon stewards for communications. It is apparent, therefore, that actual practice in these two stores bears little relation to the constitution, or that the meetings have any symbolic impact upon employees in the company.

At Grimsight, the GSM preferred to operate in an informal manner, and on the rare occasions when meetings were held, they only lasted for a short time. One of the major issues which could have been communicated at stores council were the weekly sales figures, broken down by department, but, as we have already indicated, these were conveyed by means of a notice-board near the reception area and the canteen. His previous experience with councils elsewhere in the company had convinced him that they represented an imperfect means of communication because it was doubtful whether messages ever got through to employees by way of their representatives, hence his enthusiasm for informality. The timing of meetings also led to the disenfranchisement of certain members and to clashes with business priorities. Furthermore, he felt that the council had become a forum for the submission of individual grievances and claims, rather than a place for what he termed 'constructive discussion'. Other managers at Grimsight reinforced this perspective, considering the councils to be solely concerned with trivia, and inferior to team briefing as an effective communications channel. The employees we interviewed at Grimsight were, not surprisingly, considering the irregularity of the stores council, unaware of its activities. Even the people who had sat on council could only point to fairly minor achievements when asked to cite examples of its value, although they did not believe it conflicted with the role of the union. To say that the store council had a marginal role at Grimsight might even be to overestimate its influence!

At Smalltown, council meetings were held on a monthly basis, usually lasting for about an hour; the GSM chaired most of these, although his deputy did take some, as did the Personnel Manager. The senior steward did not stand in for the GSM during our observations, even though the constitution specifies this as procedure. During 1986 and 1987, the period of our observations, the

Council meetings tended to follow a three-stage process of report-back, Chair's report, and employee concerns. In the first of these, the GSM (or stand-in) reported on the progress of matters raised by the representatives at the previous meeting, items which were usually of very specific domestic relevance, but often suggestions to improve store performance. For instance, management responded to an idea from the shop floor – suggesting that carrier bags be provided free to customers – by detailing the cost of this, before rejecting it on the grounds that this would have to be added on to prices.

The second part of the meeting consisted of the GSM's passing information to the council, on issues such as new personnel, training, dress regulations, health and safety, and 'business matters'. Some of the latter related directly to store performance over the previous period, followed by exhortations to improve or congratulations on good results. Information was also provided about new initiatives which would directly affect the store, such as the introduction of the customer care campaign or the 'employee of the year' competition. The way in which these issues were dealt with provides a feel for the character of the council, and the ability of the Chair to control the meeting. 'Employee of the year' was first mentioned by the GSM in April 1987, and he indicated that several nominations had already been received for this competition. By June, the CSM was 'disappointed' at the small number of nominations so far, whilst by July, in response to a comment that the staff were not particularly interested in the scheme, he explained

> It's an incentive to maintain customer service. Staff make the difference in the market place. People like going into some stores *because* of the people. All this is to reward staff who give good service. I'll be disappointed if someone from each department is not nominated by the end of the month. There's only one winner, but it should create an atmosphere, everyone aiming for the same goal and with a happy atmosphere.

The matter was not raised in August, since more nominations had been forthcoming, and it did not reappear during our time at the store.

'Store of the year' results were reported at the August meeting, with the news that Smalltown had come fifth in the region; 'a bit disappointing' said the GSM, 'basically we are not keeping our costs down. I'm expecting to jump up the league table next time . . . . I'm going to try and squeeze us a few points. I'll do my bit, staff must do theirs.' This almost innocent unitarism was also conveyed when he gave out advance information about a new range of confectionery products, with the instruction to 'keep it under wraps so that our competitors can't get hold of it'. The representatives, especially those who were not stewards, seemed to value this information, since it made them feel part of the company, and were equally keen on improving store performance because they conceived of their future at Smalltown; remember that these individuals were probably rather different from the mass of the workforce in that they had sought membership of the stores council in the first place. Just as at Grimsight, other employees knew little about the stores council, and seemed to care even less.

The final part of council was given over to employee representatives for their issues, and certainly at the meetings we attended all of them had something to offer, either points of their own or matters raised by their constituents. This stage of the meeting was akin to a grievance procedure/suggestion scheme, with a multitude of specific complaints or ideas for improvement. For example, one representative suggested that there ought to be an emergency procedure for ordering or cancelling foodstuffs for which demand was highly dependent upon variations in weather conditions. Other items reflected more typical grievances, such as the need for fans in hot weather, complaints about the inadequacy of equipment, customer queries which they had not been able to handle, and general housekeeping concerns. It struck us that many of these would have been more appropriately handled by their immediate boss, rather than being saved up for stores council, but the chair was prepared to take such items so they kept on appearing.

In short, therefore, the evidence from the Smalltown stores council indicates its use by management as an ideological device to promote the ethos of customer care, although it was apparent that this message did not percolate through to the shop floor from the council. In addition, it was used by the representatives as a quasi-grievance procedure with direct access to the GSM; whether this is an appropriate forum for discussing such matters in a unionised firm is open to question.

Team briefing was introduced into Multistores in 1984. The then Personnel Director had previously worked for The Industrial Society, one of the major proponents of team briefing, and was keen to implement such a system within the company. Training for the scheme was undertaken in-house, and the system became operational before a fuller review of communications strategy also led to the development of the customer care committees. The purpose of team briefing, according to a senior headquarters manager, was 'to defeat the grapevine and make management responsible for communications, not leave it to the stewards. This was not systematic before we had team briefing.' In essence, this is a fairly typical objective of any briefing system, and one which aims to reinforce the position of line managers as the focal point of downward communications.

Team briefings are supposed to take place on a monthly basis, to be held during working time, and to last about twenty minutes. The kind of information to be communicated by the system is the usual mixture of company-wide issues and items of local interest, these becoming more specific as the message travels down the hierarchy. The key role of briefing is confirmed in the Staff Handbook, in a section on 'How You Find Things Out', with the statement that

> it is very important that everyone is aware of new initiatives in the company, and how we, as a company, are performing. We also would like suggestions and feedback from you. Hence your store has a Team Briefing system, and your manager or supervisor will brief you with local and company news monthly.

Other features which are mentioned in the section are notice-boards and *Multistores News*, though not the stores councils. From this, it can be suggested that management consider team briefing to be the most important component of the communications system. Whilst the briefing system is a product of central direction, the precise information to be communicated, the exact dates and times of meetings, and even the allocation of the briefers themselves, is a matter for local discretion; the centre merely dictates that it should be done, not how. The system is formally monitored to the extent that RPMs are responsible for ensuring that team briefing proceeds in accordance with good practice, with checks on attendance, the use of *aide-mémoires*, etc. and that the message is being understood by those briefed. In assessing sites for the 'store of the year' competition, the regional controllers also ask questions of staff in order to determine the regularity of meetings as well as their effectiveness.

Given local discretion, one would expect to find some differences in the nature of team briefing between the stores. At Grimsight, although the GSM was firmly committed to the idea of briefing, he indicated that the timing of meetings did vary depending upon 'business constraints and whether or not we have anything to say'. Since store performance – one of the prime subjects for briefing – was now communicated weekly via the notice-board, this removed a key feature from the system. In addition, management in the store preferred a less structured approach to employee relations, thus producing a tendency to short-circuit team briefing in favour of continuous and more immediate disclosure of information when it came to hand. This also had the advantage, according to one of the managers, of allowing for communications without the associated disruption to normal working.

Managers at both stores found that the need to brief at a predetermined time each month often conflicted with other priorities, and they saw this as a major drawback to the system. It was, therefore, common to postpone meetings at short notice in order to deal with a more immediate demand, such as a customer complaint or visits from regional management. At Smalltown, as a means of overcoming this, the checkout operators had their briefing straight after the completion of their normal working period, say at twelve o'clock, and Multistores paid them to stay on for an extra half-hour. Although this alleviated one problem, it created another for employees with other commitments – for instance, child care – which made it difficult for them to attend; in such cases, although information could be gathered from colleagues, these workers would miss out on any attendant 'message' or 'team building' aspect of the brief. Although they appreciated the conflicts confronting line management, the store personnel managers acted as custodians of the system, monitoring team briefs periodically, and trying to persuade their colleagues who adopted a less structured approach that it was important to ensure that *all* employees had the opportunity to attend the brief, and that the information was delivered in a climate which minimised other distractions.

When held, the sessions seemed to result in two-way communications, rather than solely a structured downward information-passing exercise. A number of managers clearly saw this as a positive development, and one which they declared to be a benefit from the system. As someone who was sceptical of team briefing when it was first introduced, one of the departmental managers at Smalltown commented

> Briefing is good for the things you wouldn't really discuss in normal conversation – for example, a new marketing campaign. The most important thing is getting staff feedback, which individuals may not have the courage to say on their own. The purposes of team briefing are to get employees' views, to get over information on the everyday running of the business, and to get new ideas from the staff.

Many employees also saw this interactive approach as a positive feature of briefing, to find out information from their manager, as well as to 'get their niggles out into the open' or to air their anxieties. In some measure, therefore, briefing also acts as a more direct form of the grievance procedure (like the stores council), which effectively bypasses union representatives and reasserts the position of the line management chain. Whilst most employees spoke favourably of the system, some were highly critical of the way in which it operated, though not of briefing in principle. For example, some criticised the timing of the information received – 'We're never told anything new' – its relevance – 'It's much more useful when we talk about our department' – and even the motivation and commitment of the briefers – 'Our manager is not all that interested, he doesn't tell us anyway.' Perhaps the statement which best sums up the implicit acceptance of managerial prerogatives came from one of the sales floor personnel who said of team briefing, 'If she [our manager] has had any earache, she can tell us what wants improving.' Team briefing also seems to have an effect upon employees' awareness of their place within the company, as a number of respondents spoke of the information providing them with a better 'feel for the job'. At these two stores, team briefing has been positively received by the staff, although the form it has taken in practice clearly differs from that prescribed in the literature and within the company.

Finally, we need to refer to the customer care programme, and its associated activities, which constituted the most recent initiative within the company to foster and develop a service orientation amongst employees. In part, this was advanced through quality campaigns, but a key element of the programme took the form of various competitions which employees could enter for monetary gain; as an illustration, one of the principal tasks of the customer care committee – a non-elected body, but one whose membership encompassed all employees in the store – is to select an 'employee of the month' from a list of nominations. Staff from any part of the store are eligible for nomination, and management went to great lengths to ensure that staff knew that contact with customers did *not* represent a prerequisite for the award. Committee members other than the GSM and Personnel Manager voted each month on the candidates, and the winner received a prize of £5. More important, perhaps, is that the votes cast were carried forward, contributing to the bigger award of £500 for 'employee of the year', something which all the employees we interviewed saw as a worthwhile target.

The Grimsight Store Personnel Manager described the objective of these initiatives as 'to highlight the customer care issue, and to create models of good employees for others to follow.' Similarly, the Smalltown Customer Services Manager explicitly linked employee involvement and motivation to the service ethic:

> The customer pays our wages, and is the most important part of the store. We must be the brightest, cleanest, most pleasantly served unit, otherwise all stores are the same. Giving employees a piece of the cake motivates them. The checkout operators were already practising customer care, even though they didn't call it that. The campaign just polished it up.

In general, employees at both stores reacted favourably to the notion of customer care, although the cash benefits undoubtedly increased its attractiveness. At Smalltown, a number of bogus entries were received, but nevertheless there were ten or more serious nominations each month, and the winners appeared to be more satisfied with the accolade from their colleagues than the monetary gain. Employees at Grimsight stressed the intrinsic merits of the scheme, referring to its 'making you feel more involved in the store', or 'making customer care more visible'. They also mentioned specific substantive improvements in service which had evolved from discussions at the customer care committees. The initial assessment of the schemes clearly indicated their potential, although our research contract came to an end before any longer-term evaluation could be made.

7.7 CONCLUSION

Employee relations in Multistores is an interesting study precisely because of the differences from more conventional accounts of manufacturing industry. The whole climate is explicitly and physically market-oriented, since employees are in direct contact with customers on a day-to-day basis, and are consequently immediately aware of the fortunes of the establishment. Thus, competitions such as 'employee of the month' appear appropriate in these circumstances, whereas they might be difficult to organise and could look out of place in a manufacturing company. Once again, as with Ichem and Foodpack, it is not easy to conceive of a clear and positive role for the union in the future at Multistores, since it is so marginal to activity within the store. Irrespective of management support for the union, a combination of other factors, such as employee involvement and market sensitivity, makes an increasingly barren environment in which the union could prosper.

8 · TYPENG: BREAKING WITH THE PAST

8.1 INTRODUCTION

The Typeng site is located on the same industrial estate as Ichem, a few miles from the centre of a large northern city. Engineering work has been undertaken there since the end of the nineteenth century, and trade unionism has been a key feature of the site for almost as long. Typeng is part of much larger engineering company, Grandeng, which is itself operated on a divisional basis, and Typeng is one of four sites within the Powerco division. Grandeng employs people throughout the world, of whom about 6,000 work in the Powerco division. The Grandeng company is firmly committed to decentralised decision-making structures, either at divisional or plant level, and it sees employee relations as a site responsibility.

Although there have been some significant changes to the system of industrial relations at Typeng in recent years, at the time of our research it had not shifted as far as Ichem or Foodpack. Trade unions retained a much more central presence at Typeng, direct employee involvement had not really developed, and the impact of functional flexibility was limited. Indeed, the traditional Taylorist approach of separating the execution of work from its conception seemed to be regaining ground, and there had only been minor progress on the path to harmonisation of conditions between manual and white collar staff. Undoubtedly, the product markets within which the company operates – characterised by large orders on an irregular basis – has not helped management to develop a consistent long-term policy for employee relations.

8.2 WORK ORGANISATION

Typeng itself employs approximately 1,600 people, thus making it the largest of the sites involved in our study. Nevertheless, the size of the labour force has been declining continuously since the Second World War, and the last decade has seen a further halving in numbers employed. Although employment has been reduced right across the board, the burden of redundancy has fallen most heavily on the manual workers, so that now they form a minority of the workforce. Indeed, some of the planning departments are inundated with requests for work, largely a result of the need for rigour in tendering for scarce contracts, increasing technical control over the production process, and the greater specificity of operations by these departments. In contrast to the action taken at Ichem, for example, here no attempt has been made to share the cutbacks evenly across the site, nor has it been possible to offer any implicit guarantees of job security; rather the reverse, in fact.

Typeng has operated all manner of schemes to reduce the size of the workforce – non-replacement of leavers, early retirement, voluntary severance, and compulsory redundancy – at various times over the present decade. In 1983–4, a wave of compulsory redundancies took place on a last in, first out (LIFO) basis, whilst in 1986–7, management proposed that workers would have to be selected for severance if there were insufficient volunteers. Eventually, all but 6 of the 145 required by management were found by voluntary means, so the Works Manager agreed to close the books at this stage. From that time on, the order book improved, and no more reductions took place before the end of 1987, when we finished our research there. The Managing Director even remarked that 'for the first time in many years, we can look forward to continuity of employment.' However, recent workforce reductions have illustrated the potentially ambiguous position encountered by unions when they are faced with redundancy proposals; on the one hand, operating sanctions against the company, such as overtime bans and restrictions on contracting-out, whilst at the same time cooperating with management by encouraging certain individuals to retire early.

Redundancies apart, labour turnover on the shop floor is negligible, and long service is a customary feature of working life at Typeng. Because of previous LIFO policies, the age profile of the manual works is high: twenty-one per cent of them are over sixty, nearly three-quarters are over forty and over one-third will reach retiring age within the next decade. This is most pronounced amongst the semi-skilled sections of the workforce, and managers and supervisors in the manufacturing areas; the latter have a very high age profile with almost forty-five per cent over the age of fifty-five. Absenteeism does not run at a high level, (six per cent) compared with other employers in the area. Nonetheless it is monitored very closely by management, in line with its general obsession with quantitative control mechanisms. A manual worker told us that 'the emphasis here is on timekeeping, rather than what we do when we get here', although controls over work just happen to be less obvious.

Manual workers at the site are predominantly male, reflecting the general peacetime situation in heavy engineering industry. The production system is based on a highly sophisticated technology and, although the workforce as a whole possesses considerable skills, a Taylorist approach remains central to work organisation and the labour process at Typeng. Production control and planning are now done by computer, a 'work-to' list showing the order of priority of jobs, the machine on which it is to be done, and the time it is supposed to take. Such detailed planning clearly reduces the discretion available to manual workers, though this is not immediately apparent as employees still work to target times.

On the shop floor, there are six main production areas, covering a range of tasks from fabrication through to assembly, besides the usual array of maintenance, toolroom, inspection, and stores facilities. The fabrication shop has the reputation of being the most dispute-prone in the factory, largely because of the militancy of the welders, who opposed the recent flexibility deal, an issue to which we shall return below. Given the size of the completed product, some of the work in other parts of the production process requires extremely precise and high quality craft standards, tolerances being as low as one ten-thousandth of an inch. The two machine shops, large and small, are differentiated on the basis of scale rather than skill, and here most of the work is done on lathes and milling machines. The assembly/erection section is the only part of the operation in which the complete Typeng product is seen, ready for shipment and, subsequently, construction with products from other sites within the Powerco division. This is also one of the few departments within the factory where work is organised on a team basis. The only other group of workers easily distinguishable from the rest of the manual workforce is that of the crane drivers, largely because of their central role in the production process. During our time at Typeng, there were regular disputes between management and this group over manning and flexibility arrangements, the latter being seen by the crane drivers as an attempt to reduce their power. Overall, the workforce at Typeng possesses a higher degree of individual and craft skills, plus greater independence from management control, than at any other site within our study. However, given intense product market competition, management has been keen to encroach upon this territory.

In connection with this, at the 1986 pay negotiations, management proposed the termination of the piecework system and the introduction of more flexible working arrangements on to the shop floor. In the past, individual manual workers had negotiated the rate for each job with staff from the industrial relations department, and obviously this had led to a wide range of earnings across the factory. Following the eventual conclusion of these negotiations, the new pay scheme comprises fourteen grades, two of which cover the skilled workers in the plant, three for the toolroom, one for the crane drivers and the remainder for the other semi-skilled employees, depending upon the equipment or machinery used and the working conditions under which they labour. However, the payment system still remains more complicated than at all the other sites in our study, and significantly different in design and philosophy from that at Ichem. The other major factor in the 1986 negotiations was flexibility, and this was clearly dependent upon the removal of the piecework system, although the large number of grades remaining inevitably limits its potential. Management wanted agreement that manual workers would be willing to operate machines other than their own, that they would be mobile between hand and machine trades, and that they would be willing to assist with other duties as appropriate, for example, by helping crane drivers to sling in defined circumstances. In return, the company offered to move towards the harmonisation of conditions, although this was conditional on reductions in the rate of absenteeism.

The stewards responded to these proposals with a ban on

outworking and overtime, although their action was not solely concerned with the flexibility aspects of the deal. In the 'communications' battle which followed, improvements in flexible working formed a key part of the management letter to all manual workers, though it achieved less prominence in the union response. Management's key objective was to improve productivity so as to increase competitiveness, and this could only be brought about by cost-effective working practices. In his letter, the General Works Manager stated that 'the changes in working practices required are not demanding, there are no impossible targets being set, only the ability to get on with the job in the same way as our competitors.' In response, the Works Committee issued its own statement to make members conversant with the issue: the delegates were concerned that the flexibility proposals offered 'no guarantee of security of employment for anyone due to flexibility. This would put some groups of workers in a vulnerable position.' The unions appeared to acknowledge that agreements were possible on flexibility within trade groups, and 'in certain circumstances' between hand and machine trades, but that the strings attached to harmonisation of sick pay between manual workers and staff, namely, the reduction of average levels of sickness absence to less than five per cent before the agreement would be triggered, were unacceptable. After three more months of negotiations and two ballots of the workforce, agreement was reached on the package, including the flexibility elements.

For some groups, this seems to have caused little problem; in the toolroom, for example, the foremen and the skilled workers we interviewed regarded the deal as irrelevant to them, since they had developed greater flexibility in their shop a number of years before. In another production department, a pilot scheme had been working before 1986 and it enabled direct workers to do their own slinging, and to undertake certain inspection tasks. In addition, it had also been agreed that operatives could be trained as 'back-up' crane drivers, to be used in the event of the primary drivers being absent. Workers involved in the final erection of the product operated in teams, without any apparent demarcations between them; in fact, these employees tended to be very experienced and highly skilled men, who had generally worked throughout the factory over the course of their careers with Typeng. Two groups of employees were most resistant to flexibility, the crane

drivers and the welders, and management was particularly concerned about the former, given their key position in the workflow,
and the amount of waiting time caused by their non-availability.
This group was involved in a number of disputes with management
during 1987 about the interpretation of the agreement, and the
meaning of the word 'assist' in this; other workers are now allowed
to assist the crane drivers when the need arises. The welders'
concern reflected a long-standing feeling of status incongruency,
increased by the fact they had for years been classed as semi-
skilled, and saw flexible working as yet another threat to their job
security.

8.3 THE MARKET ENVIRONMENT

The Typeng site is responsible for building one part of the total
product made within Powerco, although other jobs are taken on at
the plant if there is little work for the highly skilled core workers.
Orders are few and far between, and the lead time for the
production of the unit is measured in years, rather than months.
Consequently, the gaining of a new order is greeted with much
satisfaction, relief and publicity, not just within the factory but in
the local community as well. The market comprises a handful of
companies across the world, with just two major competitors still
in existence in the UK. Unlike Foodpack and Multistores, but
comparable with Ichem, Typeng competes in a world market, and
is thus subject to the vagaries of exchange rate fluctuations and
political uncertainties, as well as the more typical business
concerns of price, quality and reliability. Indeed, within Typeng
(and Powerco), there is a feeling that the company has not
received adequate support from successive governments, and the
lack of firm orders in the home market has forced the company to
search overseas for new customers.

Powerco has a reputation for high quality work and advanced
technology, and this has helped it secure new contracts in a world
market characterised by potential over-supply and insufficient
demand. Products are manufactured to specific requirements, and
contract negotiations are long and arduous, involving complex
discussions about the minutest of details. The most recent order
won by the company took almost six years to conclude, and given

the strength of buyers within the market, customers are able to press for extremely exacting standards and details; for example, clauses within the last order stipulate that Typeng supplies personal details of employees who will work on the contract, that only people with more than fifteen years' service are allowed on the order, and that a representative of the customer remains on site during the completion of the job. In addition, it has been stipulated – and accepted – that the order is to be finished within eighteen months, whereas previous lead times on similar jobs have been nearer to thirty months. It is clear, therefore, that the nature of the product market can have profound implications for the way in which the labour process is managed within Typeng, both as an immediate response to the tight market conditions, and as a powerful device for management to use in restraining future worker demands.

Whilst buyers in the overseas markets are attracted by the reputation of Typeng for high quality, they are also aware of their power to cut prices, given the nature of the world market. Consequently, as one of the Typeng managers put it, 'we keep building Rolls-Royces, but we have to sell them at Ford Granada prices.' Either the company loses money on individual deals in the hope of recouping this at a later date, or management is placed under increasing pressure to find ways of reducing the cost of manufacture. Thus, in the company's view, the need for more closely monitored and controlled systems of production is easily justified. This also has implications for the way in which the production workers perceive the quality of supervision on site, and the pressure for jobs to be done quickly, rather than perfectly, leads to accusations of managerial incompetence and aggressiveness in their dealings with the shop floor. The company's market position has improved during the last few years, and the most recent orders have increased confidence about the future of the site, especially given the high start-up costs which would make it difficult for other companies to enter the market. Future market prospects are more difficult to predict than those in the retail or food sectors, precisely because they are so dependent upon gaining the very few orders which are placed each year at a price that makes it worth the company's efforts; indeed, Typeng recently lost another large order to a competitor because management was unwilling to submit to customer pressure for a sizeable price cut. There are few customers in the market, and their power over the manufacturers is made even more significant by the fact that these are often national governments. Consequently, the opportunity for individual workers to meet with customers is virtually non-existent, and it is also difficult for management to make workers directly aware of the pressures that can be exerted upon the company. Indeed, the market conditions facing Typeng and Multistores could hardly be more different, although in both cases respondents were clear about the highly competitive environment in which they operated.

8.4 MANAGEMENT STRATEGY AND STYLE

The dominant paradigm of management within Powerco and Grandeng is devolution, and this point was reiterated in all our discussions with managers at and above site level. Although staff at corporate headquarters were extremely willing to provide information for our study, there was little to unearth in the way of central direction. Grandeng does organise some management development programmes for 'high flyers', individuals who have been identified early in their careers as possessing exceptional talent, and this helps them to broaden their perspective on international affairs. Typically, corporate headquarters has also arranged courses for 'experienced' managers, but most have now been through this programme. Rather, it is suggested that the company is keen on action learning as a more appropriate vehicle to achieve personal and manager development, and that consequently individual plants are better placed to assess their own needs. Unfortunately for Grandeng, the training function has historically received a low profile at Typeng, responding to requests from individuals for specific modules or 'needs', rather than seeking to develop a more coherent and recognisable style appropriate for the site as a whole.

The Divisional Personnel Manager within Powerco was yet more adamant that the company did operate with a devolved style, with very little or no influence from his level, and even less from corporate headquarters. Meetings between the Divisional Personnel Manager and his colleagues from the different sites within Powerco take place every three months, although the former is available if needed. During our research at Typeng, personal contact between the division and the site was somewhat more than once a quarter, with telephone conversations often being held daily. However, this level of interaction could be unusual for a number of reasons; for example, the Divisional Personnel Manager only joined the company part-way through 1986, there was a reorganisation of the personnel and industrial relations function at Typeng in the middle of 1987, and the year was also characterised by a number of disputes with the crane drivers over flexible working arrangements. Nonetheless, it is clear that local management at Typeng does not appear to be overtly influenced by corporate or divisional directives, particularly in relation to any notion of 'preferred' management style. So far as we could gather, there was nothing akin to a set of 'corporate principles' of the kind which we found at some of our other sites. The lack of a corporate human resource strategy statement did not seem to concern the Typeng Personnel Manager greatly, on the grounds that, 'we're much more sharply in tune with reality than worrying about where we are on the plan.' Indeed, of all the sites involved in our research, the situation at Typeng was most reminiscent of the short-term, reactive, fire-fighting style supposedly characteristic of some sections of manufacturing industry during the 1970s. On several occasions, our discussions with staff in the Personnel Department were interrupted or postponed by more immediate pressures arising from potential disputes on the shop floor. It was only at Multistores that we experienced fire-fighting on anything like a similar scale, and there it was due to direct customer pressures or welfare issues, rather than those grounded in adversarial employee relations.

As at the other sites, however, there are also signs of a move away from this reactive style of management towards a more reflective approach. For example, the 1980 Powerco Report to Employees indicated that 'the fire-fighting techniques of solving problems, rather than preventing them, are inappropriate to modern manufacturing', and we have already described how the computerised production control and scheduling arrangements increase management control and predictability within the workplace. The management of employee relations is also undergoing a slow process of adjustment, largely, it seems, via the influence of the recently-appointed Divisional Personnel Manager. At Typeng, there has traditionally been a distinction between industrial relations and personnel, with the former responsible for negotiations, dispute resolution and the day-to-day guerilla warfare of adversarial relations. This department has its roots in rate-fixing, a system overtly characterised by continual negotiations. Conversely, the personnel department (as was) had prime responsibility for employment administration and training. During 1986 and 1987, there were attempts to dismantle some of the distinctions between the two groups, a shift which was enhanced considerably by the removal of piecework in 1986.

Typeng has also recruited graduates into the industrial relations (IR) section in recent years, there have been transfers between IR and personnel, and it is expected that the two parts of the function will merge in the next few years. The site Personnel Manager sees the future in terms of training and development, employee involvement, and continued cost reduction, language of 1980s human resource development rather than 1970s bargaining and industrial relations. The key link between the commercial environment and employee relations can also be summed up in a quote from him:

> The forward load looks quite healthy, but we need to improve lead manufacturing times and get cost reductions, whilst maintaining necessary quality standards. We can only do this with the active support of the workforce, so we have to find ways to get this via employee involvement. There is a high proportion of skilled men on the site, and we need to find a way to tap that well of information.

We shall return to this in a subsequent section.

Given the emphasis on decentralisation, it is hardly surprising that there were inconsistencies in management style within the factory. Not many respondents shared the view expressed by the Personnel Manager at Typeng, a much more common perception being one of increased direct control over employee activities. The convenor argued that recent approaches reflected a hardening of attitudes and behaviour, rather than any softening, compared with the loyalty which previous generations of managers had shown towards the workforce. 'Now', he said, 'this lot reckon that we ought to be glad that we have a job at all. I feel more like a clock number than I ever did before.' Particular criticism was levelled at the Works Superintendent (originally promoted from the shop floor), who was described as a 'bully boy', an individual who forced through changes in an autocratic manner.

According to the stewards, it had become regular practice to suspend employees if they refused to cooperate with management plans (a point also substantiated by personnel), and this was felt to be largely due to the style of this person. Another of the stewards also singled out the Works Superintendent as the prime instigator of this more 'macho' approach to employee relations, He lamented the fact that the welfare aspect of personnel work seemed less important under the current régime, and that the company no longer appeared to care about staff. 'They no longer ask us to do something, it's a take-it or leave-it approach.' The Works Manager has also resorted to direct communications with the manual workers, expressing his concern about industrial action in the context of low demand; in a recent statement to employees, he stated: 'you need only to look around our shops to understand what this will mean . . . . Nobody should be in any doubt of the seriousness of the position which we now face.'

The foremen we interviewed also thought management was attempting to tighten up on control systems, because of a need to improve efficiency in a more competitive environment. There were suggestions that Typeng was trying to change too quickly from its previous 'soft' approach, and that this made the style appear more aggressive than it actually was. In evaluating the success of this style, foremen varied in their views; for one, it had led to a reduction in union sanctions and resistance, whereas another referred to the factory as still comparable to a Butlin's holiday camp. He told us that

> we get directives to act in a particular way, but then we don't get backed up by senior management. The unions just go to the top and get decisions overturned. It's impossible for us to discipline someone here and for it to stick.

Some of the shop floor employees noted a more aggressive management style, but not all of them did; one of the manual workers from the machine shop felt there had been no real change in management style in the last fifteen years. 'They're supposed to be coming over with a harder line, but I can't see any evidence of this,' he added, although 'I'm not always sure why we get information some times and not others.' However, the limited extent of his expectations is also summed up by the following statement: 'I can't complain about management style. After all, I've still got a job after fifteen years!' A respondent from the toolroom had noted a more open and informative management style in recent years, an exercise designed to 'get away from the them and us' syndrome. At odds with the intention, however, all this had done was to make him aware of the fact that there were two sides, something which he had never seen before.

Contrary to our experience with the other companies, however, we found it more difficult to pin down a consistent management style at Typeng, although the tendency was towards hard or autocratic, rather than sophisticated or facilitative, in its approach. We did not gain the impression that notions of human resource development were prominent at Typeng, even though the stewards also castigated the newer managers for their approach as well. According to the convenor, 'they have been on courses which have trained them to be smooth and devious, to manipulate us rather than be straight.' Either way, management practice was viewed in the adversarial terms born out of a century of combat and struggle.

8.5 COLLECTIVE BARGAINING AND UNION ORGANISATION

We have already mentioned that trade unionism at Typeng stretches back to the early part of this century, being formally constituted by the establishment of the Works Committee in 1917. Currently, there are seven different unions recognised for bargaining purposes at the site, with *de facto* closed shops for the manual workers and for the draughtsmen. Table 8.1 shows the relevant details.

Despite the legislative changes in relation to the closed shop, union membership has remained at a high level, and management has continued to show its explicit support for compulsory union membership by pointing out the procedural arrangements to new employees. In fact, there has never been any formal agreement regulating union membership precisely because the tradition of unionism is so strong at the site and in the surrounding area. Commitment to the trade unions amongst the manual workers was higher than at any of the other sites involved in our study, and the

Table 8.1 Unionisation at Typeng

Union	Employees represented	Numbers covered	Union members	Density (%)
AEU				
GMBATU	Hourly-rated			
TGWU	manual workers	690	690	100
EETPU				
NUSMW				
MSF	Production control, foremen, purchasing	343	151	44
MSF	Draughtsmen	190	183	96
APEX	Clerical and secretarial	149	90	60
n/a	Management personnel	261	0	0
Total		1633	1114	68

union was seen as central to life at Typeng; amongst most of the workers we interviewed, a site without a prominent union presence was inconceivable. The manual unions work closely with each other and, from discussions with the senior stewards, we could not detect any inter-union rivalry, although subsequent developments at national level with the EETPU may alter this. At Typeng, the AEU is by far the largest union with 350 members, representing both direct production workers and skilled craftsmen. The skilled workers are members of the unions appropriate to their trade; for example, the electricians are in the EETPU, and the welders and sheet metal workers are in NUSMW.

The hourly-rated employees are represented by approximately sixty shop stewards, organised into six 'tables', each of which covers a particular section of the factory. All stewards come up for re-election every year. In addition, the stewards on each table elect a delegate from amongst their number to serve on the works committee, and these positions also come up for election on an annual basis. According to the convenor, there is little turnover amongst this group, new people only being voted on to the works committee in the event of the retirement or death of an existing member; he took this as a sign of satisfaction with existing members, rather than an indication of apathy. The six delegates form the core of trade union activity on the site, and in addition to regular meetings on their own and with management via the works committee, this group also constitutes the negotiating committee, the union side of the joint consultative committee, and any other formal team to meet with personnel and line management. At the time of our study, five of the delegates were AEU stewards, the sixth was GMB.

Although none of the shop stewards was formally full-time on union duties, the convenor spent virtually all of his time on union and related business, returning to the shop floor every now and then to, in his own words, 'keep my hand in, and give other workers a thrill to see me with my overalls on!' He also chairs a committee set up by the unions and the company to administer a fund which donates kidney machines to local hospitals, the money being drawn from voluntary deductions from employees' pay packets. Other delegates spend less time on union duties, although it is usually of the order of twelve to sixteen hours per week which, according to another of the senior stewards, management has not attempted to reduce. 'We are very trustworthy, and management like a smooth running ship', said the union secretary. At the end of our study, discussions were commencing to examine the possibility of reducing the overall number of stewards on site in line with the contraction of the workforce; the ratio of stewards to members in 1987 was less than 12:1, and the unions recognised that there were grounds for some reduction. As a sign of the company's commitment to, or perhaps acquiescence with, the unions, no formal monitoring of time-off takes place. The staff unions also have six delegates and, although no formal joint staff–works union body is in existence at the factory, the convenor is in regular contact with the Chair of the staff committee.

Both sets of stewards are heavily involved in the separate annual pay negotiations (one for the shop floor, one for the staff), since these are factory-based, as are most other aspects of working conditions. Although Powerco is ostensibly decentralised, firm control is exercised by divisional management via the mechanism of central budgeting. This lays down guidelines on the amount of money available to the local team, and it also minimises the prospect of comparability claims from the unions at the four different plants. Senior stewards across Powerco do keep each other apprised of developments but, as with any multi-establishment organisation, there is also a degree of hostility and antagonism between sites which hinders the establishment of inter-plant unity. The sites are also subject to different rates of pay, as well as payment systems, and this also limits the potential for harmonising pay and conditions across the company. Perhaps the 1986 pay negotiations best illustrate the complexity of the relationship between the site and the division; whilst the company as a whole is keen to move towards performance-related pay and individual appraisal systems, Typeng management proposed a package which bought out piecework. When one form of bonus scheme had been removed, it was felt inappropriate to try and replace this with another, quite different, pay system the following year. Powerco management did not attempt to override the local judgement on this, although the basic financial parameters were as usual set via agreement between the General Manager of Typeng and the Finance and Personnel Directors at divisional level.

So far, we have concentrated on the adversarial nature of relations at Typeng, partly because this is particularly noticeable when compared with the other companies involved in our study, but also on account of the long and well-documented history of the site. At the same time, however, despite the confrontational tone of the language employed by both parties in the negotiating and consultative arena, there is also evidence of a rather more coopera-tive stance. For example, the stewards have produced a document describing the evolution and development of trade unionism at the site up to the present day. In this, the works committee appears as a prominent feature of the period immediately following the First World War; its objectives were to bring about 'a closer association between management and the workforce, and to work in conjunc-tion for the mutual benefit of all'. The achievements emanating from works committee discussions are catalogued in detail by the manual unions, with particular emphasis on the range of social and welfare benefits, in addition to safety concerns and suggestion schemes. On disputes, the document records that 'as evidence of the strength of this feeling for cooperation ... it is considered a reflection on all sides of the company if a dispute has to be taken outside the works for settlement.' Statistics are then presented which indicate the relatively low incidence of strike action at the site since 1971, most of that due to national and official disputes. The document also mentions the importance of competitive ad-vantage, especially overseas, before concluding with the statement that 'the present committee, like those of the past, has to continue to balance the needs of its members with the needs of the busi-ness.' This document, designed for outside audiences, aims to portray industrial relations in a favourable light, but it also illustrates starkly the inherent contradictions which confront trade unionists within capitalist organisations; on the one hand, a desire for more successful companies, whilst on the other the goal of greater worker influence over management decision-making and control.

8.6 EMPLOYEE INVOLVEMENT

Of all the sites involved in our research, Typeng was the one with least in the way of direct employee involvement; indeed, aside from the introduction of manufacturing cells (a sort of quality circle) in a small number of areas, and some *ad hoc* communication arrangements initiated by individual supervisors, representative institutions remained the central (and generally sole) focus for employee relations. Management wanted this to change, and experiments with briefing groups started at two of the four factories within Powerco during 1987. According to the Divisional Personnel Manager, these sites had been chosen because their more favourable industrial relations climate increased the chances of this new approach being successful. Following this, team briefing would then be considered for Typeng, but at the time we concluded our studies in late 1987, this was not yet on the agenda. Apart from the obvious relevance of .is to EI, it also illustrates the influence of the division over the sites, the way in which senior management does actually make choices between factories, and think in terms of employee relations across the division, rather than allowing for total decentralisation, as some company statements would seem to imply. Before examining direct EI in greater detail, we shall analyse the mechanisms for representative participation. At Typeng, there are three separate long-standing committees which span the communication-consultation-negotiation continuum; the works committee, the joint consultative committee, or JCC, and the 'Thursday' meeting. We shall analyse each of these in turn.

The works committee

The works committee has the longest history of the three, having been in existence in one form or another for over seventy years. It takes place on Monday mornings, and can last for anything from a couple of minutes to an hour, but its main business is usually over within ten minutes. The meeting is chaired by the convenor, and whilst there is a standing order that agenda items should be received on the preceding Friday, it is quite usual for the Chair to accept late additions from management on the Monday morning. Such is the informality of the works committee, despite its traditions. The meeting is attended by the six delegates, the Works Superintendent, the Industrial Relations Manager and his assistant, and two production supervisors. Although the General Works Manager used to be a regular attender, he now comes rarely; one of the stewards commented that 'now, when he attends, we expect a bit of trouble.' Management presents information to the committee on leavers and starters, and provides statistics on absence, lateness and sickness. Often, this is the only agenda item, and the meeting is soon over, unless there is a clear difference between the parties on an issue or its interpretation. For instance, the convenor has questioned the validity of the statistics provided by management, arguing that they were 'conveniently selective' for the benefit of management's case. Minutes of the meeting are prepared, but these tend to be short ('with the bad language taken out') and, according to both sides, not always one hundred per cent accurate, since there is no intention of recording every disputed item. The stewards in particular are acutely aware of the broader audience for these minutes, especially at divisional level, where decisions are made about future investment. At the same time, since minutes are posted on the shop floor, and all the delegates are required to report back to their tables following the meeting, they want to ensure that their constituents realise that issues have been raised at the works committee.

Not surprisingly, few shop floor workers expressed any great interest in the meetings, leaving the detailed scrutiny of the minutes and cross-examination of the delegates to the stewards. Even amongst the participants, the works committee generated little enthusiasm, its continuation owing more to tradition and symbolism than to effectiveness and centrality. Both sides appear to concur with this assessment, but any attempt to remove it would have encountered resistance from the unions, and for this reason management preferred to leave the channels open, just in case any issues did arise for which the works committee would have served as a useful vehicle. In any event, this was unequivocally seen by the delegates as 'their own meeting', in contradistinction to the JCC, which was unambiguously defined as management's.

The joint consultative committee

The joint consultative committee was inaugurated by management in 1980 in order to provide a forum for dealing with issues relating to production and kindred matters. We were not able to find a constitution for the JCC, and no-one seemed particularly bothered about this, since they all 'knew' what the meeting was about. The JCC meets monthly on a Tuesday afternoon, usually occupying approximately one hour of works time. Once again, the trade unions are represented by the six delegates, that is, the unions have a monopoly over employee representation. The management team comprises the General Works Manager (as Chair), flanked by the Works Superintendent, a departmental supervisor, the Production Control Manager, and two from the industrial relations department.

The main item on the agenda is the business report by the General Manager in which he outlines progress against budget, the order situation (forward workload), new appointments, key visitors to the site, and as usual a variety of miscellaneous items. Detailed figures are provided by the Chair, especially about performance and orders; the latter in particular clarify the state of progress of all firm orders as well as tentative enquiries, identifying the customers by name and by the nature of the work required. During the mid-1980s, Typeng was keen to take on general engineering work in order to keep the workforce occupied, largely in anticipation of a number of large new orders later in the decade; these were forthcoming towards the end of our research period, and the mood of caution lifted visibly from the site. As at Foodpack, though without the same extensive and direct exposure, it was felt important to inform the delegates that key customers were visiting the factory. Examples of the miscellaneous items on the agenda were forthcoming social events (e.g. a fun run), arrangements for shut down working, a new share option scheme, and the reorganisation of a technical department.

The General Works Manager clearly used the meeting in order to communicate management's interpretations of events to the delegates, and through them to the shop floor. In presenting the results for the previous period to the meeting, on a number of occasions the General Works Manager commented specifically on the effect of 'poor' attendance or 'alarming' levels of sickness absence on performance. Associated with this came the plea that 'we must become more competitive.' At another meeting, following the imposition of an overtime and outworking ban by the stewards in response to a redundancy announcement, the General Works Manager expressed his 'dismay' at the decision to apply sanctions, arguing that this only meant 'jeopardising the chances of winning future orders'. In reply, the convenor denied that the unions were responsible for the present situation, and reminded the meeting that he did not want to be in conflict with management. In effect, he then offered a compromise solution to management in true negotiating style, and two weeks later this situation was at least partly resolved. A similar discussion took place regarding piecework drift, with management expressing concern at the 'unacceptable escalation in piecework prices booked in certain areas' and the convenor responding with the view that 'rate-fixers had proposed ridiculously low prices under orders from above.' Again, a compromise was recorded. At another meeting, information on the forward load was presented in the context of concerns about the failure to agree pay negotiations, and was supplemented by a statement that the 'very serious' lack of orders could lead to sizeable reductions in the available hours of work (that is, numbers employed). Although management attempts to use the meeting to reinforce its views and set the ground for subsequent decisions, the stewards were not slow to resist this by producing counter-arguments.

The delegates certainly valued the JCC because it provided them with information which they might not receive elsewhere, but they were suspicious about the timing of communications and their interpretation by management. That they were fully aware of the political nature of the information disclosed is apparent from a number of quotes from the senior stewards; for example, 'they only tell us what they want to', or 'we always get a big order announced just after we've settled a pay claim. Coincidence? No, it's management manipulation.' The most radical criticism came from one of the delegates: 'performance is always judged against budget, but who sets the budget? No-one tells us how much a piece of metal is worth when it comes into the factory, or how much when it goes out. It's a bit of noddy really!' The credibility gap between the delegates and the management is further emphasised by the fact that they check information received at the JCC with other sources. Once again, though, a cooperative orientation is also in evidence, as illustrated by a comment from another of the delegates that 'generally they (management) try to tell the truth, but they can't always, business being what it is [competitive].' Shop floor knowledge of the JCC is minimal, so far as we could gather, a point confirmed by one of the delegates who suggested that 'people may not even know it exists.' As a mechanism for communicating information to the shop floor, it is clearly not very effective.

Thursday meeting

The third representative meeting which occurs at the Typeng site is the 'Thursday' meeting, so named for obvious reasons. Like the works committee, this takes place weekly, and once again it is attended by the six delegates. The Works Superintendent and the two Industrial Relations Managers constitute the management team, thus attracting the observation from one of the delegates that 'we always put in a full team, but theirs is diluted.' The purpose of the meeting, also introduced in 1980, is ostensibly to discuss production matters, but it covers much more ground than this. According to the protagonists, it primarily provides the opportunity to let off steam, and the meetings are apparently characterised by frank exchanges, foul language, table-thumping, threats, walk-outs, and all manner of associated discourse. No minutes are distributed from this meeting, and it is held *in camera*, thus remaining immune from the researcher's scrutiny. Usually, the meeting lasts for about forty-five minutes, but it can dissolve within a few minutes or expand to well over two hours. With an open agenda, any contentious issues are hammered out, and during our time at Typeng two of the most important items were the implications of the flexibility agreement for crane drivers and the termination of heat allowance payments to welders. Both management and the delegates are committed to this off-the-record meeting, since it deals with contentious local issues within the confines of the works. Of all the meetings which the delegates attend, this is the one they would least want to lose.

Beyond site level, there is one commitee which covers the whole of the Powerco division, code-named by us the 'central review committee'. This was born out of a lost order to a major competitor in the mid-1970s, and its aim is to provide forum for four union representatives from each of the four sites, along with their general works managers, to meet with the Divisional Personnel Director. Meetings originally occurred approximately once every quarter, but in recent years these have become less common, and management is now keen to reconstitute the committee on a more formal basis, but to meet only twice per year and to include provision for non-union representation from amongst the ranks of the white collar staff. At the time of our research, this was not seen by any of the participants as a central feature of employee relations (even though we spoke with some of the key union representatives on this committee), and we therefore chose to investigate it no further.

Despite the range of procedures for communication and consultation at the factory, most of the shop floor employees we interviewed felt that they knew little about what was happening at Typeng, or about future prospects for the business. Communications were regarded as poor, both through the line management chain and via their shop stewards. In some ways, this is hardly surprising, given the lack of any formal mechanism to ensure that employees are regularly updated on issues affecting the factory; in fact, it seems that the only time when workers do receive information systematically from top management is during a crisis, such as existed when the flexibility deal was in jeopardy. At these times, the delegates felt that direct mailings from the General Works Manager did more harm than good, provoking individuals in ways which were not intended. Some of the shop floor comments about the state of communications speak for themselves:

> We don't find out about things until they are sprung on you, after they are implemented. I find out more about events and orders from the television or the local paper.

> Lots of emphasis here on secrecy, don't know why they're so secret. The idea seems to be that the less people who know the better.

> There ought to be more communication because it would give us peace of mind. There's a lot of fear of redundancy.

> Communication is terrible. Management has a very hierarchical attitude, you're *only* a shop floor worker. They don't take shop floor ideas seriously enough.

Not too bad. Foreman gives us information, but it is not company policy to have meetings because if we leave the job, it means we are not working.

Even when there were communications, it was felt that these were merely to communicate doom and gloom messages to the manual workers. It was not just the shop floor workers who interpreted events in this way, for so too did some of the line managers and foremen. One of them admitted that

communications have been appalling in the past, and via the works committee they are very bad – the lads get a warped impression from the delegates. Things are improving now, but it's unfortunate that this started to happen when the economic position was poor.

Some of the supervisors did appear to pass on the information that they received from the General Works Manager every month to the shop floor, but this tended to be *ad hoc*, and only to those the foremen defined as 'interested' in such matters. Others took the view that manual workers showed little interest in information unless 'it relates to money or orders', and yet others were wary of new EI gimmicks, since 'these had all been tried in the past to no avail.' It was clear to us as outsiders that employees at Typeng felt considerably less well informed than workers at any of the other sites we investigated; in part, this has to be a function of size, but it also owes much to the reactive style of management which predominates at the factory. Tied in with this is a lack of training for supervisors, but the age composition of this group has made this a less pressing task.

The most recent addition to the system of employee relations at the site were 'manufacturing cells', these being introduced on a limited scale in the early summer of 1987. The objective behind the cells was to increase productivity through a speeding up of manufacturing times, and in part the idea was also a public relations initiative designed to impress potential customers. The cells are teams of about eight people from various technical areas (for example, engineering, production control, supervisors, computer programming, and shop floor workers) which meet weekly to discuss particular manufacturing problems and devise solutions to them. In the toolroom, there are a number of cells, whilst other areas do not have any at all. In addition, some of the cells do not include any shop floor workers, a situation which further divides the labour force, and is bound to undermine some of the anticipated achievements from the cell system. In the toolroom, there had been several examples of successful ideas which had been implemented, and the superintendent in that department was convinced of their value on both efficiency and motivational grounds. For him, 'the lads on the shop floor have a lot to contribute. You can tap their knowledge and give them a sense of worth.' The delegates were generally rather more cynical about the cells, reckoning that they had been tried in the past, but had collapsed when money was needed to finance the suggestions. Moreover, there was an element of 'brainwashing' in the cells, according to the stewards, who claimed, 'it's just line management trying to get its own way.' We had insufficient evidence by the end of our study to make a judgement about the future of the cells, largely because of the limited coverage of the cells throughout the factory, and the short period of time for which they had been in operation. However, initial evaluations would suggest that they will have to overcome severe opposition, from both stewards and foremen, in order to gain widespread acceptance.

8.7 CONCLUSION

Overall, therefore, the data from Typeng indicate that unions are still able to exert quite a considerable influence upon employee relations within British factories, despite the broader social, economic, legal and political changes in the country as a whole. Certainly, the tradition of unionism at the site presents management with a more difficult context within which to operate, but the composition and style of management itself also holds back the rate of change in this environment. Equally, however, there were signs of change during the period of our study, as management sought to introduce elements of direct employee involvement into an environment in which both parties had traditionally favoured representative institutions.

PART III

EMPLOYEE RELATIONS IN CONTEXT

9 · UNIONS ON THE MARGIN

9.1 INTRODUCTION

Most observers of the British industrial scene are agreed that the 1980s have proved a severe test for the trade union movement. In general terms, there have been major problems: considerable losses in membership; lack of access to national forums for the discussion of tripartite affairs; the growth of non-union plants; splits within the TUC; and hostile legislation; all factors which help to undermine the position of the unions. Yet, at the same time, there is other evidence indicating that many employers continue to maintain the institutional framework which supports workplace trade unionism, on the face of it not taking advantage of the potential opportunities presented to them to weaken the unions within their own companies. Arguments such as these formed the basis of the earlier chapters of the book, when we reviewed the way in which employee relations may be undergoing change, the role that management strategy had to play in that process, and the interaction between management style and the product market environment.

Each of our case study companies had undergone some changes in employee relations over the course of the decade. Ichem had experienced the most dramatic upheaval, following its turnaround project in 1980, but by the time of our research the company's prospects for the future looked better than those at all the other sites in our study. At the opposite end of the spectrum was Typeng, not because it had not undergone significant reductions in the numbers employed at the site, but rather because of the stability in its patterns of industrial relations, and the limited impact of direct employee involvement techniques. Foodpack was the site at which the trade unions had been most notably marginalised by recent events, and it was also the plant where the management was most willing to try out new techniques and enter into new agreements, such as the three-year, no-strike deal. Multistores represented something of a paradox for the retail industry in that a union membership agreement had been signed in the late 1960s, but it also had the greatest range of techniques for communicating with employees and involving them. There were clear differences between employee relations in these plants, not only in terms of workplace union organisation, collective bargaining arrangements, and employee involvement, but also in their position within the wider corporate bodies to which they belonged. All these features provided us with the opportunity to examine more carefully a number of the arguments we outlined in earlier chapters, as well as to suggest amendments to these, as appropriate. As before, we shall proceed by addressing a series of questions:

- What are the differences, if any, between the attitudes and behaviour of independent and sponsored workplace union organisations?
- Have management attempted to 'roll back' shop steward organisation during the 1980s?
- Have bargaining structures been amended so as to reduce the scope of negotiations or the influence of unions over this activity?
- Have joint consultation and direct employee involvement been upgraded in order to undermine workplace union organisation by the 'back door', rather than head-on?
- Has direct employee involvement had any effect upon the attitudes and commitment of workers towards their employers?

Before we compare the evidence from the case studies with the relevant literature, a word of caution is required. Clearly, it is not possible on the basis of just four cases to discredit totally other theses about workplace employee relations, nor is this our intention. However, as we saw from the earlier chapters, there are some theoretical problems with this literature, which suggest that it may lack meaning in the context of specific workplaces. Moreover, these theses remain in need of more rigorous analysis in order to test their applicability in different companies, as well as in the climate of 1980s employee relations; this is our principal purpose in this chapter.

9.2 SPONSORSHIP OF UNION ORGANISATION

It will be recalled from Chapter 2 that many writers interpreted the 1970s as a decade of management 'sponsorship', in which managements assisted in the development and formalisation of workplace union organisation, not through any sense of altruism, but because it was believed that this would help them to regain control over employee relations. It was argued that managements directly promoted the growth of steward organisation by providing easier access to facilities and time off, full-time stewardships, check-off, and union membership agreements, since it was expected that these would lead to greater order and stability in the workplace. In addition, changes to payment systems and other procedures in the workplace also contributed to the centralisation of steward networks, as the latter adjusted in order to mirror management organisation. Nevertheless, we also identified a number of shortcomings with this thesis of managerial sponsorship, not least because it underplayed the influence of worker power on management actions, but also for its dubious assumptions about the consequences of management assistance for subsequent steward attitudes and behaviour.

Each of the case studies has relevance for the sponsorship debate, with Multistores providing a supposedly prime example of this in action; indeed, the reasons for management's choosing to recognise a union, and also concede a closed shop at the same time, bear a remarkable similarity to those suggested in Chapter 2. Management took its decision to offer a closed shop to the GMB in the late 1960s at a time of rapid union growth, since it was felt that the expanding company would become a prime target for trade unions. A single union deal (sole recognition agreement) was seen as appropriate since this would prevent other unions from gaining access to the company, and thus overcome any potential inter-union membership battles. The GMB was selected partly because of its presence in other parts of the company, but more important because it offered a much more attractive prospect than the competitors; a union with which management felt 'it could do business'. Discussions with respondents in the company suggested there was no real pressure from employees for union membership at the time, and this is still generally the case. There is also continuing evidence of close ties between the company and the union, which might plausibly offer support for the notion of cumulation, whereby 'responsible' unionism is the result of 'responsive' management. However, there must be doubts about the direction of causality of this correlation, since one of the reasons given for recognition in the first place was the well-known moderate stance of the union, and it is much more likely that cooperation is the product of continuing good relations between union and management.

A further limitation to the applicability of 'sponsorship' in the case of Multistores relates to the level at which the agreement with the union was concluded and, indeed, continues to operate. Sponsorship would suggest that local managers foster the development of shop steward organisation at establishment level, and are assisted in this task by the creation of other systems and procedures at the same level. Within Multistores, collective bargaining and most other procedures are centralised, and local stewards only play a minor part in the administration of employee relations. Whilst relations between senior managers and national union officials are well developed and integrative, there is little opportunity for this to occur at local level, since both parties are principally concerned with the implementation of company agreements, rather than their creation. It proves difficult to find enough stewards to occupy the agreed number of places within the store and turnover amongst them is high; as we observed at Smalltown, all the stewards were relatively inexperienced, and even the senior steward had only held office for three months, a feature which militates against management's building up close and continuing relations with stewards. In addition, the agreement specifies that shop stewards shall not be the sole channel for workforce representation on the stores council, so this makes it even more difficult for the union to maintain its profile within the store; we shall return to this below. Perhaps the lack of prominence of the union within the store is best summed up by the fact that one of the council members at Smalltown (a union member herself, of course) did not know that a new senior steward had been elected for the store three months after the position had been filled. The evidence from Multistores, therefore, does not seem to offer much support for the notion of sponsorship.

In contrast to the situation at Multistores, union organisation at Typeng can be characterised as 'independent', both in terms of its history (works committee formed in 1917) and its continuing evolution. Of all the sites in our study, Typeng was the one where the stewards had the most developed form of union organisation (via delegates and 'tables'), the greatest degree of stability (lack of steward turnover), and the lowest ratio of members to stewards (at just twelve to one compared with a typical figure some three times higher than this). In addition, adversarial relations had marked much of the history of this site, and during our research period there were a number of disputes, failures to agree, and regular fire-fighting exercises by management. The stewards bargained locally, meeting regularly with management several times each week, and certainly fulfilling Willman's criteria for independence.

But, once again, there are contradictory tendencies, as the stewards displayed cooperative attitudes and behaviour in a number of ways. Relations between the senior stewards and the personnel department were generally good, in particular with the industrial relations specialists with whom the former met several times each week. The stewards ran a fund to donate kidney machines to a local hospital, and that was seen to be an important feature of life at the plant. In addition, the senior steward spoke about the site to a variety of external audiences, and his notes demonstrated a considerable commitment to its future. Phrases such as 'a closer association', 'mutual benefit', and 'balance the needs of the works committee with those of the business' seem to be more in line with what one would expect from sponsored, rather than independent, organisations. Moreover, his notes also indicated the stewards' commitment to resolving disputes within procedure, regarding strike action as a sign of failure on both sides: more like the language of management than of independent steward organisations. In other words, the sponsorship thesis appears to be incapable of distinguishing between the subsequent behaviour of the different types of steward body, and in particular the large measure of cooperation evident at 'independent' sites.

It is rather more difficult to classify Ichem and Foodpack as either independent or sponsored, although workplace union organisation has been a prominent feature of both sites for well over twenty years. At Ichem, unions were recognised in the late 1930s, when the plant was opened, and, given the traditions of the chemical industry, it is likely that they were assisted by management at that time. All the usual facilities were on offer at Ichem, as, too, was a *de facto* closed shop arrangement. However, to assert that unions were courted by management tends to overlook the fact that Multichem chose to locate its business in an area of strong union traditions, and that it would have found great difficulty in maintaining a union-free environment in such circumstances. The Foodpack case is very similar. Both of these lend support to the view that it is impossible to disentangle the influence of management acquiescence or encouragement from that of worker pressure. It is also important to recognise that the indicators of independence which are traditionally used may be poor proxies for union strength; for example, the existence of full-time or senior stewards may be more appropriately seen as typical of large workplaces, or those in which there is provision for meaningful local negotiations over pay and other matters, than the result of the influence of independent worker organisations. Conversely, just because a particular plant commenced operations in the 1970s, and the unions enjoyed management support for their activities, this should not be taken as evidence of managerial sponsorship.

9.3 THE ROLL-BACK OF UNION ORGANISATION

If we find little support in our cases for the notion of managerial sponsorship, is there any evidence to support the thesis that steward organisations have been 'rolled back' during the 1980s? Ichem is the site at which the evidence to support roll-back is the strongest. Here, the convenor is no longer full-time on union duties, having been put back on shifts in 1984, a move which has reduced his ability to contact other stewards, as well as the amount of time he can devote to union activities during working hours. In addition, the stewards all complained that it was now more difficult for them to arrange time off for union duties, and that line managers were vetting requests for time off more rigorously. Moreover, the senior stewards all agreed that management was attempting to marginalise the role of the convenor and, more broadly, that of the unions in the workplace; the most explicit illustration of this was provided by their limited access to senior personnel management, given that their contacts with the function came through a personnel officer whose direct responsibility was confined to issues relating to the manual workforce. So far, the evidence would seem to offer support for the 'roll-back' thesis.

However, the reality is rather more complex; the Personnel Manager argued that the tightening up on time off was a consequence of other changes since the turnaround in the early 1980s, and part of a general policy to operate cost-effectively. In addition, the Personnel Manager believes that the stewards have failed to appreciate that the status of the person with whom they have contact has not changed, merely that the individual they used to deal with (namely, himself) has since been promoted. The case of the convenor is more complicated, but nonetheless reflects the intricacies of employee relations on the shop floor; before the negotiation of the New Deal, the convenor had been a shift operator, but management had seen advantages in transferring him to days for the four-year period of readjustment and turnaround, particularly in view of the fact that the workforce was to be halved between 1980 and 1984. During this time, he generally worked full-time on union duties, although no formal agreement was signed to ratify this. Following the completion of turnaround, management suggested that the convenor be put back on to shifts, a decision which he personally opposed, and which caused some resentment, though nothing else, from the other stewards. Since that time, he has been much less active, and management admits that it has tried to minimise his position in the works because it feels he is 'politically motivated'. As we have already seen, he had, during a recent pay deal, attempted to form a combine committee between the separate unionised plants owned by Multichem, but to no avail. This had failed, according not only to the stewards at Ichem but also to the convenor at another Multichem site, largely because of his approach. We also observed the willingness of his own colleagues at Ichem to conclude the annual pay negotiations in his absence; in short, other stewards (at Ichem and elsewhere) had their doubts about him, as did management, although none of the stewards was willing to oust him from the position of convenor.

Events at Foodpack offer a similar, if less pronounced,

perspective on roll-back. The role of the union, at least in terms of the amount of time stewards spend on union duties and in the regularity of their contact with management, has been reduced since the negotiation of the three-year deal in 1985. This is to be expected, considering that one of the management objectives for the deal was to 'de-hassle' industrial relations so as to provide time for the introduction of other initiatives in the field of employee involvement. The stewards used to have regular contact with the Personnel Manager and also monthly meetings with the previous Production Manager, although the latter actually ceased during 1986. On his arrival, the new Production Manager reinitiated the practice of meetings but he saw these as principally for the purpose of informing stewards of new developments and dealing with problems of a plant-wide nature. Contacts with the personnel department now occur less frequently than they used to, but this also represents part of the Production Manager's aims. Although we felt that the union representatives were not as central to affairs at Foodpack – and so, too, did management – the stewards themselves did not appear to share this view, adding yet another twist to 'roll-back'.

In both cases, therefore, the interpretation is rather more complicated than roll-back would imply. As we suggested above, the removal of full-time steward status or restrictions on time off may be caused by events other than a desire to reduce the role of the union in the workplace; a reduction in numbers employed offers one pertinent reason and another is tightening-up on costs more generally which takes in steward activity as a part of the exercise, and also the after-effects of a change in bargaining arrangements. There is a danger of mistakenly assuming that a restriction of union activity is the principal reason for change, rather than seeing it as a consequence of other adjustments.

It is also possible that we can misinterpret an attempt to marginalise the convenor as an assault on the union *per se*. At Ichem, there is little doubt that the senior stewards did see management's action as an assault on the principle of unionism at the site, yet they were still willing to reach agreements with management which further isolated the convenor within the works. The process workers we interviewed were also aware of the lessened role of the convenor, and of previous acrimonious meetings involving him and the management, but they attributed this to personality conflicts between the convenor and the Personnel Director. Management did not attempt to deny that it was trying to isolate the convenor, but vigorously disputed that this was an assault on the union, by pointing to the ways in which management continued to support its role and activities elsewhere, as was the case with the closed shop. This interpretation does have some plausibility in view of the attitudes of the Ichem stewards towards their convenor, as well as his standing with other Multichem convenors. However, as we shall see below, the role of the union may be affected by the introduction of other techniques, such as employee involvement.

In contrast to the above cases, there was no evidence of roll-back at either Typeng or Multistores. In the case of the latter, there was virtually no steward organisation to roll back; indeed, the Personnel Manager at Smalltown was attempting to develop union organisation by providing for regular bi-monthly meetings with the stewards. She was particularly keen to establish a forum whereby issues such as those relating to working conditions could be resolved to the benefit of all employees, and she had also agreed that the new senior steward could attend a series of TUC courses. The fact that union representatives occupied a marginal role within the stores owed more to the indifference of union members and other attempts to involve employees in improving customer care within the company, than it did to any concerted management strategy to undermine the unions. At Typeng, contact between management and the senior stewards had been maintained at a high level throughout the 1980s, to a large extent because management was cautious about trying to alter the institutions at the plant. Since the unions here are arguably the most powerful of all those involved in our study, it is also the plant for which a reduced role for the unions would presumably present an attractive option for management. However, management did not seem to be planning a full-scale assault, even though it was keen to reduce the number of stewards at the plant. Considering the precarious state of the principal product market, there were many sound reasons for maintaining the *status quo*, if only to minimise the risk of disruption to production. Consequently, contrary to some other survey evidence, there was no greater likelihood of a more aggressive approach towards the unions at the site with strong workplace organisation.

Although the position of the stewards was undergoing change in all of the cases, albeit in different ways and directions, we found no attempt by managements to remove the closed shop from any of the plants. None of them had organised ballots to test the strength of feeling for the closed shop, because they saw no point in destabilising an arrangement which offered them a degree of order in the workplace. Their response had been fairly standard, in that management had agreed not to ballot, but to expect new starters to join the appropriate union; in return, the unions had accepted that management would not dismiss people for non-membership. Unionism appeared most central to the lives of employees and members at Typeng, and, indeed, the closed shop here had never been formalised, precisely because it was 'natural' for new starters to join. Not surprisingly, employees at Multistores showed the least interest in the union; apart from the lack of union traditions in the industry, many of the workers were part-time, labour turnover ran at fifty per cent per annum, and collective bargaining took place at national level, all features which militate against union commitment at workplace level. However, the company handbook also advised new staff that union membership was a requirement of the job, showing its determination to keep the closed shop operative. At all the sites, even though management might have attempted to influence steward organisation, the closed shop had remained broadly intact. Although there were some fairly superficial indicators of roll-back at two of the plants, this is less plausible when seen in its wider context.

9.4 THE SIGNIFICANCE OF COLLECTIVE BARGAINING

In Chapter 2, we noted that the British system of collective bargaining was noteworthy for the diversity of arrangements, particularly in the private sector, where arrangements reflected the differing traditions of industries and companies, especially in multi-plant organisations. The notion of 'institutional separation' has been proposed as an explanation for bargaining operating at the level it does in different companies; briefly, the argument suggests that employers are keen to maintain a separation between strategic decision-makers and collective bargaining, either by conducting these at different levels in the company, or through different management functions. At the same time, even though bargaining may take place at plant level, any autonomy which this appears to offer to local managers is, in fact, illusory, since their activities are closely monitored by corporate personnel. There are a number of problems with this as an explanatory device, not least because it ignores the role which political processes play within organisations, but also because it assumes that labour relations questions are central to management decision-making. Nonetheless, it is an approach which has gained some support, so we need to re-examine it against the data from the case studies.

Institutional separation appears to have most relevance for Typeng and Foodpack. In the case of the former, collective bargaining takes place at plant level, whereas strategic decisions about the business are made at divisional (Powerco) level, owing to the integration of production between the different plants within the Powerco division. There are differences in payment systems and also in levels of pay between establishments; this conforms with the espoused policy of the company to decentralise employee relations decisions to plant management, since it is in the best position to respond to local variations in labour market conditions. To a large extent this happens in practice, although there appear to be more divisional influences than senior managers publicly admit. Trade union representatives have some contact across the plants within the division, but this is neither encouraged nor explicitly supported by management, and the stewards gave us no indication that there was any combine committee. A similar separation occurs at Foodpack, in that strategic decision-making takes place at divisional level, whilst collective bargaining is a plant activity. As at Typeng, senior management easily justifies the separation. Since there is a level of interdependence between plants, the latter manufacture their products in line with a divisional schedule, and indeed there is no marketing or selling function at the Foodpack plant. Since plants are located around the country, differing in their local labour market environments, and also in the mix of employees required, the company argues that decentralised bargaining makes sense.

Even if bargaining and strategic decision-making do take place at different levels in the company, it does not necessarily follow that this is done principally for the purpose of keeping trade union negotiators away from key strategic decision-makers. From the

company's perspective, both may make sense for the quite uncon-
nected reasons suggested above, and labour relations considerations may have played no part in the production decision. Indeed,
there is a danger that the thesis of institutional separation merely
transposes cause and effect, elevating labour relations to centre
stage when it is a secondary consideration.

The case of Multistores offers another perspective on the thesis,
in that collective bargaining and strategic decision-making both
take place centrally. The reason for this, according to senior
management, is simply that there is so little variation between the
one hundred stores around the country that it makes little sense to
allow local autonomy; costs can be more effectively controlled by
means of central buying, stores can be assessed against set criteria,
customers expect a similar range of products irrespective of location, and it is administratively easier to determine employee
relations at the centre. There may be institutional separation by
function, as negotiations are conducted principally by the Employee Relations Manager. However, all the senior management
team is housed in the same office block, and access could be
arranged if desired. Equally, the trade union officials with whom
the company meets are national-renowned figures who are unlikely to accept being 'fobbed off with the corporate monkey', if that is
how they see it. But, there is a further reason why bargaining and
strategic decision-making can coexist at the same level, which adds
another twist to the thesis; in Multistores, despite the closed shop,
the union would encounter difficulty in organising concerted and
cohesive resistance to management, as it lacks centrality and
meaning for the majority of its members, hardly surprising for the
retail trade. Consequently, there may be no need for management
to 'engineer' institutional separation since the union does not pose
a substantial threat to the company in any event. Therefore, the
thesis of institutional separation, if it does have any relevance,
may only be applicable in situations of union strength, for when
unions are weak there is little need for it to be pursued.

There are also problems in applying the notion to Ichem, where
collective bargaining and strategic decision-making both take
place at the level of the division/plant. Negotiations are led by
senior line and personnel managers, although the Managing Director keeps out of these, as one might expect. The division is a
profit centre in its own right, has marketing and selling functions

on site, and, indeed, is the sole producer of this range of chemicals within Multichem worldwide. It has also been highly profitable since the completion of the turnaround programme in 1984. All these features give the division a considerable degree of autonomy, in excess of that enjoyed by other parts of the Group, as we discovered from research elsewhere in Multichem. Although there are some similarities to Multistores, the labour factor is quite different because the unions possess sufficient local power to disrupt the works, have stronger traditions of unionism in the area, and undertake establishment bargaining. It is difficult to see how the institutional separation argument can apply to Ichem unless the hidden hand of the European HQ maintains subtle controls on strategic decision-making which by-pass the UK Group altogether. However, an alternative explanation can also be put forward, which treats pay determination as more than just the product of the negotiating arena, viewing it more positively as a device to recruit, motivate and retain workers, as well as a control on labour costs. To embroider the notion somewhat: the company which successfully keeps down labour costs, via a process of institutional separation, is hardly likely to operate effectively if it cannot recruit, motivate or retain workers at the negotiated rate. Its success in the former area is inconsequential when set against its failure in the latter. Therefore, if strategic decisions are made at the plant, rather than automatically elevating pay negotiations to a higer level, there may be advantages in retaining these in-house especially, as in the case of Ichem, if a plant-wide performance-related bonus also figures prominently in pay determination. Not only can this increase employee rewards substantially (as it did at Ichem), but it can also encourage identification with the success of the plant and discourage industrial action; it can moreover be combined with attempts to increase employee involvement, as we shall see below.

Overall then, our case study evidence casts some doubt on the applicability of the institutional separation thesis, even in situations where, on the surface, it appears to hold. Not only does it elevate labour considerations to an unrealistically high profile within organisations, by assuming that these represent the main reason for separation, but it also fails to take account of a principal purpose of pay determination, namely to recruit, motivate and retain staff. Furthermore, it makes the cardinal error of presuming that senior management is automatically cohesive and omniscient, neither of which can be taken for granted.

For a large number of companies, collective bargaining is undertaken at establishment level because, it is argued, this allows local managers the autonomy to tailor arrangements to their own specific circumstances. As we saw in Chapter 2, however, several researchers regard this autonomy as illusory, since corporate headquarters closely monitor any negotiations which occur there. Considering the word 'illusion' to be too strong, others prefer 'constraint', but in any event the assumption remains of one-way control down the management hierarchy. Of all our sites, the case of Ichem provides us with an opportunity to reconsider this in more detail. Within Multichem, the individual divisions or plants are responsible for pay determination at local level, but, as one might expect, this does not proceed without contact between management at different levels. Usually, the process would commence with the Managing Director of Ichem making the Group HQ aware of the plant's intentions, not for approval, but for information and discussion. Since he is a member of the UK Group Board himself, it would be inaccurate to portray this process as an approval-seeking exercise, but rather more as a sharing of ideas. We mentioned in the case study that managers at Group level also seek legitimacy with personnel managers on the plants, so it would be absurd to view their relationship in terms of authority down the managerial chain. There are few concerns about comparability claims across the plants, partly because of different settlement dates, but also resulting from the differences in the nature of the workforce between sites, so Group HQ is not usually obsessed with consistency. However, several years ago, this appeared to change as all the unionised plants offered very similar basic pay increases. The individual plants were able to make this similarity less apparent by negotiating plant-wide bonuses, but this did not prevent some of the unions, and notably the convenor at Ichem, from questioning whether they were still dealing with the appropriate negotiating team. Following the conclusion of the negotiations, at the next Group personnel meeting, the plant personnel directors made it known that they were annoyed about this policy, and suggested that it should not be repeated. Our contacts at Group level and various of the plants have confirmed that the centre acknowledged that there would not be a repetition of this policy, and the following year there was a reversion to local bargaining. Although the examples are different, the links between the division and the plants in Typeng were broadly similar. What these examples indicate is that the process for determining and monitoring plant pay settlements is highly complex, a product of circumstances played out within specific companies. This is not to deny that the centre does expect to be informed of, and even to try to alter, the proposed pay offers to be made at plant level, but that researchers should be more alert to the political processes operating within multi-divisional organisations. Moreover, to conceive of the links between the personnel function at the centre/division and the plants solely in hierarchical terms, is to misinterpret the nature of this relationship.

9.5 EMPLOYEE INVOLVEMENT AND WORKPLACE TRADE UNIONISM

In Chapter 2, we considered the argument that employee involvement (EI) techniques could be used by management to undermine the activities and position of trade unions within the workplace. According to this view, one method for doing this is to upgrade JCCs and feed these bodies with high level information so as to reduce collective bargaining to 'form without content'. Shop stewards, the argument continues, would be convinced by the logic of managerial presentations to the JCC, and, as a consequence, not push so hard in the negotiating arena. We expressed some reservations about this thesis, not least for its failure to locate consultation within the broader product and labour market environment of the firm. A supplementary mechanism for weakening the unions is for management to develop communications and involvement techniques direct with the workforce, rather than relying on shop stewards to do this for them. This approach, it is suggested, would 'educate' employees about business realities to the extent that they would then enforce moderation on their shop stewards. If the latter failed to express their constituents' views, they would eventually become marginal to employee relations in the workplace. Whilst some commentators see this as an accurate reflection of the 1980s, it is difficult to assess its validity, given the paucity of detailed research on the subject. Both of these views will be re-examined on the basis of the case study evidence.

Joint consultative committees were present in only two of the companies, Typeng and Multistores. In the case of the former, the JCC is one of three regular meetings between management and the six senior stewards from the various unions, the other two being the works committee and an informal (Thursday) meeting, both of which can be characterised as negotiating bodies in the sense that their brief is to resolve conflicting issues. The JCC is marginal in that it meets less often than the negotiating committees (once a month compared with weekly), and also because the results of its deliberations are not well known on the shop floor. Conversely, however, the six delegates are the sole workforce representatives on all the committees, and the Chair of the JCC is taken by the General Works Manager; the works committee is chaired by the convenor and attended by the industrial relations personnel, with only a rare appearance from the boss, whilst the Thursday meeting is highly informal. The subject matter discussed at the two sets of meetings is also quite different, with the main agenda item at the JCC being the General Works Manager's business report, in which he provides a range of financial and production information. In contrast, the other meetings are used for resolving issues of a more immediate and overtly frictional nature, and regularly erupt into more vociferous interactions. Perhaps the most fundamental difference is in the 'ownership' of the meetings, with both parties viewing the JCC as belonging to management, the works committee to the stewards, and the Thursday meeting as a much valued free-for-all.

There were clear signs that management used the JCC to communicate information which bolstered its interpretation of issues relating to the plant, particularly the link between shop floor behaviour – such as levels of sickness absence or an overtime ban – and competitive prospects facing the company. But, unlike the impression of upgraded JCCs provided by Terry and others, the 'managerial logic' in the JCC at Typeng was either openly disputed by the stewards or treated with some caution. The stewards valued the JCC because it provided them with information from the General Works Manager, which they might not have been able to secure from elsewhere, but equally they were fully aware that this was designed to serve management's purposes, and they were accordingly suspicious about the timing and selectivity of these messages. JCC minutes were also posted on the shop floor, but they attracted little interest and there was no evidence that the workforce was influenced by their contents. Whilst management may have wanted the JCC to assume a central place within the network of shop floor communications, the strength of workplace trade unionism at Typeng ensured that this did not happen. Furthermore, the delegates' monopoly of all the representative machinery at the plant meant that trade unionism and collective bargaining could not be undermined by such methods, nor could they be by-passed, as there were no other formal mechanisms through which management could systematically communicate its ideas direct to the manual workforce. In addition, the manufacturing cells had made only minor inroads on to the shop floor in terms of coverage and symbolic importance. During the period of our research, management proceeded cautiously with its attempts to increase the number of channels for shop floor communication and involvement against a backcloth of union strength. In short, rather than supporting the thesis that EI could marginalise the unions, at Typeng it was the unions which had succeeded in maintaining EI as a marginal activity.

The situation at Multistores is somewhat different. Representative consultation is embodied in the stores council, its terms laid down in the national agreement between the company and the GMB. In addition, direct EI practices are to be found in team briefing and customer care committees, so there is a range of techniques by which management can communicate its ideas to the shop floor. It should also be recalled that all negotiations take place at company level, so in a sense there is no bargaining machinery for EI to undermine. However, this does not mean that the stores council automatically assumes a position of prominence within the local regulatory network. At Grimsight, it was rare for a meeting to take place, for the General Store Manager favoured a more informal approach to employee relations, and this preference had been reinforced because of the absence of a personnel manager at the store during part of 1986 and 1987. In addition, one of the key items which could be communicated by way of the council – store performance – was published weekly on a blackboard just by the entrance to the canteen. Nevertheless, the GSM and the senior steward at the store did meet informally on a regular basis to sort out local issues, so this did not appear like an attempt to freeze the union out of a role in the store, even though that might be the end-result of his actions. In short, the stores council at Grimsight is broadly similar to the model of marginal JCCs described in Chapter 2, and it operates in a labour market context which clearly enables this role to be upheld. Not only is the JCC marginal to activities at the workplace, but so, too, is the negotiating machinery.

At the company's Smalltown store, the council did meet monthly. It was generally, though not always, chaired by the GSM, and it did publish minutes which were posted on the shop floor. According to the constitution, we should have expected the stewards to form a majority on the stores council, whereas they were a distinct minority; this was because it had never been possible to find enough stewards for the store. Of course, all the council members were in the union, but that was not their basis for attendance; in fact, one of the leading lights on the stores council was largely unsympathetic to the GMB, regarding herself solely as a spokesperson for her constituents. The stewards had only equal status with all the other representatives on the council, and they certainly did not offer a focus for establishing a cohesive and unified shop floor response, should one be needed. The council operated partly as a forum for the GSM to communicate his ideas to the representatives, and partly as an avenue through which to resolve grievances by taking them straight to the boss. In its former capacity, the council provided the GSM with a platform to cajole, criticise, exhort or congratulate the representatives, and via them their workmates, about the performance of the store over the preceding and forthcoming periods. He had some influence over this group of people, and they, unlike the stewards at Typeng, lacked the expertise and the collective organisation to oppose him had they so desired. In the latter part of the meeting, all the representatives were given the opportunity to raise issues that were causing them or their constituents concern, which they did with gusto. Their success in managing to resolve these grievances obviously improved their own and the council's standing in the eyes of the shop floor, and contributed to an even more marginal role for the formal union organisation within the company; certainly, most members displayed little interest in and commitment to the union. In other words, activities at the stores council, whilst not explicitly intended to marginalise the union, did manage to ensure that it exercised little influence within the workplace. However, it would be incorrect to view this as part of a grand managerial strategy to undermine trade unionism in the company, largely because there was nothing much to undermine, in any event. Moreover, to ascribe such conscious and intended motives to the behaviour of the GSM would not square with reality, in view of his support for regular meetings between the stewards and the Personnel Manager, and also the strength of his commitment to quite different issues, notably customer care. Nonetheless, it is difficult to conceive of a role for shop floor trade unionism in a context where the immediacy of a competitive market place continually serves to reinforce unitary conceptions of the firm.

Although collective bargaining is dealt with at corporate level, the union could still find a role in handling grievances within the store. We have already seen that much of this is undertaken at the stores council, as often by council representatives as by shop stewards. In addition, many of the items discussed at the customer care committees could also have entered the grievance procedure. Typical issues might be improvements to the equipment used at work, and environmental features such as heating and lighting. However, since customers shared many of the same conditions as employees, or were inconvenienced by inappropriate equipment, this made such issues a prime and legitimate concern of the customer care committees. Furthermore, the system of team briefing, ostensibly designed for the downward dissemination of information by management, had evolved into a two-way communication channel, one aspect of which was the resolution of grievances by immediate superiors. Indeed, a number of the employees we interviewed specifically pointed to this as a major achievement of briefing, as it provided them with the opportunity to get issues aired and if possible resolved. Managers also confirmed this as a useful, if unforeseen, development which they valued because it enabled them to tap into employee concerns in a way that would not have been possible during normal working time. The evidence from Multistores seems to confirm that managerial initiatives to promote EI are associated with a minimal role for the union in the workplace. To impute any causal connection between these factors, however, is not particularly credible in the case of Multistores for at least two reasons. First, the unions did not occupy a central place within workplace employee relations prior to EI, and secondly, EI had been introduced to foster the ethic of customer service, rather than to undermine the activities of trade unions. As we have suggested above, if workplace trade unionism does not seriously restrict management's room for manoeuvre, there is little need to find ways of minimising the union's role even further.

The complexity of this issue is more readily apparent from our studies at Foodpack and Ichem. Neither of these sites had formal consultative arrangements at the current time, nor had they in the past, but management at both plants had initiated direct EI techniques during the 1980s. In the case of Foodpack, an attempt had been made to introduce briefing in the early part of the decade, only for this to fail because of problems in maintaining the system during the hectic production period up to Christmas. On his arrival, the new Personnel Manager set about its revival, planning carefully for the formal launch in early 1987. As we saw, there were many motives for its introduction, but none was explicitly directed at undermining the unions within the workplace; more an attempt to re-establish motivation and commitment amongst staff, which he felt was missing. He was not unaware of the fact that this might have an effect upon the position of the unions, but that, in his view, would be a consequence of briefing, since employees could now understand managerial interpretations of events rather than those of the stewards alone. The new Production Manager subscribed to a similar view, although he was rather more inclined to see this as a favourable development within the plant; indeed, when combined with other initiatives, such as the weekly newsletter, and his regular communications meetings with stewards, in our view there was little doubt that the union representatives had been marginalised within Foodpack. This increase in formal communications, either in spoken or written form, had been well received by the manual workforce, who now felt management was willing to keep them in the picture about local events, such as visits of major customers to the factory or progress with the commissioning of a new production line. The shift towards a unitarist package at Foodpack is most concisely summed up in the words of the Personnel Manager himself: 'It's pushing negotiations down to consultation, and consultation to communication. You need only do the last two if you get it right because ultimately there's only one best way of running the business.' Surprisingly perhaps, the stewards themselves seemed unaware of this possibility, and for the most part warmly welcomed the plethora of new communications techniques, even though these could potentially minimise their role. Despite the fact that the institutions of unionism remained intact at Foodpack, just as they do at many other plants, we were convinced that the stewards were participating in their own emasculation. An attitude survey conducted for the company by a sponsored student confirmed this view; she found that supervisors were now considered more central to communications at the plant than the stewards, an exact reverse of the result from a similar exercise carried out two years before.

There are some similarities in the events at Ichem, though there are also a number of quite distinct differences in philosophy and techniques. In this case, the sole formal vehicle for EI is the Quarterly Review, a regular three-monthly structured communications exercise in which all employees are briefed by senior managers. The stewards collectively attended the second brief, following that for the senior managers, when they have an opportunity to hear the Managing Director outline his interpretation of company performance, and question him before the cascade of information down the hierarchy. All briefings are undertaken by senior managers, rather than first line supervisors, and often these managers are drawn from outside the department concerned; in all cases, however, a steward is present at the presentation. Both of these are indications that management wishes to ensure that stewards remain involved in the communication of information down the chain, and are available to check the validity of interpretations provided to their members in the subsequent presentations. On the other hand, although they are able to question the Managing Director, it is clear that this is not a negotiating forum. As in the case of upgraded JCCs, the stewards are merely the recipients of information of site-wide relevance, albeit of a highly confidential nature. In addition, the formal monitoring service which takes place following the Review, and which results in the Managing Director's receiving a list of questions raised, also has the potential of replicating the grievance procedure and possibly undermining the position of the stewards here as well. The stewards themselves were fully aware of the political nature of the Review and the information they received, although they also made use of it in a similar way, to provide ammunition for wage negotiations. The manual workers we interviewed were all satisfied with the principle of the Quarterly Review, and even had suggestions for minor improvements, thus demonstrating their interest in the future of the company. Overall, the fact that these managerially-initiated mechanisms for communicating with the shop floor have tended to assume predominance over those issued by the stewards, the union will progressively lose its place within the network of plant interactions, irrespective of any stability in formal institutional support for the principle of unionism and the stewards. Considering also that the convenor is becoming a more marginal figure within the plant, EI is certainly helping to de-emphasise the trade union at Ichem, even though this does not appear to be the express intention of personnel management at the company.

9.6 EMPLOYEE INVOLVEMENT ON THE SHOP FLOOR

One of the problems with research based on questionnaires sent to senior managers is that it is better at identifying intentions and aspirations than establishing the precise nature of employee relations in practice. Considerable differences may exist between intention and reality, and this is especially problematic in the field of employee involvement when one recognises that this is a focus for contemporary managerial and governmental rhetoric. Many of the current EI initiatives are aimed at increasing employee commitment to the goals of the enterprise and improving their understanding of business affairs. The means chosen to achieve this is often new communications initiatives, and it seems that a key test of effectiveness must be their impact on the shop floor. Arguably, the more that companies can encourage employees to identify with the aims of the enterprise in securing competitive advantage, the more difficult it will be for unions to influence events in the workplace even if they maintain their institutional presence. At the same time, however, if management fails to make the communications system work, either in the short or the long term, its own credibility will be damaged on the shop floor. Each of the case study companies has made some attempt to introduce new EI techniques over the course of the last few years.

As we have already seen, the impact of EI at Typeng has been minimal, restricted so far to the introduction of manufacturing cells in certain parts of the factory, and then not with the total support of the workforce in those areas. Nearly all the manual workers we interviewed were critical of management's ability to communicate with them, and a number suggested that the local paper was a better source of information about the company's prospects than were any internal mechanisms. The adversarial traditions from the past, plus recent instabilities in the product market, combined to limit the willingness and ability of management to disseminate information to the shop floor workers. Moreover, the supervisors we interviewed were sceptical of new techniques for communicating with their subordinates and doubtful about their impact, unless information related to the workers' wage packets.

There was some form of briefing system in operation at each of the other companies, and Multistores also had a customer care programme in place. We have already illustrated the manner in which the Quarterly Review system at Ichem deviated from the Industrial Society model, and indeed there was never any intention to follow this blueprint at the plant. At Multistores, the system was implemented by an ex-Industrial Society employee, in line with its broad principles, but this had not prevented team briefing from adapting its form at store level. The principal problem faced by managers operating the system was how to comply with predetermined dates for delivering their message to the shop floor, especially if this conflicted with more pressing priorities. Managers also reported that on occasion they had been forced to postpone briefs at short notice, and even terminate them mid-stream, if there was an urgent customer query or service-related problem. It is hardly surprising that such matters should take priority in the retail industry, considering the closeness of the customer, but equally it also makes employees acutely aware of their subservience to market pressures. Although the management at Smalltown had alleviated this particular problem by moving the briefs for some employees to the end of the working shift, this meant that certain workers were disenfranchised owing to other commitments. Even if the briefing system has the potential to marginalise workplace trade unionism, this is unlikely to be achieved if the briefings lack regularity and continuity, or if staff rarely attend.

Supervisors at Foodpack also complained that it was not always possible to maintain regular briefings because of the continuous nature of the production system; in some cases, the brief had to be 'squeezed in' when there was a breakdown or changeover to a new production run, demonstrating the perceived worth of the system in their eyes and in those of senior plant managers who, not surprisingly, stress production over communication if there is a clash. The distinction between espoused and operational policy, referred to in Chapter 3, is clearly relevant here, and at Multi-stores. At Foodpack, the system faced a further problem arising from the marked seasonality in demand for the product, and corporate decisions to keep stock to a minimum, which meant that for part of the year managers and supervisors found it very difficult to sustain the briefs. Suspending a production run in order to brief would have appeared quite incongruous in the circumstances, especially since some employees worked seven days a week and the factory also operated an extra shift during the busier parts of the year. Indeed, the previous attempt to introduce team briefing had failed at precisely this time of the year. In some respects, management is faced with a potentially irresolvable problem in cases such as this; if briefings are suspended, employees may question the strength of managerial commitment to the system itself, whereas if briefs continue (and production is stopped temporarily) management's ability to judge priorities could become a focus for shop floor criticism. To some extent, management at Foodpack side-stepped this dilemma, as its commitment to providing information was maintained by the weekly newsletter which contained similar material to the briefs, although most of it was of a plant-based nature. In short, management was enabled to maintain its new-found centrality to the communications system.

Improvements in the flow of information from management did appear to have had some effect on shop floor employees at Foodpack, who talked in terms of a reduction in the 'us and them' at the plant, as well as an increased willingness among managers to listen and act upon their suggestions. They certainly displayed a greater awareness of the demands which customers placed upon the company and of the position of their own plant within the conglomerate as a whole. In particular, the information contained in the weekly newsletter had increased their knowledge of activity at the plant, so that they knew more about production schedules, new equipment and visitors. All these, it was suggested, gave them a greater appreciation of what was going on. Information about visitors was seen as especially crucial, since the company had just won an order from a major high street retailer which meant that non-Foodpack personnel had moved in to inspect the workplace for hygiene; the effect of this on employee behaviour was quite significant. However, the influence of management communications on employee attitudes can easily be overstressed, as the comments in the case study chapter (Chapter 6) illustrate. As one of the engineers succinctly stated, he had not been persuaded to buy shares in the company yet.

The shop floor employees at both Multistores and Ichem were generally favourably disposed towards the communications systems at their workplaces, though for quite different reasons. In the case of the stores, all the employees with whom we spoke valued the amount of information which they received from management, though they did not always consider it to be highly relevant. Clearly, one of the problems with a briefing system in a large multi-establishment firm is that some items of a company-wide nature are of little interest to many employees, especially those who have no great commitment to the enterprise in the first place. Given also that labour turnover rates are so high, it is difficult for the company to develop long-term commitment amongst certain groups of employees. However, this also means that employees are in a better position to compare arrangements at Multistores with those at other places where they have worked; in relation to most organisations in the retail sector, Multistores was seen as a good employer. Even though there were faults with the briefing system, the amount of information which these individuals received was rather more than they would expect, considering their previous employment history and their future prospects should they go elsewhere. The reason why manual workers at Ichem are so keen to receive information through the Quarterly Review is almost the exact converse of this. These employees have built up long periods of service with the company, and in many cases expect to remain at the site for the rest of their working lives. Their commitment to the company rests to some extent upon their instrumental desire to see it prosper into the future, largely because their own careers are more likely to be intertwined with the success of Ichem. It is for this reason that detailed – and possibly confidential – information can be provided in the Quarterly Review, without much fear that it will be leaked or found irrelevant.

9.7 CONCLUSION

On the basis of these case studies, we find little explicit support for the arguments outlined in the early chapters of the book. In particular, the theses of managerial sponsorship, roll-back, institutional separation, and upgraded joint consultation are all found to over-simplify operational reality. In addition, they all tend to elevate labour relations concerns to a prominence in strategic decision-making which does not appear to accord with contemporary practice. However, with the exception of Typeng, the evidence from these cases also suggests that union representatives are now increasingly marginal to workplace employee relations, although it must be stressed that this is a consequence of other managerial actions rather than part of a concerted attempt to undermine the unions *per se*. To understand this better, we now need to reanalyse the data on management style and product market competition; this is the subject of the final chapter.

10 · EMPLOYEE RELATIONS IN A COMPETITIVE ENVIRONMENT

10.1 INTRODUCTION

The evidence from our case studies suggested that the trade unions, despite maintaining a presence in the workplace, are becoming more marginal to the management of employee relations in the 1980s. This did not appear to be part of a conscious and well-develolped strategy by employers directly to undermine the unions, but was more likely to be a consequence of other managerial initiatives within companies, principally those relating to the development of employee involvment, itself directed at the achievement of broader corporate goals such as customer service.

In this chapter, we intend to pull together the threads of the study, and focus more explicitly on the way in which the companies differed in their approach to the management of employee relations. In addition, our goal is to provide a more adequate categorisation of product markets, since these appeared to exert a considerable influence on management style. Finally, we shall outline a model which aims to theorise the links between product markets, management style and trade unions in a more explicit manner. We shall proceed as before by addressing a number of key questions:

- What is the meaning of management style, and how did this differ between the case study companies?
- How can product markets be categorised so as to allow for generalisations about the power or pressure of the market to be made?

- How can we theorise the links between product markets and management style?

10.2 MANAGEMENT STYLE

In Chapter 4, we reviewed several attempts to differentiate between management approaches to employee relations, two of which seemed particularly appropriate for further refinement. Within the industrial relations literature, Purcell and his colleagues have proposed a number of categorisations, the most recent being along the independent dimensions of individualism and collectivism; organisations may choose to focus on one or both aspects of this, although it is also possible, according to Purcell, that companies will not have a distinctive management style at all. Within the labour process school, the contribution of Friedman remains highly relevant, largely because the simplicity of his distinction between responsible autonomy and direct control reflects the basic dichotomy facing all employers, i.e. whether to allow employees to take responsibility for their own work to the extent that they effectively control themselves, or conversely to maintain close supervision over their activities with little room for employee discretion. As Friedman himself suggests, both these approaches ultimately may be impossible to achieve. Although we could see problems with both these models, we did feel they offered scope for further testing and refinement, especially since this does not appear to have been done before in the context of 1980s workplace employee relations.

Of the four companies in our study, Ichem had made the most explicit attempt to articulate a coherent management style. This was based to a large extent on the corporate principles published by the company in a booklet circulated to all employees. The influence of the European HQ was clearly imprinted on this booklet, which merely reiterated the principles enunciated by the parent, Multichem, back in the early 1970s. Furthermore, this document appeared to have a considerable influence over management at the plant, and had provided a focus for recent reviews of activity at Ichem. Perhaps more crucial is the fact that the shop floor workers we interviewed could recognise a coherent and consistent management style at the plant. In short, Ichem would certainly conform to the meaning of style advanced by Purcell, and might go further in that company philosophy also appears to be translated into supervisory behaviour at the point of production. The only other company to articulate its philosophy in written form was Foodpack, although this was a divisional, rather than a plant, initiative and the company had not gone so far as to distribute copies of this document to all employees; indeed, the only people at the plant to make explicit reference to this were members of senior management, perhaps indicating its more limited impact at the Foodpack plant compared with Ichem. The attempt to develop a corporate approach to employee relations is of much more recent origin at Foodpack, and it was clear to us that it had not yet filtered down to the shop floor in such a coherent manner as at Ichem. Nevertheless, it would be incorrect to argue that Foodpack lacked a coherent management style, merely that it was in the process of attaining prominence.

Neither Multistores nor Typeng had a published corporate philosophy or a written pronouncement on management style. In the case of the latter, the corporate headquarters was publicly committed to decentralisation in the field of employee relations, so any declaration on 'preferred' management style would have contradicted this standpoint, and possibly encountered resistance from managers at plant level. However, despite the lack of any central direction in relation to this, it does not seem accurate to conclude that management at the plant did not have a characteristic style of its own; indeed, during our time at the company, it became very apparent to us that a distinct and continuous management style could be identified at Typeng just as easily as at Ichem, and indeed rather more so than at Foodpack; given the traditions of the site, it could hardly be otherwise. Consequently it does not appear plausible to argue that the use of the term 'style' is only appropriate in circumstances where a set of corporate guiding principles can be identified, which subsequently influence action at individual plants within a large enterprise. It seems to us that to define style in such a restrictive way effectively renders it inapplicable to diversified conglomerates, and that this reduces the analytical value of the term yet further.

The case of Multistores offers another perspective on this debate, particularly in view of the highly centralised system for handling industrial relations in the company. Although there is no corporate philosophy for employee relations, or a published document on preferred management style, our interviews with personnel practitioners at regional and national level indicated that there had been a distinct shift in approach since the mid-1980s. This revolved around an attempt to reorientate the way management conceived of the labour force, encouraging a resource-centred rather than a cost-based perspective on employees. But the adjustment to management style had its roots in the customer care programme developed by the company, and it was only by implication that employee relations philosophies and practices were seen to require adaptation. In other words, the change in style which is permeating from the top of Multistores is a clear consequence of other aspects of business policy, and as such conforms well with Purcell's definition of style. However, there are also limits to the ubiquity of this style, even in such a highly centralised company, since in our research we found clear differences between the way in which the stores were managed. At Grimsight, the preferred style tended to be more informal than at Smalltown, largely because of the influence of the GSM over relations at the stores. In addition, geographical location can also have a significant influence over the styles adopted in the different stores, not least because of the variation in customer profile and physical surroundings of the site. To expect no variation between different establishments is probably to stretch the meaning of style too far, and discount the element of choice which undoubtedly exists at all levels within large organisations. Equally, however, this is not to argue that a coherent management style cannot be defined just because there are deviations from the model, but to suggest that notions of style cannot be read off from interviews with senior management. Style, if it is to mean anything, needs to be identified in distinctive practices on the shop and office floor, since these are presumably the points at which it is directed, and where senior management anticipates changes in performance. This is particularly pertinent at Multistores in view of the extent of direct contact between subordinate employees and customers. We believe, therefore, that management style is a concept which can have meaning in all workplaces, irrespective of policy pronouncements, and further that it needs to be examined in relation to its impact on the practices and behaviour of managers within indi-

vidual establishments, rather than on the basis of senior management intentions and announcements alone.

Having analysed the *meaning* of style, we can now turn to an
evaluation of its dimensions. As indicated in Chapter 4, Purcell's
individualism axis spans the range from labour control (commod-
ity-status) to employee development (resource-status), with paternalism in the middle. Ichem displays a number of features which
would place it at the development end of this axis, given the
company's corporate principles (which generally stress the notion
of employees as a key resource to be developed), in addition to its
commitment to training for all employees (an average of seven
days per year per employee), its policies on harmonisation (removal of clocking, sick pay for all employees), and its attempts to
develop teamwork and some operator control over the production
process. In addition, the Security of Employment Agreement also
demonstrates the willingness, and the ability, of the company to
offer assurances to the core manual workers remaining on site
after the dramatic reduction in numbers employed during the early
part of the 1980s. Typeng, as in so many other aspects, is at the
opposite end of the individualism dimension; management feels
unable to give any guarantees about job security because of the
continuing uncertainty of the product market, clocking is maintained, there is little in the way of harmonised conditions, separate canteens, for example, and recent technological developments have tended to reinforce the separation of conception from
execution in the performance of shop floor tasks. According to the
plant Personnel Manager, Typeng is attempting to move away
from this approach towards a resource-based perspective, but this
had made little impact by the end of our research. Both Multistores and Foodpack were part-way along the individualism dimension, each having clearly identifiable elements of labour control
and employee development; at Multistores, for example, management was attempting to encourage increased commitment to the
company through customer care and team briefing, yet at the same
time labour turnover levels were approximately fifty per cent per
annum and the company maintained strict controls on dress and
behaviour at work. In addition, the form of words used on the
posters in the training room made explicit the link between
customer satisfaction and security of employment, features which

emphasised the labour control elements of management style. Foodpack was also in the process of strengthening the employee development aspects of its style.

Although we found it relatively easy to locate these companies on the individualism dimension, we had more difficulty in attaching the specified labels to the particular approaches adopted in each case. This was most apparent for the companies in the middle of the range, to which the label of paternalism is supposed to apply. There were certainly elements of a welfare paternalist perspective at Multistores and Foodpack, specifically in the way in which information was communicated down the hierarchy, and in the provision of cheap and healthy meals on site for employees, for example, but this did not seem to be the dominant theme which underlay management behaviour; indeed, given the emphasis in paternalism on 'looking after' employees, and on the development of close relations and shared experiences, it would prove difficult to sustain such an approach in Multistores because of the high levels of labour turnover amongst managers and staff. The inadequacy of the paternalist label is even more apparent if we attempt to apply this to companies which are in the process of change. As we mentioned above, Typeng did exhibit some signs of the development/resource pole of the individualism dimension. Let us suppose that this trend continues and Typeng moves further in that direction, but not as far as Ichem. Considering the adversarial character of employee relations at the company, it would hardly seem plausible to describe Typeng as paternalist in character, though it would clearly be incorrect to assign it to either of the alternative categories. Perhaps paternalism is better seen as a possible *example* at the mid-range of the individualism dimension, rather than constituting the mid-point itself.

More seriously, we had doubts about the whether the end points of the axis were mutually exclusive, so that a management which aims to develop its employees therefore fails to consider them as costs or seeks to control them as well. Surely, all employers are concerned about controlling labour costs or enhancing efficiency on the shop floor, but at the same time some also aim to treat employees as resources to be developed, whereas others do not. In short, it may be more appropriate to view this dimension in terms of the degree to which managements adopt an 'investment-orientation' towards labour, consequently accepting that all will seek to control labour costs. Furthermore, this also casts doubt upon the accuracy of the term 'individualism', since this suggests a discrete aspect of style which does not seem to have meaning for managers themselves. They are more likely to view this as indicative of a general approach to the management of labour, rather than as an attempt to develop individualism *per se*. This also appears to be more in tune with the kind of language used by employers themselves. From our studies, we did not detect that managers conceived of activity designed to develop employees or treat them as commodities to be indicative of an individualist strategy on their part, nor could this be simply differentiated from any collectivist strategies. Consequently, we shall relabel this dimension as 'management's approach to employees', with high and low investment-orientation as the poles.

We encountered even more difficulty in applying the collectivism dimension to our cases, largely because of the way in which it had been conceptualised in its original form. It will be recalled that two separate aspects were seen to constitute this: first, the existence of structures for employee participation, with the term being used in its broadest sense to encompass collective bargaining; and, second, management's approach to operating these structures. Consequently, the employer who espoused a commitment to trade unionism, fully accepting it as a legitimate channel for employees, would be further along this dimension than would the employer who tolerated unions via a constitutional relationship. The unitary employer, who neither accepted trade unions nor other avenues for employee participation, would be seen as demonstrating least commitment to collectivism.

One of the problems with this is its failure to consider the reasons why employers should want to deal with trade unions in the first place, or whether they would prefer, if the circumstances permit, to operate without unions. We have already seen that trade unions can contribute to the maintenance of order in the workplace, and management may facilitate this by developing a cooperative relationship with the unions. Employers recognise trade unions, either because worker pressure leaves them with no other realistic option at the time, or because they see little alternative to unions in the future. To regard this as a commitment to collectivism seems to miss the point, because all that employers are doing is to find a mechanism for maintaining and securing order in the workplace. In much the same way, to adjudge the continuation of relations with trade unions as evidence of managerial commitment to collectivism also seems wide of the mark. Employers may choose not to derecognise unions either because current arrangements deliver a high degree of order and do little to inhibit their room for manoeuvre, or because they are fearful of the consequences should they attempt to initiate change.

In all four of our cases, union membership remained at a high level and the personnel managers espoused their continuing commitment to the principle of trade unionism at the establishment. In our initial interviews at each site, as well as those with more senior managers beyond the level of the establishment, the companies' commitment to trade unions was continually reiterated. It was only later in our study that we became more aware of the marginality of union representatives, and began to question the depth of managerial support for the position of the unions. Management in all the cases could quite legitimately argue that the company remained committed to trade unionism on the site; after all, no convenors had been sacked, stewards retained direct access to management, new starters were encouraged or required to join the appropriate unions, more information was provided to workplace representatives than had previously been the case, and so on. But at the same time, union representatives were marginal to workplace employee relations, either because they no longer represented the dominant channel of communication with the workforce following the growth of direct EI, or because management was less willing to deal with individual union representatives on personality grounds.

In trying to place each of these plants on the collectivist dimension, it was difficult to determine whether they should appear as cooperative or unitary, as there were elements of both in all cases; apart from the case of Typeng, they could not be categorised as adversarial collectivism. Typeng was the only plant where union representatives had managed to maintain a monopoly over meetings with management and the central role in communications with the workforce; but even here, management was attempting to develop a system for briefing workers which, should it be successful, could lead to competing messages within the works. Perhaps a further clue to the lack of union centrality to employee relations can be found from the two companies (Ichem and Foodpack) which operated according to a set of corporate principles; in neither case were unions explicitly mentioned in the sections on employee relations. This is not particularly unusual and is in line with the analysis of the policy/philosophy statements by Purcell, in which 'support for trade unions' formed by far the least mentioned key words (approximately two per cent to four per cent of all items). What it does seem to indicate, however, is the limited value of the collectivist dimension of management style as it is currently conceived.

We propose therefore that the collectivist dimension should also be refined, partly as a result of our doubts about the appropriateness of the dimension itself, but also because it has proved so difficult to apply in this study. In its place, a more relevant dimension would appear to be management attitudes and behaviour towards the trade unions in the workplace, and the degree to which a 'partnership orientation' is pursued. Obviously, all employers will regard trade unions to some extent as opponents in the workplace, especially when they dispute management's plans or put forward counter proposals. In some workplaces, management's behaviour towards unions is even more antagonistic, particularly when unions are not recognised, derecognised or kept at arm's length. As with the other dimension, however, differentiation is possible in relation to the absence or presence of support and consideration for the activities of the other party, in this case the unions. The question of whether or not to recognise a union is consequently rather less important than management's behaviour towards the union if one is recognised.

We have applied this refined version of management style to our cases, and the graphical representation of this can be seen in Figure 10.1. Two sets of cautionary comments must preface this, however. First, all our companies recognised trade unions, and although we detected some attempts to reduce the role of workplace representatives in each case, it is certain that there are many more aggressive approaches in other places of work. For example, our studies did not include analyses of assertively non-union companies, nor those much publicised examples of macho management, so there is a likelihood that we have exaggerated the distinctions between the companies on the 'trade union' dimension. Similarly, even though we have categorised some of our companies as having a low 'investment-orientation', this will also

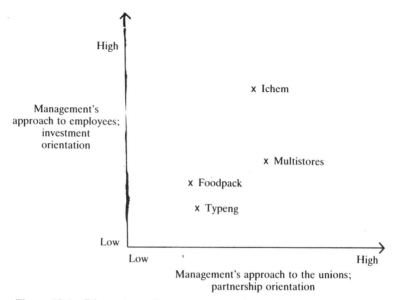

Figure 10.1   Dimensions of management style

over-exaggerate their position compared with a representative sample of all UK employers; undoubtedly, many small business or 'sweat shop' employers would regard management's approach towards employees at Typeng (the company we felt tended to treat employees least as investments) as exceptionally light-handed. Secondly, we need to reiterate that the position of a company on either axis is meant to indicate the dominant element, rather than the only component, in its style. Just because we suggest a company tends to treat the unions as partners, this is not to imply that they are never seen as opponents, merely that the dominant approach tends towards partnership. Similarly, because management tends to treat employees as 'investments', this is not to say that it pays no attention to labour costs, or that no attempt is made to ensure that labour is employed cost-effectively.

These cases have already been discussed at some length in this chapter, so we intend only to make a brief mention of their respective positions on Figure 10.1 at this stage. Ichem clearly demonstrated the greatest commitment to employee development, although it should also be recalled that this policy has been more consistently applied following the turnaround programme in the early 1980s. Conversely, Typeng management was the least likely to treat employees as resources to be developed, and was the most explicitly Taylorist in its approach to labour relations in general. Both Foodpack and Multistores were attempting to move further in the direction of an 'investment' approach towards employees, the food company because of divisional influences on management style, the superstore because of its growing commitment to customer service and higher quality employees. Even at Typeng, there was some evidence of managerial initiatives to shift towards the investment end of the dimension, although this was also offset by contradictory forces to increase technical control over the production process. There were fewer differences between the companies on their approach to trade unionism, although we felt that Multistores management was the most likely to view the unions as partners, particularly at company level. At store level, their willingness to work with the union representatives may also owe something to the relative lack of challenge which management could expect from employees collectively. Management at Foodpack was the most explicit in its attempts to marginalise workplace union representatives, but this should not be overstressed, since the stewards remained party to regular disclosure of information from the Production Manager. Typeng and Ichem were in between these two; we classed the engineering plant as less partnership-oriented than the chemicals factory, only because of the formal and adversarial nature of relations at the site. In the case of Ichem, it should be recalled that the principal opposition management mounted against the unions was, in fact, directed at the convenor, himself a somewhat isolated figure within the plant shop steward network, as well as with convenors in the other unionised establishments within the company. Having examined the way in which styles may vary between establishments, we can now turn to an assessment of why they may differ, especially in relation to the product market context.

10.3 PRODUCT MARKETS

We have already seen from Chapter 4 that there is no shortage of research findings which relate product market conditions to the management of employee relations. Some of this is rather superficial, merely being used to set the context for an examination of particular cases, but much of it is rich in detail. What it all lacks, however, is a precision that allows for a comparison of product market circumstances between different companies or industries. Our principal purpose in this section therefore, is to provide a framework for that task, and to categorise product markets according to their 'power' over the employer. Or, to put it another way, to analyse how far the product markets in which companies compete allow senior managers room for manoeuvre in their choice of how to handle employee relations. Drawing upon the literature discussed in Chapter 4, and the data collected in the four case study companies, we have condensed the range of different aspects of the product market into just two separate components – competitive pressure (or degree of monopoly) and customer pressure (or degree of monopsony) – both of which contribute to the overall power of the market.

Competitive pressure; degree of monopoly power

This measures the degree to which the company is able to dictate terms to the customer where a lack of suitable alternative suppliers exists, or, conversely, the extent to which the company feels constrained to follow the general trend within the market as a whole. Added to this is the ease with which other firms may enter the market, that is, whether or not there are barriers to entry in terms of factors such as high initial capital investment costs or markets protected by patent or other restriction. Competitive pressures are likely to be least in the case where demand is growing, because the company's share of the market is likely to be on the increase, and other companies find it difficult to establish a presence in the market. In such circumstances, management should generally have considerable room for manoeuvre, both in terms of influencing the direction of the market and in choosing appropriate responses to market pressures. Conversely, if demand for the specific company's product is in decline, and this is exacerbated by the entry of new competitors, senior management is likely to feel under increasing pressure from the market. Within such a context, the 'power' of the market may be seen by management to decrease its opportunity for choice and make it appear that the market determines management action; in this case, management may see its primary task as engineering the 'best fit' with external contingencies. However, to generalise from this and take the view that the product market constitutes an exogenous variable which determines management action in all cases, would be a gross misrepresentation of the way in which markets and management style are interrelated.

Of the four cases, Ichem is the company which faces the lowest degree of competitive pressure, largely because its share of a growing market has been maintained, and in some segments this has grown as well. There are two major products manufactured on site; one of these accounts for approximately eighty per cent of the company's sales, and the market for this product has recently been growing as a result of its increasing value as a safety device; the other range of products, a new initiative for the plant, is in a highly buoyant position in the overseas market, and production at Ichem has been expanding rapidly over the decade. Both markets are oligopolistic, with Ichem being one of a small number of major producers, and there is considerable liaison between the competitors, who all value market stability. As we saw in the case study, the decision by one of its major customers to place a complete annual order (rather than a part of it) with Ichem caused some concern amongst senior managers, fearful of what might happen with the next order. In addition, there are considerable financial obstacles that prevent other companies from entering the market, since the cost of capital investment in a new product (research and development, and building new plant) is massive. In general, although Ichem managers report a more competitive environment, the pressure from the market is not high when compared with many other industries.

The position at Foodpack is rather more complex; although the principal product market is mature, the company's brand is a household name, to a large extent synonymous with the product itself; indeed, within the branded market, this product accounts for over fifty per cent of all sales in any one year. There are a small number of other large producers, but Foodpack certainly leads, rather than follows, the market in this field. In addition, the company now manufactures other flavours of the principal product, and this has also had an effect upon the market, as too, does a more recent decision to manufacture a new product range on site. Although the financial barriers to entry in this market do not compare with those in the chemical industry, it is not easy to start production in this part of the food market, partly because of the high cost of plant and machinery which is now used within the industry, but also because of the increasingly stringent hygiene standards which now govern manufacturers.

There are some similarities between the situation at Typeng and those just described; there are few companies which compete in this part of the heavy engineering market, which is now predominantly worldwide in character, and Typeng is one of the leaders, along with a number of American and Far Fastern enterprises. The cost of setting up new plant and equipment also makes this a difficult market for new companies to enter, added to which is the reputation that companies manage to develop over a considerable period of time; both of these place Typeng in a strong position in relation to other competitors, and the company prospered in a secure market slot for much of this century. However, since the mid-1970s, there has been considerable overcapacity in the world market and, although the company has broadly maintained its market share, this has meant a significant decline in demand over the last decade. Since all the other major firms in the market are in the same position, this has resulted in a considerable increase in competitive pressures, and has even driven Typeng to tender for small engineering jobs in order to keep its craft workers occupied. In short, competitive pressures seem greater to managers at Typeng than they did in the previous cases.

Multistores is confronted by a similar level of competitive pressure, but for quite different reasons; demand in the retail market as a whole has been increasing for the last decade, and with it so has that for Multistores' goods and services. The company has expanded its outlets at the rate of at least ten per year, and at the same time older stores have been revamped in order to improve the image of Multistores. However, the company is not one of the market leaders, although senior management is keen for the company to be rather nearer the top by the early 1990s. Compared with the other companies in our study, entry into the retail market is relatively easy, although it is rather more difficult to move into the superstore league, given the high costs of building and operating new stores and the inability of small companies to match the buying power of the large retail chains. In the short term, the high level of competition between the large operators is

offset by the increase in overall market size, which means that
there are sufficient customers for all the major retailers. However,
it is predicted that the market will become saturated before the
end of the century, thus emphasising the importance of the dash
for new outlets at the current time, and the potential insecurity of
the longer-term future.

Customer pressure; degree of monopsony power

As well as experiencing pressures from competing producers,
companies also come under pressure from customers. Demand for
the company's products may fluctuate over time by year, month,
week or day, or it may be relatively stable from one period to the
next. Similarly, there are also variations in the degree to which this
is predictable in advance. Clearly, a pattern of demand which is
regular, stable and predictable provides management with rather
more room for manoeuvre than one which is subject to considerable variability in its pattern of demand. In the latter case, managers are more likely to feel the pressure of the market, be forced to
adapt continually to changing circumstances, and feel that their
actions are determined by the nature of the product market
environment. In addition, the structure of the customer profile can
also vary. A single customer who buys from a range of competing
producers is clearly able to exert more pressure on the company
than is an uncoordinated group of individual consumers who
purchase from a monopoly producer. Again, in the former instance, the market will appear to leave managers with little room
for manoeuvre, whereas in the latter it would not make sense to
conceive of this as market determinism.

Of the four cases in this book, Typeng management faced the
most serious customer pressures, as there had recently been
considerable uncertainty about future prospects. As we have
already seen, the company even took on small engineering contracts so as to keep the skilled workforce occupied, in the expectation that larger orders would eventually materialise; within the
United Kingdom, Powerco, the divisional parent company, is
heavily dependent on government orders, but political uncertainties meant that firm contracts were continually deferred. There are
few customers in this part of the heavy engineering market and
this, combined with the irregular pattern of demand for goods in

the industry, also means that suppliers are under considerable pressure to meet customer requirements. For example, of the orders that Typeng has recently won, the customer has been able to demand reduced production times, lower prices, high quality, and other concessions which have not traditionally been part of conventional practice. All these factors can obviously have a substantial effect upon attitudes and behaviour within the plant, such that management feels the market leaves it little room for manoeuvre in its approach to employees or the trade unions. Nevertheless, market prospects never became quite so bleak as in other heavy industries such as UK shipbuilding or steel in the early 1980s, and towards the end of our research new orders offered the promise of a more prosperous future.

Ichem is in a similar position to Typeng to the extent that the bulk of its output is supplied to a small number of customers, but there is also a range of differences between the two companies. Most obvious is the lack of variability in production, partly caused by less fluctuation in demand and a more predictable market environment, but also caused by the ease with which throughput can be adjusted without serious manpower implications. The amount of labour required to manufacture this range of chemicals is largely independent of production levels, since valves can be opened (or shut) to increase (or decrease) the flow of product through the plant. Moreover, once an order is gained, this can guarantee steady production levels for long runs, a situation quite different from that at Typeng where, depending upon the state of the order book, different parts of the factory can be over-stretched or under-stretched at the same time. Of course, in common with the other cases, customers are now more demanding in their requirements, but in relative terms this is a less pressurised environment than elsewhere.

At Foodpack, the pressure from customers is increasing, largely from the substantial buying power of the superstores and high street multiples. Since these companies buy similar products from a range of manufacturers, they are in a strong position to demand concessions from them, specifying high quality goods, precise delivery dates, competitive prices, and exacting hygiene standards. Producers are given less room for manoeuvre, and are less able to dictate terms to the market than was previously the case. At the same time, demand varies considerably over the course of the year, with distinct peaks and troughs at certain – albeit predictable – times; as we described in the case study chapter (Chapter 6), production levels during the run-up to Christmas can be five or six times as high as at other times in the year. However, this massive variation in production output is not solely the result of market signals, since senior management (at divisional level) has decided not to iron out production runs and stock pile finished goods because this is estimated to be a more costly alternative. Furthermore, the company has also attempted to reorientate the pattern of consumer demand by its recent moves to introduce on to the market new flavours which have less of a seasonal character, and to manufacture new products altogether. In other words, even within a market which is subject to substantial variability, management retains some room for manoeuvre in its choice of appropriate solutions. Significantly, however, Foodpack is also able to rely upon its branded market leader as a source of stability *vis-à-vis* customer pressure.

Whilst all of the other companies in our study sell to commercial, industrial or government customers, Multistores is rather different in that it supplies the domestic consumer. Clearly, each of these individuals has relatively little power as a single consumer, although the success of environmental pressure groups in achieving modifications to the range of goods available in the superstores shows that this population does not lack power completely. Demand is instant and more variable than at all the other sites, fluctuating over the course of the working day, week, month and year, but it is partially predictable in advance. For example, Multistores is aware that there will be more customers during the late afternoon than in the morning, or more towards the end of the week than at the begining, and this enables store management to plan labour requirements accordingly. As we indicated in the case study, an objective of the company is to control queue lengths, so the degree to which this is fulfilled places extra pressures on the system of employee relations: greater flexibility in working hours and practices being the obvious implication of this. But Multistores, like its principal competitors, is also attempting to extend the range of goods on sale at its stores, and to 'educate' the public into viewing the superstore as the source of most products, thus indicating once again the two-way relationship between markets and management strategy/style.

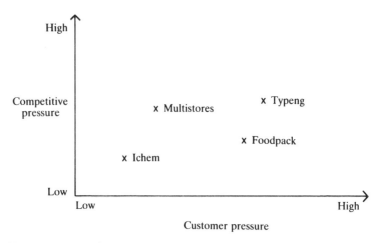

Figure 10.2 Product market pressures

Graphically, we can locate the four companies according to their position on the two dimensions of competitive pressure and customer pressure as shown in Figure 10.2.

10.4 MANAGEMENT, EMPLOYEE RELATIONS AND MARKET POWER

Up to now in this chapter, we have tested and refined previous attempts to increase our understanding of management style and product market circumstances. In this section, we shall put forward a more integrated model for conceptualising the link between these two factors. It also incorporates an analysis of employee reactions to the market, the role of trade unions, and takes account of product character. This is outlined in Figure 10.3. Whilst it must be stressed that this graphical representation of the model inevitably oversimplifies the complexity of the relationship, it does have the value of clarifying the interaction between these different factors.

The product markets within which companies compete influence the nature of employee relations in the enterprise, to some extent through the responses of management at different levels to these circumstances, but also through the direct effect of the market on employees. We noted above that the room management may have for choice in its approach to employee relations is greater when market power, but especially the pressure exerted by customers, is lower. In the converse situation, when managers feel that market power is significant, they perceive little room for manoeuvre in ways of handling employee relations and regard their actions as contingent on and flowing directly from a market which is beyond their control. But there are many instances when the relationship is not solely one way, and senior managers can possess considerable power to influence the character of the markets within which the company operates. They can, for example, choose the kind of products to be manufactured or sold, the location of facilities, the geographical markets in which to compete, as well as the precise range of goods available to the customer. However, once the decision to compete in a certain range of markets has been made, management at establishment level is more often left with the task of responding to the market, and consequently choosing appropriate styles to manage employees in order to satisfy broader corporate objectives. Of course, management can also 'blame' market forces in order to legitimise decisions which it wishes to make in any event, thus aiming to absolve itself from criticism.

Of our case study companies, we have already seen that Ichem experienced the lowest pressure from the market, both customers and competitors, whereas Typeng was confronted by the most

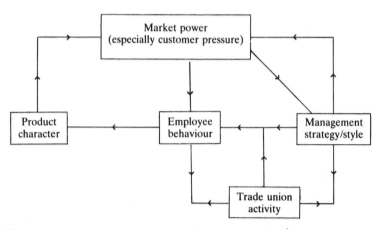

Figure 10.3. Management, employee relations and market power

difficult situation. The market was a source of much concern for management and employees at Typeng, and we believe this exerted a powerful influence on the character of employee relations at the plant. Market prospects have been highly insecure during most of the 1980s, and this led management to adopt a style which was more adversarial than at any of the other sites. Of course, we also need to recall the history of the site, especially the Taylorist traditions and the emergence of trade unionism in the engineering industry. Given this history and the uncertain market conditions, any attempt to develop an investment-orientated style for managing employee relations did not seem appropriate to the supervisors and many of the line managers in the factory, although the head of personnel could see the value of this in the longer term. Consequently, the tougher style seemed entirely justified to them in view of the unpredictability of the environment. The style at Ichem was almost totally different, but again much of this can be related to the more favourable market environment within which the plant had operated since the turnaround of the early 1980s. Such a context allows management the time and the opportunity to develop a resource-based style, and to introduce a range of policies which enhance the status and security of employees. Furthermore, management's practical commitment to a job security agreement does not need to be tested in such circumstances, provided that the market is signalling stability and growth, and labour costs contribute a relatively small amount to the total costs in the industry. In short, it has been much easier for Ichem management to develop an investment-orientated style than it has for their counterparts at Typeng. However, this is not to argue that favourable product market circumstances necessarily and automatically lead to an approach of this kind, and it is equally feasible that management could choose to operate a less resource-based style, provided it had the desire and the ability to make this work. What lower levels of market pressure seem to facilitate is more room for managerial choice in determining an appropriate style, of whatever character this may be. Conversely, it is rather more difficult for managements who feel under greater market pressure to adopt anything other than a traditional, cost-based style.

Of course, although the product market typically impacts more directly on managers, they are not the only people to be influenced by the nature of the product market, and employees are also likely to receive messages from this quarter, either directly or via management interpretations. Some of this will occur outside the workplace, through social contacts or media influences, but many of the pressures are apparent from the jobs on which employees are engaged. To take one example, the quantity of work which flows through a department can give employees some idea of the current state of the order book, as can informal conversations with colleagues or friends from other companies competing in the same product market. In some industries, such as those in the service sector, employees experience customer pressure through direct contact with consumers, whereas in others it is to a large extent mediated through management interpretations of the product market and the results of decision-making at higher levels of the organisation. In the former situation, especially if pressures are high, management may need to do little to reinforce the messages which are received from the market, since employees are already aware of the potential force of customer power. If employees are not generally in direct contact with the consumer, management may initiate schemes to increase their awareness of the market through exposure to key customers; for example, in one of the plants previously investigated, shop floor employees were used to demonstrate and market the product at sales launches. In many companies, the possibility of increasing direct exposure may prove difficult especially if the part the product plays in a finished article is hard to identify. In these circumstances, management becomes the major factor in interpreting customer and competitive pressures to employees, and may use the threat of market forces in order to legitimise decisions which they would want to make in any event; the case of mediated 'Japanisation' to which we referred in Chapter 4 is a prime example of this.

Of our case studies, the employees at Multistores were most directly and continously exposed to the customer, especially those who worked on the shop floor, either as checkout operators or performing other tasks in the front of the store itself. Those behind the scenes, such as butchers or warehouse operators, whilst not in immediate contact with customers, are nevertheless relatively close to the point at which sales are made and often experience direct customer pressure from complaints or demands for restocking. The employees we interviewed at Multistores were highly aware of potential customer power, and to a lesser extent that of the competition, and even revelled in the thought that they were more in tune with customer needs than were the managers in the store. Despite employee awareness of the competitive environment, management tended to reinforce this message at all times. In the stores council, for example, the Chair (the General Stores Manager) used part of the meeting to remind representatives of the importance of customer care, and similar messages were communicated via team briefing as well. In addition, the principal purpose of the customer care committees, 'employee of the month,' 'store of the year' and even the weekly update on store performance on the Grimsight 'blackboard', all served to reinforce a culture in which customer service appears to be accorded priority over all other features. Perhaps the best illustration of this climate was the language used on a poster in the training room, which explicitly and unambiguously linked security of employment to levels of store performance: 'customers make pay-days possible'. At the same time, however, the company was attempting to create a resource-based management style in order to develop higher quality employees who possessed the skills to provide a better level of customer service. Similarly, team briefing had been introduced, amongst other things, in order to increase employee awareness of the reasoning behind management decisions, in the context of the company's position in relation to customers and competitors.

Since all the other plants were manufacturing products for commercial, industrial or governmental outlets, contact with customers did not form a substantial, or even a minor, part of these employees' jobs. At Typeng, a handful of the skilled workers from the assembly/erection part of the factory could come into contact with customers, but since most of the finished goods were exported – often to developing countries – this was not a common occurrence. Given also the size of the completed product, the time it took to make, and the fact that it was fabricated from work at several sites within Powerco, it was extremely difficult for any employee at Typeng to identify his or her contribution to the totality of production in the company. Management made some attempt to encourage a broader awareness of this but, as we have already seen, its communications were not regarded as particularly effective by those on the shop floor.

Management at both Ichem and Foodpack had made some

attempt to expose their employees directly to customers; at Ichem, the company had initiated a scheme whereby manual workers were sent overseas to assist with the commissioning of new systems which utilised products from the plant. In addition, the Quarterly Review contained information which focused on orders from major customers, comparisons of sales performance over time, and future prospects, all of which were designed to illustrate the links between customer service, product quality, and employee relations. It was somewhat easier for management at Foodpack to raise employee awareness of customer service, since the complete product was manufactured on site, over a relatively short period of time, and was also highly visible to employees when they themselves visited shops. Yet that had also led to complacency, according to some of the new managers, since long-serving employees had grown accustomed to the company's dominant position in the market. In recent times, with the advent of own-label products from the superstores, the company had started to make employees more aware of the power of the major customers over activity at the factory; consequently, the weekly newsletter always devoted about half its space to providing advance information on visits by these customers, and the employees were made aware of the importance of these visits for future market prospects. Moreover, because of these visits, management had been able to legitimise its decision to place a much greater emphasis on hygiene throughout the whole factory, even though the customers were only interested in inspecting certain lines. The relative lack of direct contact between customers and shop floor employees puts management in a key position to interpret market signals for employees, and consequently persuade them that managerial solutions offer the best response to external pressures.

In a non-unionised environment, it is extremely unlikely that employees would challenge these managerial interpretations of the product market, especially if they also lack direct contact with customers. Even in situations where they are personally exposed to the market, employees will find it difficult to contest management decisions in the absence of collective organisation. In all our case study companies, however, trade unions were recognised, and, moreover, at each site there were high levels of union membership. Potentially, this provides employees with the opportunity to dispute managerial interpretations of market signals, and put forward their own alternative perspective on appropriate responses to customer power. For instance, through an alternative information network, such as a combine committee or a trade union research department, union representatives can check the accuracy of the arguments used by management to justify decisions, and attempt to discredit them if appropriate. Furthermore, as we have seen on a number of occasions already, management style does not develop in isolation from the influence of trade unions, and the willingness of management to make concessions to employees is also highly dependent upon the actual, potential, or anticipated power of trade unions. In short, even allowing for the lack of centrality of the unions, the model would be incomplete if we were to ignore their role altogether.

We have already illustrated the way in which management style varies between the different companies involved in this study. Whilst the state of the product market influences the style adopted by management, so, too, does the activity of the unions in the workplace. Thus, the more adversarial and commodity-based style at Typeng is a reflection of similar behaviour on the part of the union representatives, not just at the present time, but also over the preceding decades. Neither side has been prepared to drop its defences in order to reach a new understanding about industrial relations, and consequently managerial initiatives to develop employee involvement have so far made little impact on the shop floor. It was at Typeng that managerial interpretations of events were most readily challenged by shop stewards, and 'messages' from the JCC were treated with considerable scepticism. Union representatives were fully aware that the release of information to the shop floor was carefully timed to coincide with broader management objectives, for example in relation to annual pay negotiations. Within the works, senior union representatives retained a monopoly over formal communications from management to the shop floor, and were therefore able to reinterpret messages to suit their own perspective. All the shop floor workers we interviewed at Typeng were scathing about the quality of communications in the factory, and of management attempts in particular, thus indicating the degree to which the unions had managed to maintain a relatively central position within the works. Union organisation was somewhat less well developed across the different sites within Powerco. Although the senior stewards had established some links with their colleagues at other plants, and could gather information about the state of the market and management strategies affecting the division as a whole, this association was neither particularly strong nor cohesive. Consequently, whilst it was easy for union representatives to query management interpretations of events, it proved rather more difficult for them to reject these altogether.

Trade unions occupied a more marginal position within the other workplaces, having rather less influence over the evolution of management style. At Ichem, the investment-orientated approach owed much to the individual preferences of the Managing Director, who actively sought to operationalise the corporate principles of the multinational parent company. Although the plant continued to give substantial support to the principle of trade unionism, as well as to its practical expression in a variety of ways, management had also successfully marginalised the convenor within the workplace. Whilst the shop floor workers whom we interviewed remained committed to the unions, management had undoubtedly achieved a new prominence within the network of workplace communications, and employees appeared to accept their messages on the shop floor. However, since market signals tended to be positive, in that future prospects appeared favourable, it is unlikely that the unions would find much need to question these interpretations in any event. Moreover, since union representatives had also been able to secure sizeable wage increases in recent negotiations, to some extent all workers had shared in the company's success in the market. In short, it could be argued that management's responsive and investment-orientated style had been rewarded by a more responsible approach on the part of employees,. It is impossible to judge, however, whether such a cosy relationship could be sustained in more hostile market conditions.

Trade unions were even less central to employee relations at Multistores and Foodpack, especially in the former at store level. Even if the unions had wanted to, it would have been difficult for them to challenge managerial interpretations of the market, considering the representatives' lack of expertise and resources at local level. The stores council at Smalltown tended to resemble a management seminar about the character of the product market, the need to provide high quality customer care, and the ever-present threat of the competition. Rather than challenge these interpretations, stores council representatives usually elaborated on them, thus reinforcing the power of the managerial message to their constituents. In much the same way, the senior stewards at Foodpack tended to accept managerial evaluations of the market, as did most, if not all, of the employees we interviewed at the site. Given that the weekly newsletter also contained information about market prospects, the fact that this was so well received on the shop floor further strengthened the power of the management message. In these two cases, the trade unions' influence on management style has been insignificant.

The final part of the model deals with the link between employees and the market, through the character of the product or service which their company provides. A key feature of recent attempts to improve the competitive performance of British companies has been the focus on customer care and product quality, both of which are substantially dependent upon employee actions. Whilst this link is most apparent in the service sector, where employees come into direct contact with customers, it has also become more central to the labour process in manufacturing companies. Techniques such as TQM (Total Quality Management) have as their primary objective the improvement of quality *within* the company, and rest upon a philosophy which encourages all employees and all departments to regard themselves as providers or customers of other employees and departments. The ultimate consequence of this is meant to be a greater awareness of customer needs more generally, leading to improvements in quality or reductions in the cost of finished products. However, as we have already seen, employees may just as readily use their tacit skills in order to thwart the objectives of employers as they may to benefit the company as a whole. Since even the most unskilled of employees have at their disposal the ability to influence the character of the product – in either direction – some managements have seen the value of developing an investment-orientated style in an attempt to harness these capabilities and elicit worker commitment. Conversely, others have sought to minimise employee discretion through policies designed to standardise product character, and further separate the execution of the task from its conception. Whatever the intention or the outcome, however, it is clear that in most cases individual employees possess the capacity to influence the nature of the market, albeit in minor, yet often immediate, ways.

Multistores is the company where employees can have the most immediate impact on the product market, since they have the greatest likelihood of direct contact with customers, through the quality of service provided in the stores. In addition, they are clearly 'closest' to the customer in a variety of ways, and their actions, or inactions, have immediate implications for the character of the product sold, and relate to their own job security within the store. The attempt by Multistores management to move towards an investment-orientated style, and to encourage employee identification with the company, is more readily appreciated in this context; if employees feel little attachment to the company, they are unlikely to care much about the quality of customer service, since they will be prepared to look elsewhere for jobs if the product market collapses. In the context of a more buoyant labour market, the company will suffer the greater loss unless it can persuade employees to identify their own future with that of the company. This accounts for the shift in management style in the company.

Ichem and Foodpack management have also recognised the influence that shop floor operatives can wield over the finished product, in terms of quality and hygiene. In the case of Ichem, employees in the production plants can affect product quality by failing to operate controls at the correct time or by sabotaging the process, whilst the attractiveness of product packaging is dependent upon conscientious performance by those in the warehouse. Continuous flow of product through the system, a key feature of this kind of chemical factory, also rests to a considerable extent upon the work undertaken by employees in the maintenance function. Although it is less apparent than at Multistores, management at Ichem is nevertheless heavily reliant on manual employees for the completion of a high quality task; once again, the investment-orientated and teamwork style offers management considerable benefits in such an environment, not the least of which is the generation of employee commitment to the plant/division. The situation at Foodpack is somewhat similar to that at Ichem, especially in the contribution which employees make to product quality, and the serious revenue implications of oversights by workers in this area.

Consequently, recent attempts to develop resource-based management styles can be more readily understood once the contribution of tacit skills to product quality is recognised.

Yet again, Typeng is the exception, not because employee influence over product character is not significant, but rather on account of the lesser willingness of workers to use their skills for the benefit of the company, and the considerable pressure exerted by customers to keep down prices and reduce lead times. As we saw in the case study, shop floor workers at Typeng probably possess higher levels of skill than at any of the other plants in our research, in view of the extreme precision with which they have to manufacture parts for the total product. At the same time, minor errors can have significant consequences for the performance of the product as a whole. However, although quality is seen as a key component of the finished product, management now feels obliged to accord it lower priority than reduced costs or shorter delivery dates. Not surprisingly, highly skilled workers find this ranking of priorities difficult to appreciate, and management has not been able to convince them otherwise through existing communications networks. In this case, therefore, managers are attempting to minimise the influence of shop floor workers on product character through greater controls on costs and performance.

10.5 CONCLUSIONS

In this chapter, we have demonstrated the complexity of the links between product markets and the management of employee relations. Because private sector employers are increasingly concerned with competitive advantage, and product quality appears to be a prime consideration in this quest, we have argued that an investment-oriented approach to employee relations can offer them substantial benefits over a more 'macho' stance. It is also apparent that certain product market conditions facilitate the adoption of an investment-oriented style, because these give employers more room for manoeuvre than when competition is severe. In the latter circumstances, management is likely to feel under considerable pressure from the market, and see little option but to adopt a more aggressive stance in order to achieve change. Of course, it is perfectly feasible that employers will adopt a more aggressive style in a favourable market situation, although none of the companies in this study did. What this does suggest, however, is that the degree of choice available to management is itself a matter for empirical investigation.

We have a number of more general conclusions to this book. The evidence from our study does not support the contention that private sector employers automatically seek to take advantage of favourable labour market conditions in order to increase direct control over employees. On the contrary, all the organisations were moving towards an investment-oriented approach, albeit at different speeds and with differing rates of success. Nor does it suggest that employers are actively pursuing strategies designed to undermine the position of the trade unions in their companies, whether by the dismissal of senior shop stewards or general restrictions on union activity; indeed, in one case, management was even attempting to bolster the position of the union. At the same time, however, it was also apparent that unions were not on the whole central to workplace employee relations, and in some cases their role was becoming more marginal. This factor did not, however, arise from any concerted management strategy directed specifically at labour relations, but was more appropriately seen as a consequence of other actions taken in pursuit of wider corporate goals – in particular, to increase employee commitment to product quality and customer service.

A second feature that we wish to stress is that, despite the well-publicised examples of macho management, employers still appear to proceed with extreme caution when seeking to make changes in their employee relations practices. Some of this has to do with a lack of desire to achieve change, considering that current relationships can provide employers with a degree of order and stability which they see little point in jeopardising. A related issue is that employers may be rather more concerned with building employee commitment to corporate or, at least, establishment goals to be bothered with a fight with the unions, especially at a time when the latter appear more willing to cooperate with the process of change. However, it is also likely that many employers still feel they lack the ability to force through changes, partly because labour market signals do not necessarily feed through to the individual plant, and partly because the product market context can make it risky to chance a confrontation. Perhaps the employer who is in a dire competitive position feels that there is nothing more to be lost – and much to be gained – by adopting an aggressive approach. Conversely, employers who are in a relatively favourable product market position may recognise the part which employees can play in maintaining this advantage, through the contribution of inherent skills to the achievement of a high quality product. Either way, achieving change is not as straightforward as macro conditions might imply.

Finally, we need to reiterate that the practice of employee relations on the shop floor rarely conforms with policy pronouncements or intentions espoused at corporate headquarters. In this study, the disparity was most apparent in relation to team briefing, which deviated from the model in all the sites where it operated. Most significant was the manner in which it had developed into a forum for two-way communications, an opportunity for line managers to discover the grievances and concerns of the people who worked for them, rather than to inform employees about developments in the company. The fact that this seemed to go down well with the participants is also of interest, and demonstrates the resilience of shop floor institutions to directives from above. It also means that we should take care in assuming that change is in fact taking place, just because senior managers tell us that it is. Moreover, it is also confirms that, despite the trend towards quantitative surveys, there is no substitute for detailed, qualitative investigations of shop floor practice if we are to establish whether or not patterns of employee relations are actually changing in Britain.

BIBLIOGRAPHY

Ackroyd, S., Burrell, G., Hughes, M. and Whitaker, A. (1988) 'The Japanisation of British industry', *Industrial Relations Journal*, vol. 19(1), pp. 11–24.

Advisory Conciliation and Arbitration Service (1981) *Improving Industrial Relations: A Joint Responsibility*, HMSO, London.

Advisory Conciliation and Arbitration Service (1988) *Labour Flexibility in Britain*, Occasional Paper no. 41, HMSO, London.

Ahlstrand, B. and Purcell, J. (1988) 'Employee relations strategy in the multi-divisional company', *Personnel Review*, vol. 17(2), pp. 3–11.

Analoui, F. (1987) 'An investigation into unconventional behaviours within the workplace', unpublished PhD thesis, Cranfield School of Management.

Armstrong, M. (1987) 'HRM: A case of the Emperor's new clothes', *Personnel Management*, August.

Armstrong, P. and Goodman, J. (1979) 'Managerial and supervisory custom and practice', *Industrial Relations Journal*, vol. 10(3), pp. 12–24.

Armstrong, P., Goodman, J. and Hyman, J. (1981) *Ideology and Shop Floor Industrial Relations*, Croom Helm, London.

Astley, W. and Van de Ven, A. (1983) 'Central perspectives and debates in organisation theory', *Administrative Science Quarterly*, vol. 28, pp. 245–73.

Atkinson, G. (1977) *The Effective Negotiator*, Quest Publications, London.

Atkinson, J. (1984) 'Manpower strategies for flexible organisations', *Personnel Management*, August.

Atkinson, J. (1987) 'Flexibility or fragmentation? The United Kingdom labour market in the eighties', *Labour and Society*, vol. 12(1), pp. 87–105.

Atkinson, J. and Meager, N. (1986) 'Is flexibility a flash in the pan?', *Personnel Management*, September.

Batstone, E. (1984) *Working Order*, Blackwell, Oxford.

Batstone, E. (1988) *The Reform of Workplace Industrial Relations*, Clarendon Press, Oxford.

Batstone, E., Boraston, I. and Frenkel, S. (1977) *Shop Stewards in Action*, Blackwell, Oxford.

Batstone, E., Boraston, I. and Frenkel, S. (1978) *The Social Organisation of Strikes*, Blackwell, Oxford.

Batstone, E., Ferner, A. and Terry, M. (1983) *Unions on the Board*, Blackwell, Oxford.

Batstone, E., Ferner, A. and Terry, M. (1984) *Consent and Efficiency*, Blackwell, Oxford.

Batstone, E. and Gourlay, S. (1986) *Unions, Unemployment and Innovation*, Blackwell, Oxford.

Beaumont, P. (1986) 'Management opposition to union organisation', *Employee Relations*, vol. 8(5), pp. 31–8.

Beaumont, P. (1987) *The Decline of Trade Union Organisation*, Croom Helm, London.

Beaumont, P., Thomson, A. and Gregory, M. (1980) 'Bargaining structures', *Management Decision*, vol. 18(3).

Beaumont, P. and Leopold, J. (1985) 'Public sector industrial relations: recent developments', *Employee Relations*, vol. 7(4).

Beynon, H. (1973) *Working For Ford*, Penguin, Harmondsworth.

Black J. and Ackers, P. (1988) 'The Japanisation of British industry? A case of quality circles in the carpet industry', *Employee Relations*, vol. 10(6), pp. 9–16.

Blauner, R. (1964) *Alienation and Freedom*, University of Chicago Press, Chicago.

Blyton, P. and Hill, S. (1988) 'Temporal flexibility in Britain: engineering, coal and teaching', paper presented to the 6th UMIST/Aston Labour Process Conference, Birmingham, March.

Bradley, K. and Hill, S. (1983) 'After Japan; the quality circle transplant and productive efficiency', *British Journal of Industrial Relations*, vol. 21(3), pp. 291–311.

Bradley, K. and Hill, S. (1987) 'Quality circles and managerial interests', *Industrial Relations*, vol. 26(1), pp. 68–82.

Brannen, P. (1983) *Authority and Participation in Industry*, Batsford, London.

Brannen, P., Batstone, E., Fatchett, D. and White, P. (1976) *The Worker Directors: A Sociology of Participation*, Hutchinson, London.

Braverman, H. (1974) *Labour and Monopoly Capital*, Monthly Review Press, New York.

Brewster, C., Gill, C. and Richbell, S. (1983) 'Industrial relations policy; a framework for analysis', in Thurley and Wood (eds) *Industrial Relations and Management Strategy*, pp. 62–72.

Brewster, C. and Connock, S. (1985) *Industrial Relations: Cost Effective Strategies*, Hutchinson, London.

Brown, W. (1973) *Piecework Bargaining*, Heinemann, London.

Brown, W. (ed.) (1981) *The Changing Contours of British Industrial Relations*, Blackwell, Oxford.

Brown, W. (1986) 'The changing role of trade unions in the management of labour', *British Journal of Industrial Relations*, vol. 24(2), pp. 161–8.

Brown, W. (1987) 'Pay determination', *British Journal of Industrial Relations*, vol. 25(2) pp. 291–4.

Buchanan, D. (1986) 'Management objectives in technical change', in Knights and Willmott (eds) *Managing the Labour Process*, Gower, Aldershot, pp. 67–84.

Bulmer, M. (ed.) (1975) *Working-Class Images of Society*, Routledge and Kegan Paul, London.

Burawoy, M. (1979) *Manufacturing Consent; Changes in the Labour Process under Monopoly Capitalism*, University of Chicago Press, Chicago.

Burns, T. and Stalker, G. (1961) *The Management of Innovation*, Tavistock, London.

Cappelli, P. (1985) 'Competitive pressures and labour relations in the airline industry', *Industrial Relations*, vol. 22(3), pp. 316–38.

Cappelli, P. and McKersie, R. (1987) 'Management strategy and the redesign of workrules', *Journal of Management Studies*, vol. 24(5), pp. 441–62.

Chadwick, D. (1983) 'The recession and industrial relations; A factory approach', *Employee Relations*, vol. 5(5), pp. 5–12.

Chandler, A. (1962) *Strategy and Structure*, MIT Press, Cambridge, Mass.

Child, J. (1972) 'Organisational structure, environment and performance: the role of strategic choice', *Sociology*, vol. 6(1), pp. 1–22.

Child, J. (ed.) (1973) *Man and Organisation*, George Allen and Unwin, London.

Child, J. (1977) *Organisations, A Guide to Problems and Practices*, Harper and Row, London.

Child, J. (1985) 'Managerial strategies, new technology, and the labour process', in Knights *et al.* (eds) *Job Redesign*, pp. 107–41.

Clegg, H. (1970) *The System of Industrial Relations in Great Britain*, Blackwell, Oxford.

Clegg, H. (1976) *Trade Unionism under Collective Bargaining*, Blackwell, Oxford.

Clegg, H. (1979) *The Changing System of Industrial Relations in Great Britain*, Blackwell, Oxford.

Collard, R. and Dale, B. (1985) 'Quality circles: why they break down and why they hold up', *Personnel Management*, February.

Commission on Industrial Relations (1973) *The Management of Industrial Relations*, Report no. 34, HMSO, London.

Coombs, R. (1985) 'Automation, management strategies and labour process change', in Knights *et al.* (eds) *Job Redesign*, pp. 142–70.

Cooper, B. and Bartlett, A. (1976) *Industrial Relations: a Study in Conflict*, Heinemann, London.

Cousins, J. and Brown, R. (1975) 'Patterns of paradox; shipbuilding workers' images of society', in Bulmer (ed.), *Working-Class Images of Society*, pp. 55–82.

Cressey, P. and MacInnes, J. (1980), 'Voting for Ford: industrial democracy and the control of labour', *Capital and Class*, vol. 11, pp. 5–33.

Cressey, P., Eldridge, J. and MacInnes, J. (1985) *Just Managing*, Open University Press, Milton Keynes.

Curson, C. (ed.) (1986) *Flexible Patterns of Work*, Institute of Personnel Management, London.

Cuthbert, N. and Whitaker, A. (1977) 'The rehabilitation of joint consultation: a recent trend in the participation debate', *Personnel Review*, vol. 6(2), pp. 31–6.

Daniel, W. (1987) *Workplace Industrial Relations and Technical Change*, Frances Pinter/PSI, London.

Daniel, W. and Millward, N. (1983) *Workplace Industrial Relations in Britain*, Heinemann, London.

Denzin, N. (1970) *The Research Act in Sociology*, Butterworths, London.

Dickens, L., Jones, M., Weekes, B. and Hart, M. (1985) *Dismissed: a Study of Unfair Dismissal and the Industrial Tribunal System*, Blackwell, Oxford.

Donovan, Lord (1968) *Royal Commission on Trade Unions and Employers Associations: Report*, Cmnd 3623, HMSO, London.

Dunn, S. and Gennard, J. (1984) *The Closed Shop in British Industry*, Macmillan, London.

Edwardes, M. (1984) *Back from the Brink*, Pan, London.

Edwards, P. (1985) 'Managing labour relations through the recession', *Employee Relations*, vol. 7(2), pp. 3–7.

Edwards, P. (1986) *Conflict at Work*, Blackwell, Oxford.

Edwards, P. (1987) *Managing the Factory*, Blackwell, Oxford.

Edwards, P. and Scullion, H. (1982) *The Social Organisation of Industrial Conflict*, Blackwell, Oxford.

Edwards, R. (1979) *Contested Terrain*, Heinemann, London.

Elliott, J. (1978) *Conflict or Cooperation? The Growth of Industrial Democracy*, Kogan Page, London.

Evans, S., Goodman, J. and Hargreaves, L. (1985) *Unfair Dismissal Law and Employment Practice in the 1980s*, Department of Employment Research Paper no. 53, HMSO, London.

Fidler, J. (1981) *The British Business Elite*, Routledge and Kegan Paul, London.

Flanders, A. (1975) *Management and Unions*, Faber and Faber, London.

Fox, A. (1966) *Industrial Sociology and Industrial Relations*, Royal Commission Research Paper no. 3, HMSO, London.

Fox, A. (1974) *Beyond Contract: Work, Trust and Power Relations*, Faber and Faber, London.

Fox, A. (1985) *History and Heritage*, George Allen and Unwin, London.

Friedman, A. (1977) *Industry and Labour*, Macmillan, London.

Friedman, A. (1984) 'Management strategies, market conditions and the labour process', in Stephen (ed.) *Firms, Organisation and Labour*, Macmillan, London, pp. 176–200.

Friedman, A. (1986) 'Developing the managerial strategies approach to the labour process', *Capital and Class*, vol. 28, pp. 97–124.

Gennard, J., Dunn, S. and Wright, M. (1980) 'The extent of closed shop arrangements in British industry', *Employment Gazette*, January.

Gill, C. (1974) 'Industrial relations in a multi-plant organisation: some considerations', *Industrial Relations Journal*, vol. 5(4), pp. 22–35.

Goldthorpe, J., Lockwood, D., Bechofer, F. and Platt, J. (1968) *The Affluent Worker: Industrial Attitudes and Behaviour*, Cambridge University Press, Cambridge.

Goodman, J., Armstrong, E., Davis, J. and Wagner, A. (1977) *Rule Making and Industrial Peace*, Croom Helm, London.

Gospel, H. and Littler, C. (1983) *Managerial Strategies and Industrial Relations*, Heinemann, London.

Gregory, M., Lobban, P. and Thomson, A. (1985) 'Wage settlements in manufacturing, 1979–84: evidence from the CBI databank', *British Journal of Industrial Relations*, vol. 23(3), pp. 339–58.

Gregory, M., Lobban, P. and Thomson, A. (1986) 'Bargaining structure, pay settlements and perceived pressures in manufacturing 1979–84: further analysis from the CBI databank', *British Journal of Industrial Relations*, vol. 24(2), pp. 215–32.

Grummitt, J. (1983) *Team Briefing*, Industrial Society, London.

Guest, D. (1987) 'Human resource management and industrial relations', *Journal of Management Studies*, vol. 24(5), pp. 503–21.

Hakim, C. (1987) 'Trends in the flexible workforce', *Employment Gazette*, November.

Hart, M. (1979) 'Why bosses love the closed shop', *New Society*, 23 February.

Hickson, D., Hinings, C., Lee, C., Schneck, R. and Pennings, J. (1971) 'A strategic contingencies theory of intraorganisational power', *Administrative Science Quarterly*, vol. 16, pp. 216–29.

Hill, C. and Pickering, J. (1986) 'Divisionalisation, decentralisation and performance of large United Kingdom companies', *Journal of Management Studies*, vol. 23(1), pp. 26–50.

Hill, F. (1986) 'Quality circles in the UK: a longitudinal study', *Personnel Review*, vol. 15(3), pp. 25–34.

Hrebiniak, L. and Joyce, W. (1985) 'Organisational adaptation: strategic choice and environmental determinism', *Administrative Science Quarterly*, vol. 30, pp. 336–49.

Hyman, R. (1972) *Strikes*, Fontana, London.

Institute of Personnel Management (1988) *Annual Reports – Employee Involvement Statements*, IPM, London.

Jackson, M. (1977) *Industrial Relations*, Croom Helm, London.

Jones, B. (1982) 'Destruction or redistribution of engineering skills? the case of numerical control', in Wood (ed.) *The Degradation of Work*, Hutchinson, London, pp. 179–200.

Joyce, P. and Woods, A. (1984) 'Joint consultation in Britain: towards an explanation', *Employee Relations*, vol. 6(2), pp. 2–8.

Kelly, J. (1985) 'Management's redesign of work: labour process, labour markets and product markets', in Knights *et al.*, (eds) *Job Redesign*, pp. 30–51.

Kelly, J. (1987) 'Trade unions through the recession, 1980–84', *British Journal of Industrial Relations*, vol. 25(2), pp. 275–82.

Khandawalla, P. (1977) *The Design of Organisations*, Harcourt Brace Jovanovich, New York.

Kinnie, N. (1985) 'Changing management strategies in industrial relations', *Industrial Relations Journal*, vol. 16(4), pp. 17–24.

Kinnie, N. (1986) 'Patterns of industrial relations management', *Employee Relations*, vol. 8(2), pp. 17–21.

Kinnie, N. (1987) 'Bargaining within the enterprise: centralised or decentralised?' *Journal of Management Studies*, vol. 24(5), pp. 463–77.

Kirkbride, P. (1985) 'Power in industrial relations research', *Industrial Relations Journal*, vol. 16(1), pp. 44–56.

Kirkbride, P. (1988) 'Legitimising arguments and worker resistance', *Employee Relations*, vol. 10(2), pp. 28–31.

Knights, D. (1987) 'Subjectivity and the labour process', paper presented to the 5th Annual Labour Process Conference, Manchester, April.

Knights, D. and Collinson, D. (1985) 'Redesigning work on the shop floor: a question of control or consent?', in Knights *et al.* (eds) *Job Redesign*, pp. 197–226.

Knights, D., Willmott, H. and Collinson, D. (eds) (1985) *Job Redesign*, Gower, Aldershot.

Knights, D. and Willmott, H. (eds) (1986) *Managing the Labour Process*, Gower, Aldershot.

Kochan, T. McKersie, R. and Cappelli, P. (1984) 'Strategic choice and industrial relations theory', *Industrial Relations*, vol. 23(1), pp. 16–39.

Lawrence, Paul and Lorsch, J. (1969) *Organisation and Environment*, Richard D. Irwin, Illinois.

Lawrence, Peter and Lee, R. (1984) *Insight into Management*, Oxford University Press, Oxford.

Lazonick, W. (1983) 'Technological change and the control of work', in Gospel and Littler *Managerial Strategies and Industrial Relations*, pp. 111–36.

Legge, K. (1978) *Power, Innovation and Problem Solving in Personnel Management*, McGraw Hill, London.

Littler, C. (1985) 'Taylorism, Fordism and job design', in Knights *et al.* (eds) *Job Redesign*, pp. 10–29.

Littler, C. and Salaman, G. (1982), 'Bravermania and beyond; recent theories of the labour process', *Sociology*, vol. 16(2), pp. 251–69.

Littler, C. and Salaman, G. (1984) *Class at Work*, Batsford, London.

Lupton, T. (1963) *On The Shop Floor*, Pergamon, London.

McCarthy, W. (1964) *The Closed Shop in Britain*, Blackwell, Oxford.

McCarthy, W. (1966) *The Role of the Shop Steward in British Industrial Relations*, Royal Commission Research Paper no. 1, HMSO, London.

MacDonald, D. (1985) 'The role of management in industrial relations and some views on its conceptualisation and analysis', *Journal of Management Studies*, vol. 22(5), pp. 523–46.

MacInnes, J. (1985) 'Conjuring up consultation', *British Journal of Industrial Relations*, vol. 23(1), pp. 93–113.

MacInnes, J. (1987) *Thatcherism at Work*, Open University Press, Milton Keynes.

Mackay, L. (1986) 'The macho manager: it's no myth', *Personnel Management*, January.

Mansfield, R. Poole, M. Blyton, P. and Frost, P. (1981) *The British Manager in Profile*, British Institute of Management, London.

Manwaring, T. (1983) 'The motor manufacturing industry in Britain: prospects for the 1980s', *Industrial Relations Journal*, vol. 14(3), pp. 7–23.

Manwaring, T. and Wood, S. (1985) 'The ghost in the labour process', in Knights *et al.* (eds) *Job Redesign*, pp. 171–96.

Marchington, M. (1975) 'A path model of power generation', University of Aston Working Paper Series, no. 36.

Marchington, M. (1979) 'Shop floor control and industrial relations', in Purcell and Smith (eds) *The Control of Work*, Macmillan, London, pp. 133–55.

Marchington, M. (1980) *Responses to Participation at Work*, Gower, Aldershot.

Marchington, M. (1982) *Managing Industrial Relations*, McGraw Hill, Maidenhead.

Marchington, M. (1987a) 'A review and critique of recent research into joint consultation', *British Journal of Industrial Relations*, vol. 25(3), pp. 339–52.

Marchington, M. (1987b) 'Employee participation', in Towers, B. (ed.), *A Handbook of Industrial Relations Practice*, Kogan Page, London, pp. 162–82.

Marchington, M. (1988a) 'The changing nature of industrial relations in the UK and its impact on management behaviour', in Dluglos, Dorow and Weiermair (eds) *Management under Different Labour Market and Employment System*, de Gruyter, Berlin.

Marchington, M. (1988b) 'Conflict, collaboration and commitment in British industrial relations', *European Management Journal*, vol. 6(1), pp. 61–7.

Marchington, M. and Loveridge, R. (1979) 'Non-participation: the management view?', *Journal of Management Studies*, vol. 16(2), pp. 171–84.

Marchington, M. and Loveridge, R. (1983) 'Management decision-making and shop-floor participation', in Thurley and Wood (eds) *Industrial Relations and Management Strategy*, pp. 73–82.

Marchington, M. and Armstrong, R. (1983) 'Shop steward organisation and joint consultation', *Personnel Review*, vol. 12(1), pp. 24–32.

Marchington, M. and Armstrong, R. (1985) 'Involving employees through the recession', *Employee Relations*, vol. 7(5), pp. 17–21.

Marchington, M. and Armstrong, R. (1986) 'The nature of the new joint consultation', *Industrial Relations Journal*, vol. 17(2), pp. 158–70.

Marchington, M. and Parker, P. (1988) 'Japanisation: a lack of chemical reaction?', *Industrial Relations Journal*, vol. 19(4), pp. 272–85.

Margerison, C. (1969) 'What do we mean by industrial relations? A behavioural science approach', *British Journal of Industrial Relations*, vol. 7(2), pp. 273–86.

Marginson, P., Edwards, P., Purcell, J. and Sisson, K. (1988) 'What do corporate offices really do?' *British Journal of Industrial Relations*, vol. 26(2), pp. 229–45.

Marples, D. (1967) 'Studies of managers – a fresh start', *Journal of Management Studies*, vol. 4(3), pp. 282–99.

Marsden, D., Morris, T., Willman, P. and Wood, S. (1985) *The Car Industry: Labour Relations and Industrial Adjustment*, Tavistock, London.

Meulders, D. and Wilkin, L. (1987) 'Labour market flexibility: critical introduction to the analysis of a concept', *Labour and Society*, vol. 12(1), pp. 3–17.

Miller, P. (1987) 'Strategic industrial relations and human resource management – distinction, definition and recognition', *Journal of Management Studies*, vol. 24(4), pp. 347–61.

Millward, N. and Stevens, M. (1986), *British Workplace Industrial Relations, 1980–1984*, Gower, Aldershot.

Mintzberg, H. (1973) *The Nature of Managerial Work*, Harper and Row, New York.

Mintzberg, H. (1978) 'Patterns in strategy formation', *Management Science*, vol. 24(9), pp. 934–48.

Nichols, T. (1969) *Ownership, Control and Ideology*, George Allen and Unwin, London.

Nichols, T. and Armstrong, P. (1976) *Workers Divided*, Fontana, London.

Parkin, F. (1972) *Class Inequality and Political Order*, Paladin, London.

Peach, L. (1983) 'Employee relations in IBM', *Employee Relations*, vol. 5(3), pp. 17–20.

Peters, T. and Waterman, R. (1982) *In Search of Excellence*, Harper and Row, New York.

Pettigrew, A. (1985) *The Awakening Giant: Continuity and Change in ICI*, Blackwell, Oxford.

Piore, M. and Sabel, C. (1985) *The Second Industrial Divide: Possibilities for Prosperity*, Basic Books, New York.

Pollert, A. (1988) 'Dismantling flexibility', *Capital and Class*, vol. 34, pp. 42–75.

Poole, M. (1986a) 'Profit sharing and employee share ownership schemes', *Employee Relations*, vol. 8(5), pp. 45–50.

Poole, M. (1986b) 'Managerial strategies and styles in industrial relations: a comparative analysis', *Journal of General Management*, vol. 12(1), pp. 40–53.

Porter, M. (1979) 'How competitive forces shape strategy', *Harvard Business Review*, March–April.

Purcell, J. (1979) 'Applying control systems to industrial relations', *Journal of the Operational Research Society*, vol. 30, pp. 1037–46.

Purcell, J. (1981) *Good Industrial Relations: Theory and Practice*, Macmillan, London.

Purcell, J. (1983) 'The management of industrial relations in the modern corporation; agenda for research', *British Journal of Industrial Relations*, vol. 21(1), pp. 1–16.

Purcell, J. (1985) 'Is anybody listening to the corporate personnel department?' *Personnel Management*, September.

- Purcell, J. (1987) 'Mapping management styles in employee relations', *Journal of Management Studies*, vol. 24(5), pp. 534–48.

Purcell, J., Dalgleish, L., Harrison, J., Lonsdale, I., McConaghy, I. and Robertson, A. (1978) 'Power from technology; computer staff and industrial relations', *Personnel Review*, vol. 7(1), pp. 31–9.

Purcell, J. and Gray, A. (1986) 'Corporate personnel departments and the management of industrial relations: two case studies in ambiguity', *Journal of Management Studies*, vol. 23(2), pp. 205–23.

Purcell, J. and Sisson, K. (1983) 'Strategies and Practice in the management of industrial relations', in Bain G. (ed.) *Industrial Relations in Britain*, Blackwell, Oxford, pp. 95–120.

Purcell, J. and Smith, R. (eds) (1979) *The Control of Work*, Macmillan, London.

Rainnie, A. (1984) 'Combined and uneven development in the clothing industry: the effects of competition on accumulation', *Capital and Class*, vol. 22, pp. 141–56.

Ramsay, H. (1975) 'Firms and football teams', *British Journal of Industrial Relations*, vol. 13(3), pp. 396–400.

Ramsay, H. (1977) 'Cycles of control: worker participation in sociological and historical perspective', *Sociology*, vol. 11, pp. 481–506.

Ramsay, H. (1980) 'Phantom participation; patterns of power and conflict', *Industrial Relations Journal*, vol. 11(3), pp. 46–59.

Roberts, C. (1984) 'Who will bite the closed shop ballot?', *Personnel Management*, October.

Roots, P. (1986) Collective bargaining: opportunities for a new approach. Warwick Papers in *Industrial Relations*, no. 5, April.

Rose, M. and Jones, B. (1985) 'Managerial strategy and trade union responses in work reorganisation schemes at establishment level', in Knights *et al.* (eds) *Job Redesign*, pp. 81–106.

Rothwell, S. (1984) 'Company employment policies and new technology in manufacturing and service sectors', in Warner (ed.), *Microprocessors, Manpower and Society*, Gower, Aldershot, pp. 111–33.

Royal Commission on Trade Unions and Employers Associations (1967) *Productivity Bargaining*, Research Paper no. 4, Part 1, HMSO, London.

Rubery, J., Tarling, R. and Wilkinson, F. (1987) 'Flexibility, marketing and the organisation of production', *Labour and Society*, vol. 12(1), pp. 131–51.

Sisson, K. (1987) *The Management of Collective Bargaining: An International Comparison*, Blackwell, Oxford.

Smith, C., Clifton, R., Makeham, P., Creigh, S. and Burn, R. (1978) *Strikes in Britain*, Department of Manpower Paper no. 15, HMSO, London.

Smith, G. (1986) 'Profit sharing and employee share ownership in Britain', *Employment Gazette*, September, pp. 380–5.

Spencer, B. (1985) 'Shop steward resistance in the recession', *Employee Relations*, vol. 7(5), pp. 22–8.

Sproull, A. and MacInnes, J. (1987) 'Patterns of union recognition in Scottish electronics', *British Journal of Industrial Relations*, vol. 25(3), pp. 335–8.

Storey, J. (1983) *Managerial Prerogative and the Question of Control*, Routledge and Kegan Paul, London.

Storey, J. (1985a) 'The means of management control', *Sociology*, vol. 19(2), pp. 193–211.

Storey, J. (1985b) 'Management control as a bridging concept', *Journal of Management Studies*, vol. 22(3), pp. 269–91.

Storey, J. (1986) 'The phoney war? New office techonology: organisation and control', in Knights and Willmott (eds), *Managing the Labour Process*, pp. 44–66.

Storey, J. (1988) 'The people management dimension in programmes of organisational change', *Employee Relations*, vol. 10(6), pp. 17–25.

Sturdy, A. (1987) '*Coping with the Pressure of Work*', paper delivered to the 5th Annual Labour Process Conference, Manchester, April.

Terry, M. (1977) 'The inevitable growth of informality', *British Journal of Industrial Relations*, vol. 15(1), pp. 76–90.

Terry, M. (1978) 'The emergence of a lay elite? Some recent changes in shop steward organisation', *Industrial Relations Research Unit*, Discussion Paper no. 14, University of Warwick, November.

Terry, M. (1983) 'Shop stewards through expansion and recession', *Industrial Relations Journal*, vol. 14(3), pp. 49–58.

Terry, M. (1986) 'How do we know if shop stewards are getting weaker?' *British Journal of Industrial Relations*, vol. 24(2), pp. 169–80.

Thomason, G. (1981) *A Textbook of Personnel Management*, Institute of Personnel Management, London.

Thomason, G. (1984) *A Textbook of Industrial Relations Management*, Institute of Personnel Management, London.

Thompson, P. (1983) *The Nature of Work*, Macmillan, London.

Thompson, P. (1986) 'Crawling from the wreckage; the labour process and the politics of production', paper presented to the 4th Annual Labour Process Conference, Aston, April.

Thurley, K. and Wood, S. (eds) (1983) *Industrial Relations and Management Strategy*, Cambridge University Press, Cambridge.

Timperley, S. (1980) 'Organisation strategies and industrial relations', *Industrial Relations Journal*, vol. 11(5), pp. 38–45.

Torrington, D., MacKay, L. and Hall, L. (1985) 'The changing nature of personnel management', *Employee Relations*, vol. 7(5), pp. 10–16.

Towers, B. (ed.) (1987) *A Handbook of Industrial Relations Practice*, Kogan Page, London.

Truman, C. and Keating, J. (1988) 'Technology, markets and the design of women's jobs: the case of the clothing industry', *New Technology*,

Work and Employment, vol. 3(1), pp. 21–9.

Tyson, S. (1987) 'The management of the personnel function', *Journal of Management Studies*, vol. 24(5), pp. 523–32.

Watson, T. (1977) *The Personnel Managers*, Routledge and Kegan Paul, London.

Wedderburn, D. and Crompton, R. (1972) *Workers' Attitudes to Technical Change*, Cambridge University Press, Cambridge.

Werther, W. (1985) 'Job 1 at Ford: employee cooperation', *Employee Relations*, vol. 7(1), pp. 10–16.

Whitaker, A. (1986) 'Managerial strategy and industrial relations: a case study of plant relocation', *Journal of Management Studies*, vol. 23(6), pp. 657–78.

Wickens, P. (1987) *The Road to Nissan: Flexibility, Quality, Teamwork*, Macmillan, London.

Wilkinson, B. (1983) *The Shopfloor Politics of New Technology*, Heinemann Educational Books, London.

Willman, P. (1980) 'Leadership and trade union principles; some problems of management sponsorship and independence', *Industrial Relations Journal*, vol. 11(4), pp. 39–49.

Willman, P. and Winch, G. (1985) *Innovation and Management Control: Labour Relations at BL Cars*, Cambridge University Press, Cambridge.

Wilson, D., Butler, R., Gray, D., Hickson, D. and Mallory, G. (1982) 'The limits of trade union power in organisational decision making', *British Journal of Industrial Relations*, vol. 20(3), pp. 322–41.

Winkler, J. (1974) 'The ghost at the bargaining table: directors and industrial relations', *British Journal of Industrial Relations*, vol. 12(2), pp. 191–212.

Wood, S. (1979) 'A reappraisal of the contingency approach to organisation', *Journal of Management Studies*, vol. 16(3), pp. 334–54.

Wood, S. (1982a) 'The study of management in British industrial relations', *Industrial Relations Journal*, vol. 13(2), pp. 51–61.

Wood, S. (ed.) (1982b) *The Degradation of Work?* Hutchinson, London.

Wood, S. and Kelly, J. (1982) 'Taylorism, responsible autonomy and management strategy', in Wood (ed.), *The Degradation of Work*, pp. 74–89.

Woodward, J. (1965) *Industrial Organisation: Theory and Practice*, Oxford University Press, Oxford.

Young, K. (1986) 'The management of craft work: a case study of an oil refinery', *British Journal of Industrial Relations*, vol. 24(3), pp. 363–80.

INDEX